Sales Readiness:
A Template for Success

SALES READINESS:
A TEMPLATE FOR SUCCESS

Paul Fornelli

ISBN: 0692579095
ISBN 13: 9780692579091
Library of Congress Control Number: 2015957661
P Performance Publishing, Scottsdale, AZ

TABLE OF CONTENTS

INTRODUCTION

We are all products of our experiences. My most significant ones were in 2008, when the mortgage and financial services world was grinding to a snail's crawl. My former employer, HSBC, was in the midst of closing down its wholesale entity altogether, and I was lucky enough to have secured a sales management role with its biggest local competitor: Barclays. They appeared to have the kind of platform and commitment that would weather what would surely be a turbulent set of events to come…but in reality the reckoning was at hand and no company was safe. Not long after I was hired, my boss called me one morning while I was on my way to work to let me know my job had been eliminated, and the future of the company as a whole was in doubt.

Surprisingly, I accepted this news calmly, mostly because I had three things: plenty of money in the bank, free and clear assets, and confidence that finding a new job would be simple for someone like me. I had twenty years of sales and sales management experience with a well-documented history of success and advancement. I had an MBA and a glowing resume.

I had also always wanted a higher purpose and deeper meaning to go with my work, and in truth I was not getting either in my current career. In fact, I was almost thankful to be finally released from the bonds of my high-level salary and overpaid commissions, from all the trappings and false sense of security that went with them. Push me out into the world, I thought, where I would find a position that better addressed my internal passions and desires—where I would do more than simply pass papers from one place to the next.

The problem: I had no idea where I would find such a job, and no clear vision for how to attain my higher sense of self-actualization. But I did have that confidence, so I was convinced that once the world got a look at me, it would be falling all over itself to swallow me up. The gates were going to open and the keys to the kingdom would be bestowed upon me. I would be the problem solver, the liberator of even the most gravely troubled corporations. Just a glimpse at my resume and earnings history would have employers fighting for my services. Bring on the pink slip, I thought. Let's get this new show on the road!

Of course this was false bravado, and I found out pretty quickly that I was going to need a lot more than a resume, some juicy W-2s, and an overinflated sense of my own value. In fact, I would eventually lose all the wealth generated from those W-2's and all the false confidence that went with them. I would for too long be mired in the sludge of procrastination in the false hopes that the good times would somehow come back. I made one bad career decision or non-decision after another. I was broken in both my pocket book and my spirit. But in all of that loss and despair, I would eventually gain more than I ever dreamed possible. It took me a long while to get there. So first things first.

I needed tools—though what they were and where I would get them was elusive to me at the time. I was a sales professional and primarily wanted to stay in that field, though I was open to switching verticals if it meant finding a place to feed my passions and utilize my talents and skills. But I had no idea how to do that. All my experience was in financial service sales. How would I convince anyone I could do anything else?

Just as I was unemployed as a result of the great recession, so were most of my fellow sales professionals from the wholesale banking world. This was a main theme in all the conversations I had with them: It was seemingly impossible to cross verticals. Prospective employers and recruiters would not return calls or e-mails. Resumes were going out but getting no replies. Even when someone was lucky enough to get an interview, the common response was, "Sorry, we really need someone with direct hard-skill experience in the field."

Many people I knew just gave up trying and accepted their fates. They settled into jobs that either they were overqualified for or hated, and I knew I was headed down that path as well. This country is filled with dispossessed and dissatisfied workers. It's sort of the American way. Some statistics say at least 80% of workers are dissatisfied.

But I was determined to reverse my course. All I had to do was find a way to relate my relevance and foundational value to employers in fields in which I had no prior hard-skill experience or knowledge, but were in alignment with my passion and sense of purpose. Nobody believed I could do it; I might as well believe in unicorns too, they said. But I knew it wasn't a fantasy, and it wasn't about luck. It would take some hard work and introspection, but I was convinced—I was *confident*—I could create a framework for success to help myself and others cross verticals in multiple spaces and compete for the most highly coveted jobs.

And I did it. Despite hardship and a lot of sleepless nights, I eventually found the inner voice, vision, and inspiration for creating a set of tools, templates, and exercises—what I've come to call Paul's Pyramid of P's—that helped me overcome the challenges of relating my relevance and value, and achieving successful cross-vertical migration. I found also that these tools, templates, and exercises—all of which are covered in this book—have relevance for more than existing sales professionals who want to rediscover and refocus on the basic processes that create sustained success, or those who want to enter the field and need a sales education in creating a framework for success.

Rather, they're a communication template for all who are currently or have ever been dissatisfied or dispossessed in their work experience. They're for all who desire to find work that satisfies their inner passion and purpose but don't know how to do it or don't think it's possible. They can lead to

- A job search devoid of anxiety.
- A successful job migration into an industry you never thought possible.
- Finding a job that satisfies your deepest sense of passion & purpose.

- Recognizing your skills that you hadn't even understood existed and utilizing them in ways that improve performance and affect outcomes in ways you never would have imagined.
- Creating a true career based framework for success designed to last a lifetime.

Beyond that, the Pyramid will work as a sales readiness template for an individual or an organization because it's designed to be flexible, meaning it can apply to any type of sales, methodology (SPIN selling, strategic selling, conceptual, Challenger, etc.), or vertical and portable, meaning all employees, even new hires, will adhere to the same framework for building action plans and ensuring sustained, long-term success.

The unexpected and difficult experience of having to overcome and adapt to a changed environment, along with the process of self-reinvention and discovery, have changed me forever both personally and professionally. If the financial services world hadn't collapsed and I hadn't lost my job, the Pyramid of P's and the concept of transferable relevance may have never come to my mind. All the hardships I went through while trying to find a new job and the new realities I faced forced me to perform that internalization exercise, and it was from those experiences that led me to create the Pyramid as both a communication template and a sales readiness template.

I now believe that each one of us has a built-in framework for success. Each one of us has a foundational value. The original goal of this book was to help you understand how to internalize your transferable and foundational relevance's so you can achieve an optimal level of alignment between your professional objectives and your inner purpose and passions. This book provides that. However, as with all ideas, they sometimes evolve into much more.

The Essence of this Book

This book is called Sales Readiness A Template for Success, and the concept of transferable relevance is a primary topic throughout the book. However, the true essence of this book is **SALES EDUCATION**. There are a million and one books out there that give you "The 10 latest, greatest and newest ways to cold call", or others that have discovered and designed the latest and greatest sales related methodology that will help you think, walk, talk, and act better on your way to sales success. Most of those books focus primarily on the strategic and the tactical elements for sales related performance improvement. Some are good and some are not. In either case, those were not the topics I wanted to focus upon in my book. In my opinion most of those sales books center upon what might work today or in the very near term. I wanted to write a sales related educational book that focused upon the foundational sales elements that lasts forever.

Although I do describe and offer some strategic and tactical elements throughout this book, I wanted to focus primarily on the structural elements of sales. In my opinion the greatest man made structures on the planet earth are the Great Pyramids. They are 5000 years old and still standing strong. They stand strong because their makers and engineers understood the value of having a sound STRUCTURE. They based their design template with the objective that their structures would last forever. That anything built to last has to have at its core, a sound structural template if it holds out any hope of having sustained success. That's why this book focuses on structure. And my sales structure is a pyramid, and I designed it to last forever.

This book brings to life some fundamental sales based education for both individuals and businesses. I wrote this story as a labor of love, and I did it through a combination of a lot of research and some story telling. Please note that I took some poetic license with the historical research and depiction of events. If at least one person out there learns something and is helped by it, then it will have been worth the 3 years it took me to write this book.

Although I do mix in some real facts, real places, and real businesses within the body of the story telling, none of the characters or events is meant to be anything other than fiction.

GLOSSARY

Boom and bust cycle: A period of high economic growth followed by an economic crash. These cycles are commonplace throughout the history of the American economy.

Communication template: A tool designed to help job seekers recognize, understand, internalize, and effectively communicate the relevant aspects of their work histories to improve their chances of success when applying for a job.

Globalization: The process of creating an integrated global economy. The Information Age and the ability to travel efficiently to all points of the globe have created a more interconnected world. This means added competitive pressure for job seekers in the United States, as jobs can always be done remotely.

Hard skills: The quantifiable skill set requested or required to perform a job. For example, typing, experience with specific software, writing, or having a specific degree or certificate.

Keywords: Words or a set of words that indicate something in your work background that an employer will covet because it represents a hard-skill match. Keywords tell the story of your work history on your resume. Today's talent acquisition world relies upon keywords a great deal to match work talent with its needs. The result is a myopic approach to talent valuation and overreliance on hard-skill matching. Online talent acquisition and job searching utilize keywords as a primary tool, which has led to a narrower mindset within these processes.

Sales Audit: An internalization exercise for businesses. The sales readiness template is utilized to evaluate and measure a companies infrastructure as it relates to its readiness to effectively adopt the prescribed sales methodology and ultimately its ability to effectively sustain and support the goals and objectives for the sales force.

Sales Readiness Template: A structural framework designed to act as a guideline and blueprint for sustained sales related success.

Self-audit: Also interchanged with the term **internalization exercise**. It's a critical step for the job seeker wanting to make a vertical migration for that dream job. It's an individual exercise designed to help a person recognize, discover, and understand not only what is relevant about their past work experience, but even more importantly what aspects of that work experience ultimately can serve their internal sense of passion and purpose. In other words, it gets to the heart of not only "what" you have done, but also "why" you want to do the things you do.

Soft skills: Subjective skills related to not just how you interact with other people, but also why you do. These are sometimes referred to as your emotional IQ. For example, a person's ability to easily assimilate within a group. A person's ability for sizing up a situation quickly and accurately, and then adapting to it. These are the intangibles often relating to the social sciences and are not easily identified on a resume. They also include a person's work ethic and general attitude.

Space: A subset of a vertical. For example, there might be a patient monitoring space within the medical vertical.

Talent silos: In the real world, a silo is typically defined as a structure or container that holds a specific product such as wheat or corn. For the purposes of this book, these structures (silos) hold very specific jobs within them. I have given these structures the name Talent Silo's. They are used more as a symbolic term to metaphorically give context for the inability of job seekers to find jobs in industry's, verticals, and spaces outside of their hard skill related job experience. These silos are a prominent feature in a fictitious world called Myopia. Only those with direct experience evidenced by specific keywords on a resume are given entrance into these job containers.

Transferable relevance: The idea that one's sales related skills (hard or soft) in one vertical can be utilized just as efficiently and effectively in a different vertical.

Vertical: A category of job. For example, medical, transportation, construction, or banking are all verticals.

World of Myopia: A fictitious world in this book that serves as the symbol for all things that makes finding a job difficult today, especially for anyone hoping to have crossover vertical success. A place for very narrow thinking. You can find talent silos littered throughout this land.

Part I: Playing the Game

CHAPTER 1

CROSSING VERTICALS

I grew up in a middle-class suburb of Chicago in the 1980s. At the time, the city had a relatively large manufacturing base, and my family's friends ranged from self-employed carpenters, union workers, and blue-collar factory folks to businesspeople working at the Chicago Mercantile Exchange.

I would hear about factory closings, and I had friends who moved away as a result. The men and women who work in factories often possess very specific skill sets and thus can be very migratory in nature, meaning they follow the work. As the overall economic landscape began to shift to a more service-related base in the 1980s, many of those skilled factory workers, machinists, and tool-and-dye guys struggled to find ways to adjust. It must not have been easy for them to transfer their very unique skill sets to new and unfamiliar jobs—sort of like playing quarterback your whole life and then being asked to play defensive tackle in the next game.

The transition was difficult, as were the options: adapt or leave. Not everyone chose to move; some did indeed find ways to reinvent themselves and change with the fluctuating economic environment. But it was also not uncommon to move away and look for more familiar work. That upheaval caused many families a lot of stress, anxiety, and depression.

At that time, I didn't give a lot of thought to this dynamic, but I do now, especially in regard to those skilled workers who chose to stay. How did they find ways to learn something new? Did anyone even give them a chance? Was it any easier to cross verticals back then than it is today? How about one hundred years ago, or one hundred and fifty? Was it easier then?

It's always difficult comparing eras, but that doesn't mean we don't try. It's a common debate in sports: Was it easier to hit the ball in the majors in the 1920s than it is today? How has available technology improved our swings, our dunks, and our strokes? I ask myself similar questions as they relate to finding a job: Was it somehow easier in the past than it is today? If so—and that seems to be the case—what was different about the search and hire process then?

When comparing job-searching capabilities in different eras, the first thing we wonder is how people did it in the past without the Internet. How did they survive without access to instant information, LinkedIn, CareerBuilder, Monster.com, Indeed.com, and the countless other digital job boards? Maybe they were better off not having them. Maybe these so-called advances just get in the way; they cause us to narrow our focus too much. I feel certain of this conclusion: Finding work before the existence of the online world and interconnectivity on a global scale had to be a much more open-minded process for all participants than it is today, because it was not tied to matching hard skills to a job title. There were more opportunities for branching out, for applying the hard and soft skills you had to an area that was new to you.

Maybe in the past it was easier to gain access to open-minded employers and find ways to cross verticals than it is today because the recruitment and talent-acquisition process was different. Hard-skill matching has always existed, but there used to be a much more balanced approach to the evaluation process and interaction. The job search used to be a face-to-face, people-to-people process; today it is much less of both. We no longer even need to meet in person for job interviews. All we need is a computer or Smartphone and Skype.

Somewhere along the line, the talent-acquisition world narrowed its philosophy, and hard-skill matching became the dominant influence on hiring decisions. A person's soft skills, passion, and purpose were no longer among the decision criteria, or at least their importance was set at a very distant second. Was it people? Had the DNA of human beings changed? Or was it something more tangible and technological in nature that created a new platform for the job seekers, brokers, and holders?

In researching this topic, I came to find out pretty quickly that it wasn't people that had changed. As is often the case in history, the introduction of new technology ushered in unheard-of competitive barriers. For example, the Internet has brought competition for jobs to a global level, and those without online access or the skills to use it are at a profound disadvantage. Without the Internet, one is likely to be unable to find a job at all. The days of poring over the newspaper classifieds are long gone.

In this sense, the job search itself has become a very insular process in which the talent acquisition vertical is overwhelmingly reliant upon technology for job alignment at the expense of face-to-face interaction and a broader or deeper level of talent evaluation. This means a potential employer wants to see only your resume—your list of credentials and the hard skills you can do—and is not so much interested in how your management experience in mortgage sales can work just as well in consultative sales, or your personal passion for helping people understand their available opportunities and reach optimal solutions. All he wants to know is if you have the right degree and if you know how to run the software his company uses.

I call this inability to see the bigger employment picture the World of Myopia, and I found myself stuck there during my own job search. It seems like a nice place at first, with plenty of jobs to go around. But then you find out that unless you have the right keywords—that is, the right hard skills—none of them is open to you. Instead, they're locked up tight inside talent silos, or verticals that include only one specific job and are off limits to anyone without hard-skill experience in that job. Soft skills, much less your passions and interests, have no place here.

Still, I thought, no problem. Surely with all my sales and management success, I possessed any number of keywords that could unlock the talent silo, and find a job that was right for me. This would have happened if I'd been interested in staying within the same vertical. I'd started out in mortgage and financial services, and I had plenty of hard skills I'd learned there: B2B wholesale, mortgage underwriting, loan and financial analysis, mortgage processing, outside and inside sales prospecting, presentations, territory management, third-party vendor relationship building, recruiting, training, and management for the full employee life cycle of sales professionals. But what if I had wanted to change verticals and try my hand at medical sales or software sales? Would these keywords transfer with me?

Sadly, I found the answer was no. While those factory workers I knew in my youth could have taken their hard skills and potentially used them to land jobs in different fields, today the Internet and the infrastructure have changed the talent-acquisition business and mindset completely, creating a much narrower and more myopic process to the detriment of many. The lack of personal interaction within the job-search process and the facelessness of the talent silos have left little room for a worker to cross verticals, or to change professions to one rooted within his or her passions and specific sense of purpose.

In short, the good old days of interactive, in-person interviewing are gone. Expediency has become king. Interviews are no longer in-depth conversations about business in general and the potential employee's abilities and insights.

The end result has been a shift favoring hard-skill matching at the expense of soft-skill alignment, and the lost opportunities for both workers and employers are immeasurable. It was this shift in mindset that created the World of Myopia and gave rise to the talent silos.

World of Myopia

No Experience
No Entry

And what will break us out of this narrow shell? Nothing short of a paradigm shift on the part of the private sector. Those who are searching for jobs need opportunities to be heard, and that's a big challenge for companies. Not all will be willing to take on the risk or make the investment such change would require, only smart and unique employee-centric organizations that ultimately believe it's their people that make the real difference. My hope is that with this book I can contribute to an atmosphere in which we can marry the passion and purpose-filled job seeker with like-minded employee-centric businesses that are willing to invest their time in a more offline and in-depth hiring process that measures value beyond a hard-skill match denoted by a keyword on a piece of paper.

CHAPTER 2

THINGS CHANGE

We are living in a transitional period of history. Finding a job today is different and more challenging than it has ever been for a variety of reasons. Technological innovation has always disrupted the employment landscape. It was true for the buggy-whip salesman when the automobile went into mass production and for the agrarian worker when our country transformed into an industrial-based society. New entrants into the workforce have always created competitive pressure, such as when the U.S. experienced mass migration to our great cities or when women began working in large numbers. War too has always created upheaval for the U.S. workforce, from the Civil War, World War I, World War II, and Vietnam to the wars in Iraq and Afghanistan. Wars often create work related upheaval because once they end, there is typically a massive flood of returning veterans searching and competing for a limited number of jobs available. Last, there have always been economic boom and bust cycles that affect how we live and work in a myriad of ways.

The fundamental common thread between all these factors is that some workers adapt to the changes and overcome the obstacles and others do not. Sometimes this is due to the workers' wills; they simply do not want to change what they've been doing for so long. Sometimes they can't change because they lack the resources to do so—the training or equipment needed in order to progress to new careers. Those who are willing and able to adapt, however, don't have it much easier. They still face sometimes-insurmountable odds while trying to stay relevant, and it's only their tenacity and inner drive that keep them from giving up.

So what poses a greater challenge today than anything we've faced before? Why is changing verticals so much harder than it used to be? Technology may be to blame, but every generation has new inventions to assimilate into the culture. Wars have been going on since the dawn of time, so nothing's too new there. Really, any factor we've listed here could be seen as nothing new. There will always be boom and bust cycles, and there will always be new people or groups of people entering the workforce. None of these things are new to this country or to world's history in general, and they will always continue to serve as obstacles for dispossessed and dissatisfied workers.

What then makes adapting to today's competitive pressures so different from adapting to the pasts?

To answer that question, we first must understand the historical context of what has come before us to better understand where we are today and, to some extent, figure out and prepare for where we are going tomorrow.

Boom and Bust Cycles

A boom and bust cycle is a pattern over time wherein high prices in a particular market eventually spill out into the broader economy, followed by a flood of speculation by a great mass of people. Typically, in the beginning they find great success, and that attracts an even greater mass of people. The exuberance during the boom portion of the cycle is irrational—a concept made famous by Alan Greenspan, an economist and former chairman of the Federal Reserve. But the resulting glut of product ultimately fulfills the demand and even exceeds it, which drives the prices down and ends in a loss for most; needless to say, this kills the buzz the boom had created.

An example is the Great Recession that began in 2008, which was in large part the result of a classic boom and bust cycle in the financial services sector. The general public is most aware of the hyperinflation of home prices at the time and the subsequent crash of the real estate market. However, the boom and bust included far more than just mortgage-backed securities; it also included a wide range of very complex financial institutions that nearly destroyed the entire world economy overnight.

The United States is not alone in experiencing boom and bust cycles. They are in fact prevalent throughout world history. The most famous one, and in many respects the first one, was called the "tulip bubble," which occurred between 1636 and 1637. At the time, people in Europe were going crazy for tulips, and so demand for their bulbs was high. With that demand came a rise in prices; consumers were paying ridiculous amounts for a few flowers, and the sellers, mostly from the Ottoman Empire, were getting rich. However, what was true then is still true today: In the middle of the boom, the vendors thought (mistakenly) that the prices of tulips would never go down. But after a while, the flowers went out of vogue, and the majority of individuals and businesses selling the bulbs went bust.

History never ceases to repeat itself, and people and businesses will always believe the illusion that prices will continue to go up forever. See, for example:

- The railway mania of the 1840s
- The nineteenth-century era of the robber barons
- The Florida speculative-building bubble in 1926
- The American economic bubble of 1922 to 1929
- The dot-com bubble of 1995 to 2001
- The Asian financial crisis of 1997
- The United States housing bubble of 2007
- The commodity bubble of 2008

The cycle continues to repeat.

New Technology

Technology is often the catalyst for a boom and bust cycle. Inventions have always brought with them new jobs and innovative ways to do those jobs. The workers who understand how to adapt fare well, and others who cannot are left behind. Workers have always been challenged to redefine themselves, develop new skills, and adjust to the new demands and changes in their industries and eras.

Take a look at history. In the early twentieth century, Americans began to migrate from the farmlands to the cities, in large part because of their adaptation to new technology and the new markets it brought. This included the invention of steamboats to navigate the nation's rivers and railroads to connect towns to one another. People and goods could move from place to place quicker than they ever had, and with the ease of movement came an enormous amount of innovation and commerce.

During this transition we experienced a great number of boom and bust cycles, with ebbs and flows in employment, mass foreign migration, world wars, and an unprecedented degree of technological change. The workforce in this country was constantly challenged, but as difficult as the situation became for the American worker, at least the competitive pressures remained within our borders. The industries were new but the process of finding work remained the same, as most of these transitions happened before the advent of computerization and globalization.

Consider also inventions like planes, trains, and automobiles. With these came explosive growth in new jobs, and those who could make themselves relevant and valuable continued to thrive. All the buggy-whip sales jobs were lost with the mass production of the automobile, but the loss was more than made up for in opportunities revolving around the car business.

Technological innovation has a cycle. Something is invented, it takes years for it to become part of general society, and then it inevitably declines in use because something new comes along. Workers must follow this same cycle: If they're working in the vertical that serves that technology during its rise, they fare well when the technology remains profitable over a long period of time. When the jobs associated with that technology and the vertical serving it decline, some workers will find ways to relate their relevance to something new or similar. Others are not so lucky.

Consider next that globalization was possible only because of the invention of perhaps the ultimate technological platforms: the computer and the Internet. The combination of this new technology and its boom and bust cycle would forever change the talent acquisition space. For the purposes of this book, we are focusing on its effects on job searches and the talent acquisition space for the American worker.

The rise of the Internet and dot-com companies in the mid-'90s represented one of the biggest booms in our history until the so-called "dot-com bubble" became a bust in 2001. The boom created a massive amount of wealth for many, and the bust created just as much loss. In past booms and busts revolving around technology for specific job verticals, substantial amounts of workers were typically displaced and forced to adapt to a new way of making a living. In this instance, that trend did not come to pass. Unlike with other technologies, this boom and bust cycle did not leave in its wake a massive amount of unemployment. In fact, the technology was what gave rise to talent silos and helped form the current World of Myopia in which we operate.

When the bubble burst, it left behind an enormous technological infrastructure that stood ready and able to absorb the workforce that had very specific and valuable knowledge: the technology workers who had helped create the "dot-com bubble." This specific phenomenon created the talent silo. Those technological workers had the keywords required by employers that needed very specific hard-skill sets to add value to their organizations. The rise of the silos and their inherent databases full of hard-skill matches proved to be a great solution for a vertical demand needing highly skilled, ever-changing, and flexible workers. This was an era of data management, big data, demographic targeting, analytics, decision support, and a number of other solutions all designed to deliver targeted data at an effectiveness and speed never before imagined. That efficiency would prove to be extremely valuable for so many verticals but also had the unintended consequence of creating the World of Myopia, the rise of the talent silos and their keywords, and an inevitable mindset change in how workers would come to be valued by the job-search and employer community. Expediency over value would become our generation's opportunity cost.

The high-tech space is one area in which talent silos are perfect for brokering human talent, and the use of keywords is the perfect formula for it. The problem today is that the rest of the business community searches the World of Myopia for nearly all jobs.

Globalization

American workers have always faced competitive pressures for jobs at home because of immigration, but globalization, largely facilitated by technology, has posed new and unique challenges. Never before have we had to compete with the world's population in such a way.

Before the age of the Internet, U.S. workers could at least count on having to compete only with other U.S. workers. Globalization brought about a shift in power between workers and businesses by creating a much larger pool of potentials from which employers could choose. There was more supply than demand. The result was a weakened position for the American worker, who now had to compete against people all over the world.

Ironically, globalization has led employers to become increasingly narrow minded in their searches for new employees. Because the talent pool is so large, they can and even must be choosier, since looking at every candidate would take too long. This means they will be more likely to look for hard-skill matches instead of soft-skill experience, and expediency wins out over quality. That mindset, along with employers' use of the Internet platform for the entire talent-acquisition process, is what sends job seekers right into the World of Myopia.

A job that can effectively be done anywhere in the world is no longer a phenomenon. The Bureau of Labor Statistics, in fact, estimates that one fifth of U.S. workers are in industries subject to off shoring. This is another way in which technology, as always, has created new ways of doing things, and workers in general have had to adapt. The remote workforce is growing, and technology continues to innovate in a global economy; we can expect it to remain as a means of competitive pressure in the future.

Economic Turmoil

Globalization brings added competitive pressure and innovation forces adaptation, but economic calamity is another factor with which the workforce in general must contend. We live in a market society, and the world has seen its share of cyclical economies; depressions and recessions are not new to the United States. The lengths of the cycles have been shorter in more recent times, mostly because the growth of government services and our position in the world have acted as buffers against longer, more painful cycles. Our modern government is better equipped than it used to be to handle the harsh effects brought on by bust portions of the cycle.

The Great Recession of 2008 was a traumatic event in our history, but it was not unique. The Great Depression followed the crazy exuberance of the stock market in the roaring 1920s. As in other boom and bust cycles, people thought the stock market would never go down—until it did. How little had changed almost eighty years later, when—with 1920s-style exuberance—many people in this country thought that home prices would not possibly drop. The bust came in the form of financial weapons of mass distraction: modern-day innovations and instruments such as CDO's, derivatives, deregulation, and a legislative landscape that favored and supported home ownership. All these factors worked together to create the perfect storm for a classic boom and bust cycle.

Just how often do we suffer through economic turmoil? Some economists say there have been as many as forty-seven recessions in the United States since 1790. Some last just a few months, while severe recessions can go on for years. In general, people become fearful, anxious, and spend less. The net result is that joblessness goes up; unemployment is one of the most recognizable indicators that we are in a recession. With the Great Depression, the U.S. unemployment rate jumped to 25%; in other areas of the world, it went as high as 33%. Fortunately, joblessness in the United States during the Great Recession peaked at 10%.

War

Just like booms and busts, recessions and depressions, new technology and innovation, and the competitive pressure brought upon us by foreign migration and globalization, war is an unfortunate cyclical and common obstacle for the American worker.

War has often served as a trend marker for the unemployed and the dispossessed, and tends to follow a classic boom and bust economic cycle. War is actually good for an economy, at least while it is being waged. The recession of 1913 and 1914 came to an end in large part because of the onset of World War I and the ensuing huge international demand for American-made goods. However, that war came to an end in 1918. What followed? A recession, in part because the supplies we manufactured for consumers around the world were no longer needed. In addition, the market became flooded with job seekers because the U.S. soldiers came home and had to find work to support their families. Our military employed 2.9 million people in 1918 and just 380,000 two years later—meaning an additional 2.52 million men and women were back at home and looking for employment opportunities.

Which leads one to wonder: Where did those 2.52 million dispossessed and unemployed soldiers go to find work? What was the job search experience and process like for them? How was it different from or similar to today? I wonder if employers looked at a veteran's hard skills—assembling and firing rifles, for example—as measures of his or her value. If not, then how did the former soldier relate and transfer value? Was it difficult to define and communicate back then?

Eventually, the unemployment rate skyrocketed, but fortunately didn't last long; by 1923 it had dropped to just 2.4%, thanks in some part to the federal government, which came to the aid of U.S. workers by creating job programs with the leaders of industry. At the time, it was a great means of easing the pain of the American workforce, but it would become the template for future employment problems.

The record-low unemployment rate in 1923 gave everyone the sense that life would be great forever—irrational exuberance, for sure. But the war to end all wars was over, and the economy was on fire. Why would they have thought anything else?

Then came the crash of 1929, which cost investors millions. Never before or since did this country suffer so much. Unemployment skyrocketed to as high as 25%, and millions of people lost their savings and their jobs. The New Deal and other government programs provided some relief, but only the onset of World War II brought us back into the boom phase of the cycle. Again there was demand for American-made goods, as this new and bigger war in Europe erupted. The world needed American factories, and the manufacturing and technological demands of the world changed the makeup of the American workforce forever.

At that point in time, agricultural work was still a big part of our economy. But big business, big machines, and big cities would serve as platforms for a changing and transitioning workforce. While people like my grandfather went to war, Rosie the Riveter and Farmer Joe went to work in the factories and in doing so learned new skills. How different the talent acquisition landscape must have been! Demand was enormous, and I doubt there was any time to spend in the World of Myopia, pursuing only candidates with exact hard-skill matches. Jobs had to be filled, and employers were willing to hire based on soft skills and train in the hard ones. Talent silos had yet to emerge; a worker could demonstrate his or her relevance with a handshake and the promise of a hard day's work.

In 1944, as WWII raged on, the unemployment rate in the United States was just 1.2%. The world was on fire and Europe was in ruins, but American workers had no problem finding their jobs of choice.

New Entrants into the Workforce

The mass migration of immigrants and women into the U.S. workforce was a competitive obstacle as the face of the work landscape changed. At the turn of the twentieth century, immigrants were coming to the shores of the United States in droves. During the depression of the 1890s, we'd welcomed only 3.5 million immigrants into the country; that number jumped incredibly to 9 million during the first decade of the 1900s, mostly from Eastern and Southern Europe but also from Canada and Latin America. After that, immigration saw its own booms and busts depending upon the economics of the times, wars, and the immigration restrictions our government imposed during the 1920s.

Still, immigrants became a vital sector of the American workforce. Since many were leaving their own countries to escape religious, racial, or political persecution; famine; or poor economies, they came here willing to work, and so they did. Immigrants have long been known for building this nation's railroads and farming its lands, though many also crowded into our already crowded cities hoping to find the American dream for themselves.

Likewise, women joined the workforce out of basic necessity. Though women had been working in factories, textile mills, and assembly lines since the nineteenth century, by the beginning of the twentieth century, their roles in society had changed, and they were no longer viewed as viable workers; according to the National Bureau of Economic Research, in 1900 women made up less than 20% of the entire U.S. workforce; they were meant to marry, have children, and to be arbiters of society's morality.

At the same time, educational opportunities for women were opening up, creating a new class of women who were much savvier than their predecessors and ready to step into employee roles. When World War I brought increased demand from Europe for goods produced in America, more women found themselves working outside the home and happily accepted factory and assembly jobs; at the end of the war, some returned to their homes and family responsibilities, but many went on to stay in the workforce as salespeople, secretaries, and other "lace collar" workers.

World War II had a similar affect on women in the workforce—who can forget Rosie the Riveter and her "we can do it" attitude? More than ever before, women were vital to the American economy as they filled in the sixteen million jobs left vacant by men. When the war ended, two million of them lost their jobs to returning veterans and layoffs, but many more continued, keeping female employment at an all-time high.

By 1953, women made up 31% of the overall American workforce. Today, they make up nearly half. Unlike earlier in the twentieth century, women remain in the labor force during displacement and compete for jobs on nearly the same level as men do—an improvement to be sure, but a reality with which our ancestors did not have to contend.

The hard facts

According to a 2012 Society for Human Resources Management (SHRM) industry survey, 63% of employees learn the skills required to do their jobs while on the job. Approximately 38% of companies said they cross-train employees to develop skills not directly related to their jobs, down from 43% in 2011 and 55% in 2008.

The bottom-line trend is that companies have been cutting their employee training programs to save costs. The net result is that they are more likely to search the open marketplace for hard-skill matched talent as opposed to cross-training and developing talent from within. That unfortunate trend is a major factor in creating the newer phenomenon of the long-term unemployed in modern times and a contributing factor to the World of Myopia and its fields of talent silos. Companies are leaving behind a generation of talent that could in many instances provide more complete, long-term matches.

Employers used to hire the person and train for the skill. I think we would all be a lot better off if we could somehow get back to that mindset. Employers would benefit from rewarding and supporting passion and sense of purpose in their existing employees and prospective new hires. People who are willing to put in the preparation and planning necessary to reinvent themselves represent the very best of soft skills, which can be every bit as valuable as hard skills. Workers can be taught the hard skills needed to make them effective. Employers simply need to be less myopic in their hiring and have the longer-term mindset that hiring the right person is worth the short-term investment in training.

In today's job market, there has been a shift in what is deemed valuable as it relates to prospective employees. Toward the end of 2012, just over 40% of the unemployed had been looking for work for at least twenty-seven weeks, near the record of 45.5% from about a year and a half earlier. The average between 1987 and 2007 was just above 16%, and during previous recessions it was between 20 and 25%. Why the huge jump? I've already mentioned the attitude of today's business community and its penchant for placing less emphasis on training and more on hard-skill matching through talent-silo searching. We are living in a time of transition, and the level of difficulty in finding jobs of choice is higher than it has ever been before.

Certain skills always become obsolete as technology evolves; workers in the United States have always been insulated by the fact that our jobs remained within our borders. That is no longer true in this age of globalization and a fully developed, Internet-based job market. Some jobs can now be done from anywhere in the world. Globalization is in full force, and the private sector has chosen to ignore the value of the dispossessed and dissatisfied. Those workers have been locked out of the World of Myopia and its talent silos, left to drift aimlessly in the Internet, never to be seen because they lack the keywords, which are the keys to the kingdom.

I don't contend that there is anything inherently wrong with talent silos. In fact, I think their designed efficiency makes fantastic business sense and serves a great purpose for a wide variety of needs through-out the greater economic landscape. Some job profiles simply require very specific skill sets, especially technology-based positions. Talent silos are perfect for those. I contend only that the unintended consequence has been that the silo effect is acting as a barrier against the greater workforce that include a large number of dissatisfied and dispossessed American workers.

CHAPTER 3

APPLES AND ORANGES

When I was very young, a business professional told me that the key to success in sales was to recognize and understand the differences in people. That wise man was my uncle Attilio, who owned a very successful gold and jewelry distributorship based out of Milan, Italy. He retired before he turned fifty and now splits his time between his mountain home, the Italian Riviera, and Spain, living comfortably off his investments.

In his time, Attilio acted in a wholesale B2B capacity, and sold his merchandise as a supplier to various retailers throughout Italy. The decision to buy his product was not a complex one; it was primarily a short sales cycle, but it was built upon his ability to create and maintain relationships over the long term—his second key to foundational success, the core element of which was his ability to recognize and understand the differences in people. He understood that needs and expectations are different from person to person and from business to business and that how he positioned himself based on those differences would mean success.

Not everyone could do my uncle's job; even having experience in selling gold or jewelry would not translate to automatic success. But that is the way the online talent-acquisition landscape would prioritize. Say there were two resumes. One had hard-skill alignment keywords such as the following:

- Sales
- Wholesale
- B2B

- Relationships
- Short to medium sales cycle
- Territory building
- Hunting and farming
- Years of experience in a sales capacity within a gold and jewelry distributorship business

And the other focused more on soft skills:

- Passion for gold and jewelry
- Enjoys working with a tangible product as opposed to a conceptual idea or service
- Prefers to know who his customer will be on a day-to-day basis
- Prefers a narrow sphere of influence for the sales process
- Prefers selling to business owners
- Appreciates interactions with professionals as opposed to laymen
- Strong work ethic and attitude
- Is most comfortable working within a repetitive set of processes

To which do you think the employer would assign more weight? Probably the hard skills, but it would be to his or her detriment to discount the soft skills. That approach could end poorly and cost the prospective employer far more in the long run because even a perfect hard-skill match might not be the right person for the job. The cost to onboard and train someone is expensive, and too many companies today are okay with taking that risk. The end result might be a lost generation of quality value alignment, all for the sake of expediency.

The simple tenet "recognize and understand the differences in people" has stayed with me all of my adult life and has become part of the framework from which I built my own template for success. This key and an in-depth level of self-awareness are the foundation for knowing how to position you for success in sales and in business. A person's foundational values, passions, and desires, when properly aligned with the basic needs and expectations of a like-minded organization, represent the true value and opportunity for transferable relevance, or the idea that one's skills (hard or soft) and passions in one vertical can be utilized just as efficiently and effectively in a different vertical.

The problem that exists today is that the talent-acquisition and decision-making processes are inequitable and out of balance as they relate to a person's true value. Today's dissatisfied or dispossessed worker will rarely if ever get a chance to communicate and relate his or her relevance to anyone. The World of Myopia and its talent silos have become increasingly impenetrable because the technological infrastructure favors expediency over quality analysis. The reliance upon hard skills at the expense of soft ones is creating a massive loss of opportunity and increase in cost for both employees and employers. Never before has there been such a large disconnect.

Like-Minded Organizations

What percentage of the population would like to have a chance to do something else for a living? Some studies indicate that up to 80% of workers are dissatisfied with what they are currently doing. Even if you exclude all the people who perhaps don't like to work in general, it's still a huge indication that there may be a massive misalignment between the work people do and the work they might actually like doing. How many people would like an opportunity to step back, take an internal self-awareness assessment of their foundational skill sets and values, and match them with their highest sense of inner purpose and passion? How many people would like the chance to have a conversation with a like-minded organization that is willing to evaluate their true value in a more in-depth and equitable way that goes far beyond a hard-skill keyword match?

A like-minded organization puts people at the heart of what makes the business a success. These organizations take the long view and have a heavy emphasis on investing in their employees. They would rather take the time to pick the right person and are willing to forgo expediency for the sake of enduring value. Turnover is lower here than at the average company, as these organizations invest heavily in training and a culture in which leadership takes its share of responsibility in the success or failure of the people it hires.

I wish I could say that like-minded organizations are typical in our society. However, the overall pattern of today's talent-acquisition vertical shows that most companies believe investing their time and resources in the World of Myopia is most efficient for their bottom lines. To do otherwise would fly directly in the face of their own self-perceptions.

In some instances, organizations just may not know what they don't know, and that's how they end up in Myopia, pulling talent from the all-too-narrow talent silos. These organizations invest a far greater amount of time and resources into a narrow hiring process. They sometimes end up losing out on higher-value match targets that ultimately may transfer into a greater return on investment (ROI). Just think how well that investment might be if they took their time and hired the right person.

Apples Need Not Apply

Let's look at this idea of transferable relevance in terms of apples and oranges—the proverbial standard for how important it is to appreciate our differences.

In one sense, apples and oranges are essentially the same thing: They are both fruits. Similarly, someone working in wholesale can be counted in the same class as a B2B salesperson. Both come from the same industry but have found their niches in one particular silo.

Could an apple do the job of the orange? If we're looking just at hard skills, the comparison is easy. Both apples and oranges

- Are round
- Are fruits
- Are juicy
- Taste good
- Are good for you

At a very basic, foundational level, these are the five things both jobs—that of being an apple and that of being an orange—require. The only difference between an apple and an orange, then, is the keyword. If you are looking for a job in a talent silo full of oranges, having *orange* on your resume will be the equivalent of hitting the lottery; for *apple*, not so much. A business pursuing expediency and short-term cost savings will look only for the keyword it desires, following the myopic process at the detriment of its long-term ROI.

I ran into a very smart apple one day at a local coffee shop. We talked about the weather and sports, and then, of course, we talked about jobs. He asked me if I'm one of those people who think apples can't do what oranges do.

I told him, "On the contrary, I think they can."

He agreed, saying he'd always wanted to do what the oranges do— that in fact his inner passion and purpose were more closely and deeply aligned with some of the oranges' jobs than the oranges' were! He'd been adequately compensated for the work he'd done in his life, but deep down he'd always felt unfulfilled. He felt certain that doing the job of an orange was the only thing that could satisfy the void inside him.

The biggest problem, though, was that he couldn't get anyone to hear him out. "If you're not an exact match for the prototype profiled in the job description, you have no chance even to be heard," he told me.

I asked him, "What would you tell these hiring companies if you had the chance?"

He replied, "I would tell them five simple things: I'm round, I'm a fruit, I'm juicy, I taste good, and I'm good for you. Now, what can an orange do that I can't?"

The apple felt strongly that if he were simply given an audience in the World of Myopia, he could effectively convey his transferable relevance across the continuum of value. He was positive that his level of passion, purpose, and desire could differentiate him from most oranges.

He concluded, "Anything an orange can do, an apple can do too, and may even do it better."

At that, I had to smile. "I think you're right," I told him. All he wanted was a chance to align his inner purpose and passion with an organization that was open to hearing what he had to say. And all he needed was something to help him recognize his true foundational value and provide a template for communicating his transferable relevance for the position of his choice.

PART II: THE PYRAMID

CHAPTER 4

PAUL'S PYRAMID OF P'S

I believe that each of us has a built-in framework for success and a foundational value. As mentioned, the original goal of this book was to help you as individual job seekers understand how to internalize your transferable relevance so you can achieve an optimal alignment between your professional objectives and your inner purpose and passions. I achieved cross-vertical success, and I want other people to know they can do it too.

Then, as usually happens as we grow and gain new experiences, my thoughts on the topic evolved into taking a deeper dive into providing the basis for structural sales education. As the book is educational in nature, it focuses on 3 primary areas. The Pyramid acts as a communication template for job seekers, a sales readiness template for sales people or those wanting to be one, and then also acts as the guideline or parameter for any company willing to do an internal sales audit of it's sales related infrastructure and processes. I realized this tool I was developing based on years of success and experimentation crossing multiple verticals—called Paul's Pyramid of P's —could serve multiple purposes:

1. The Pyramid can act as a key **communication template** to help individual job seekers understand how to recognize, internalize, and convey their transferable relevance for job profiles that are rooted within their very specific sense of passion and purpose. The template also serves as the guideline for the **self-audit** exercise as well.
2. The Pyramid can act as a **sales readiness template** for individual sales professionals and organizations.

3. The Pyramid as a sales readiness template also serves as a **sales operating system** from which any sales methodology can be prescribed and applied. It is the science and architecture behind creating a framework for long-term, sustained success.

4. The pyramid and template could also serve as the perfect guideline and tool for any business willing to perform an internal **sales audit.** The sales audit is a means for evaluating its current infrastructure as it relates to measuring its ability to actually support the expectations placed upon the sales force in a sustainable way. Companies today too often prescribe the wrong sales methodology and at the same time do not take the time to ensure that their infrastructure is actually capable of meeting the sales objectives.

Each level of the pyramid, which will be discussed in subsequent chapters, works exactly the same for each of these entities: job seekers, sales professionals, those who want to be sales professionals, and businesses that want a sales readiness template so their sales professionals will have a ready-to-go, built-in framework designed to ensure sustained success.

Paul's Pyramid of P's is not a magic formula. It cannot and will not act as a replacement for hard work and attitude. The Pyramid can't force you to wake early up in the morning, work late, or take the time to differentiate yourself from others with the preparation it takes to achieve success. Nobody can force you to write a business plan in preparation for an interview, or do the level of study required to convey the in-depth knowledge necessary for targeting a job or vertical. The tools and exercises cannot force a sales professional to make one more stop, one more call, or to leave the house earlier than the competition.

The attitude that you are willing to do whatever it takes and the work ethic to follow through are a combination of what your parents taught you, your DNA, and your personal desire. However, I can guarantee that Paul's Pyramid of P's can act as an incredibly impact-full communication template and structural model—a blueprint for your current and future success—whether you're an individual seeking a job, a sales professional looking to refocus your basic processes, or a business entity willing to perform an internal sales audit as it seeks to create sustainable success for its sales force.

Paul's Pyramid of P's™

- Positioning — The Key To Context
- Pricing
- Product — Performance Equation =
- Process
- Present — What You Do Every Day
- Profile
- Prospect
- Planning — Off Peak Time
- Preparation

Paul's Pyramid of P's and all of the associated ideas, concepts, and tools are designed for sales-related activity, and the Pyramid can be applied to much more than a single sales vertical. However, it's always easier to understand the context of a solution if you can envision it within real-world examples, so for simplicity's sake I have chosen to focus the solution as narrowly as possible on sales in the transportation vertical. In the coming chapters, I will present each level of the P's as seen through the eyes and the experiences of a single family over the course of several generations. I'll demonstrate their discovery and ultimate implementation of the Pyramid of P's, along with a number of other associated exercises and tools as they attempt to overcome the obstacles unique to their historical eras. We will explore their challenges and actions as they adapt to changing technology, economic turmoil, the upheavals of war, and other competitive forces as they attempt to overcome the barriers presented when crossing job verticals.

This country is no stranger to ups and downs, booms and busts, war and suffering, and technological innovation. In short, we have gone through and continue to go through our fair share of change. If we've had one constant, it's the American worker's ongoing need to adapt to all these changes and more, from new job responsibilities due to a changing market to reentry into the workforce upon returning from a war or sharing one's workspace with an influx of newcomers to the field. Whether you're an individual sales professional needing a sales readiness template, a business needing to create the same for employees, or a job seeker looking to relate your relevance, your ability to adapt will play an important role at every level of the Pyramid—and determine how successfully you are able to implement it as a whole.

Although the idea remains the same—that no matter the obstacle, there will always be something to which we must adapt—I will argue that the modern-day challenges facing dissatisfied and dispossessed workers are in many ways harder than ever. Out of all possible modes of change an individual salesperson, job seeker, or business might encounter, today's technological advances are among the most challenging. Technological change itself is nothing new; our forefathers had to change from using horse-drawn buggies to steamboats to railroads to meet their business-related transportation needs. Technology always has been and always will be a major component of sales-related activity in the past, in the modern era, and in the future.

In the midst of this ever-changing world, the Pyramid is a solid, constant platform from which you can create your own success. The key is simply learning to recognize, understand, and truly internalize your existing or chosen work environment in a fundamental way, as outlined by the P's, so that when it comes time to prescribe and utilize the most applicable sales methodology for your particular vertical, your likelihood for sustained success is high. The Pyramid is a static, unchanging framework on which you will build, no matter in what direction you decide to take your life. Regardless of what you fill in your framework with—SPIN selling, or Miller Heiman's strategic selling, or The Challenger Sale for example—it remains the same. People and businesses change their buying strategies, but the fundamentals of positioning a process, product, or price have not changed a bit. The framework for success—and thus the Pyramid—always remains the same despite the obstacles one faces, whether it's the rise of the rivers, the rise of the rails, the rise of the roads, or the rise of the silos. In each instance, these venues brought us a new highway for commerce, but it was not until the rise of the cyber highway that American workers lost their visibility and their ability to communicate their relevance when traversing those roads.

Many would argue that for all the complexity we attribute to the art of sales, and however complex the selling and buying processes become, the science of sales does not fundamentally change. My P's are a great illustration of that point. We can find an endless parade of new psychologies and methodologies on bookstore shelves and in classrooms, telling salespeople that this latest and greatest way of talking, walking, listening, and influencing is the new key to success for today's modern problems. And some of it is great; I don't mean to knock it all. The way salespeople engage and interact does indeed change over time, and the art of the sale does matter. However, the ultimate constant yesterday, today, and tomorrow, is adherence to the science. The Pyramid is that science.

My Pyramid of P's makes it obvious that there are universal basics and foundational values that are transferable across the continuum of sales, from the most basic to the most complex of sales processes and circumstances. Within Paul's Pyramid of P's are the keys to Myopia, to the silos, and to anywhere outside those silos. You just have to apply the science of the P's and get ready to search, evaluate, talk, and work. The key to building your framework for success is really as simple as that.

CHAPTER 5

PREPARATION

Preparation is the big-picture stage; it creates the foundation for everything that will come. All levels of the P's will leverage the information you obtain during the preparation process, which is the same for the sales professional, the business, and the job candidate seeking to relate his or her relevance. In each instance, the sales readiness template, which begins with preparation, is done with knowledge aforethought that everything you do and gather will define the true essence of how you or the company you work for or want to work for will be positioned in the marketplace. When a salesperson has an in-depth understanding of how he or she is positioned in a marketplace, all the related activity going forward will increase in efficiency and effectiveness. The goal is to make all of your day-to-day and long-term activities as optimally effective as possible and translate them into sustained success.

But what is preparation? What does it look like in real terms? Let's look at an example.

Say it's the year 3035, and somehow Alien life forms have found a way to live on the moon. So you're up there, and you're looking down at the Earth, and you're thinking, *Hey, there are a lot of rocks around here. I bet people back on Earth—those who don't live on the moon—would like to have some.*

Thus you've created your sales objective: to get to Earth and find a market for selling some really cool moon rocks. Now your first choice exists:

1) Get in your rocket ship and fly to Earth without giving it much thought—basically the attitude is *I'll figure it out when I get there.*

What can happen in this scenario? You can hit the Earth's atmosphere and burn up. You can smash into a mountain and explode. You can crash into this weird substance called ocean water, sink, and drown. You can fall into a jungle and perhaps be eaten by a tiger or maybe even cannibals.

Even if you land safely, you might find out that you can't breathe Earth's oxygen, and you forgot your breathing apparatus. The end result is failure as a space sales alien. Oh, and you're dead.

Picture the human sales role the same way: A person can walk into a building, pick up a phone, send an email, meet a person on the street or at an event, and just start talking. The problem is he or she may be the wrong person to talk to, and you may be saying all the wrong things in a very poor way. The result here will be that you have wasted your entire day; you made no impressions, or bad impressions on people who may or may not care; and in a very short amount of time, you may likely go broke and be fired.

So, flying a spaceship to Earth by the seat of your pants is the same thing. The missing ingredient is *preparation.* And in either scenario— whether you're selling moon rocks or yourself as a potential employee— it's always wiser to make the second choice:

2) Have the proper attitude and work ethic. Make an investment in yourself, and differentiate yourself with a willingness to take the opportunity in front of you seriously. Make a conscious decision to **prepare.** It's going to make an impression on anyone you engage with, whether you're an existing sales professional, a business that believes in having sales readiness as part of its infrastructure, or a job seeker looking to relate your relevance to an employment opportunity.

When beginning the process of preparation, all salespeople, job seekers, and business representatives must think about the quality of engagement they are going to have with their prospects, their employees, their clients, or, in the job seeker's case, the hiring managers. Too often, the common thread between the three groups is a failure to prepare. If your objective is to find success, then take a step back and make an investment in the preparation process and yourself. That preparation will help ensure that all of your future engagements at every level will be worthwhile for all involved.

Preparation is a comprehensive, deep-dive discovery process of gathering information on a vertical, space, and company in which you are interested in seeking employment; in which you are currently employed in a sales capacity and interested in improving your performance; or in which you are the existing leadership and are looking to create a readiness template or framework that can ensure long-term, sustained success for any current or future salespeople. Whether it's today or in 1840, a sales professional, a job seeker, and any business hoping to have success has to go through the exhaustive process of researching, gathering, evaluating, and filtering through as much data as possible from as many sources as possible, using whatever means or platforms that are available for the respective era. The means and methods of preparation have evolved over time, but not the value nor the process of preparation. The task of research, the task of gathering, the task of aggregating, and the task of filtering the data has not changed. The research platforms have evolved and as an example, the tools used today provide the same results, albeit at lightning speed.

Today the most important tool we have for this information-gathering phase is the Internet, which allows us not just to collect, but also to disseminate and utilize data at speeds unheard of prior to its creation. Online resources we can use to find out about companies or verticals in which we are interested include search engines such as Google and Yahoo! Along with information brokers such as Hoover's or other data aggregators. And when we are through gathering, there are more tools to support us in recording, studying, analyzing, and evaluating the information.

In the past our preparation phases have relied on various platforms for gathering and filtering data. The tools change over time. Today for example, our tools include but are not limited to the following:

- Programs like **Word** and **Excel** are often used for documentation. These applications can serve as storage files for what we've learned as we begin the organization process. That process will eventually lead to the evaluation and analysis portions of the preparation stage.
- **Databases** that can hold unlimited amounts of data (especially if they're in the cloud) that can be accessed at lightning speed from all sorts of platforms, including mobile devices. Databases give sales professionals easy access to information that can help them identify ideal profile sales targets, while job seekers can get up-to-date access on particular companies in which they are interested.
- **Social media** such as Facebook, LinkedIn, and Twitter are invaluable in the preparation phase and in fact throughout Paul's Pyramid of P's. Job seekers can use social media to research organizations that maintain active presences on these and other online forums. Sales professionals can use them as tools to generate sales and gather data on competition and potential customers. Businesses can utilize social media sites for the same purposes and to explore if these are viable outlets that will help them increase sales.
- **Outsourcing** works for just about any task at any level of the Pyramid. Outsourcing is actually a tactic more than it is a tool. Outsourcing can be especially valuable during the preparation stage, as resources such as virtual assistants can be utilized not only to help with research and gathering data, but also to remove tactical burdens such as phone calls and emails, so you can concentrate on your revenue producing strategic objectives.

A good salesperson, candidate for hire, or organizational decision-maker will start the preparation phase with his or her own discovery process. This means reading everything you can find having anything to do with the vertical, the space, and the company in which you will be interacting. Some of the modern-day factors to be considered are included in the following list, which represents a small sample of the kind of information one would want to research, collect, and evaluate. The list is by no means complete and comprehensive.

- **The vertical**: For example, medical. What are the micro and macro trends? Is the vertical mature? Is it growing? Is it in decline? What are some of the common strengths, weaknesses, opportunities, and threats?
- **The space within the vertical**: For example, patient monitoring. What are the common macro and micro trends? How does this particular space compare to other spaces within the vertical? Does this space fall in line with your overall short-and long-term objectives? Why and why not? What is the history of this particular space on both national and local levels? What are some of the strengths, weaknesses, opportunities, and threats?
- **The specific company in which you're interested**: For example, a medical device supply company. Whether you're going to try to sell to it, already work for it, or it's your own company, there are certain things you must know. How is it structured? Does it have the tools and all the major technology of the day (e.g., sales automation, CRM, marketing support, technical support, service support) in place to succeed? You'll want to perform a full external sales audit and evaluation of the marketing, sales, and operations departments, including evaluations of their abilities to communicate across the continuum. Is each department communicating the branding and messaging in lockstep and in a coordinated way? If so, you can rest assured that the organization knows and understands who it is and probably has a good sense of its positioning in the marketplace. That's a good thing in most circumstances.

    Further, what are its history, objectives, trends, goals, mission, and vision? What kind of reputation does its culture have? What can you expect from a compensation standpoint? How many, if any, of these things are aligned with your personal and professional objectives? A full SWOT analysis of the company in scope is a must. An in-depth evaluation of its performance equation, its positioning, and differentiators as they relate to their products, processes, and price points is a must.

- **Any competitors**: Study all of this company's direct competition. For example, if you are seeking a job selling anesthesia machines to hospitals, evaluate other medical device companies selling the same. Go to their websites. Go to their trade shows and networking events. Talk to people who work at those companies and people who do business with those companies. Read their case studies, white papers, and reviews. Talk to former employees and anyone you can find who has something to say about it. Perform a full SWOT analysis of the primary competition to evaluate strengths, weaknesses, opportunities, and threats not just for competitors but also for yourself, and determine your overall positioning in the marketplace. Evaluate the competitor's processes, products, and pricing to get an overall understanding of the value proposition based performance equation and positioning in the vertical and the space.

- **Any indirect competitors**: Not all competitors are direct; just because they don't sell the same widget does not mean they are not in competition with you or the company in which you are interested. Indirect competitors sell within the same vertical and space and perhaps sell different products, but they still pose threats because you each compete for the same budget dollars and resources. For example, one company sells plastic tubing for oxygen administration to hospitals; another sells the tanks that store the oxygen. Different products, but both companies are competing for the hospital's dollars. This makes them competitors. As you can't study every single indirect competitor in the universe, narrow it down just to the ones you know are selling to your target base and profile. Take the same approach as you did to gathering data and researching.

- How and to what extent the company utilizes **analytics and decision support software applications**. As a job seeker or current sales professional looking to migrate to a different vertical, I want to know how the company at which I want to obtain a position would use these tools to help me create sales opportunities. As a business I would want to evaluate whether I should invest in such technology to help my current or future salespeople.

- The methods and tools the company utilizes in **lead generation**. Does it generate consumer interest for its products or services online? Does it rely more heavily on offline tools such as personal referrals, cold calling, advertising, or events? As an individual job seeker, I want to know if the hard or soft skills I already possess align with the company's current practices; as a business, I want not only to keep abreast of how and what the competition is doing but find out what I can do to get a few steps ahead. As a sales professional, I am very interested in evaluating their processes and methodologies for opportunity creation. Does the company support me with marketing and/or telemarketing? Does that distinction even make a difference in this vertical, this space, and this particular company? These are the typical questions I will be researching in order to evaluate the results.

- To what extent the company utilizes **search engine optimization (SEO)**—a modern-day tool to raise the level of awareness for search results online. Does SEO matter for your chosen vertical, space, and company? It might make a big difference for a small company with little brand-name recognition but would perhaps not matter to a large brand name like Coca-Cola. Again, the point is to put the time into researching, evaluating, and internalizing useful information so you can use the results to meet your personal and professional objectives.

However, just for the sake of example, let's assume your target company operates within the small-business widget space and has very little or no widespread brand-name recognition. As a job seeker, you'll want to evaluate whether the company in which you're interested is serious about SEO and using it to its full advantage as a gauge of its commitment to helping their employees create sales. As a sales professional, you can investigate what SEO is and how it works in order to judge if it can help you in your efforts to create sales. And as a business, you want to know how keeping up with SEO best practices can help your current and future salespeople and your company as a whole.

- How the company uses **advertising** to generate business. Here you would evaluate the company's advertising model not only for effectiveness but also for importance. Not every business needs to rely on a heavy marketing budget for advertising campaigns. But again, for just example's sake, let's assume you are researching a small company that does rely on its marketing and advertising team for success in supporting its employees' efforts in sales opportunity creation. Does it utilize affiliate networks, ad exchanges, and other digital online tools? Or does it go the old-school offline route? As a business owner or decision maker, what tools would *you* use to create a market where you can sell your goods and services? As a job seeker, of course, you want to evaluate a potential employer's advertising efforts to ensure you're going for a company with proven methods to create high visibility and opportunity creation.

- How the company handles **customer relationship management (CRM)**. There are many configurable and customized ways for individuals and businesses to support their sales efforts. For example, cloud systems such as Salesforce and Sage can support sales professionals' prospecting efforts with email campaigns, tracking opportunities in the pipeline, managing their contacts, etc. Does the company you're researching have a CRM? If so, which one? If not, does that really matter? Say your targeted account is extremely small; you might not care whether or not there's a CRM in place because a small account base might be more easily and efficiently managed without one. The key here is to research all of the proper questions so you can evaluate the companies and your overall positioning properly and utilize that knowledge to make good choices.

As an individual applying for a position, these are things you want to know in order to ascertain if you have any hard- or soft-skill matches; if they use Salesforce, and so did you at your previous job, that is a relevance you can and should relate. If you're in a business, look into CRM to determine if you need to make an investment in it for your salespeople. (Not every business needs one.) That's part of the research and discovery process—finding out if we need one or not.

- The company's experience with **sales automation.** Does it have, for example, a customized interface linking its CRM system to an external firm that provides an email delivery service? Does that even matter? If not, why not? How does it remove the burden of manual, mundane tasks from its employees so they can focus on what's most important: selling? Job seekers should evaluate this area, as it's favorable to work for a company that excels at automation. Current salespeople can evaluate if and what kind of sales automation will help them make more sales. Perhaps it provides tracking mechanisms and a package that includes software applications for analytics to give you meaningful feedback on effectiveness. You can then use that information to create better ways to automate sales-related activity and thus create a system for more effective repetitive processes. These are things you could research and evaluate during the preparation phase. If you represent a business, you'll want to evaluate the marketplace as a whole to determine if sales automation is worth the investment—will it help their existing and future salesforce increase their output?

A sales-professional, job candidate, or business representative will call, visit, and communicate however possible (verbally or written) with other sales professionals in the vertical, space, and target or subject company he or she is exploring. He or she will also solicit any and all applicable information from customers, prospects, direct competitors, indirect competitors, and those in his or her network. The sales professional or job candidate will do as much verbal discovery as he or she can in this open-end questioning stage. You don't want yes or no answers; you want conversations. Asking questions designed in advance for soliciting useful information that will help you move the ball forward will help toward this end.

During these interviews, you will record all information and then analyze it, evaluate it for prioritization, and categorize it strategically so you can drawn upon and leverage it as you work through the levels of the P's in your quest to build the optimal sales readiness template. Once you've gathered and written down all the data, you'll need to put together a report that categorizes and makes sense of it all—possibly using Word and/or Excel, two modern-day tools you can use to organize the information you gather during the preparation stage. This can be done in the form of an in-depth executive summary that categorizes, prioritizes, and filters the information in a way that can eliminate what is unnecessary, leaving only what will be most useful in all your efforts going forward for all levels of the P's. This database must be manageable; as it will be what you leverage for everything else you're going to do.

The process of preparation—and, indeed, all levels of the Pyramid— is the same whether you are an individual salesperson, a business, or a job seeker looking to relate your transferable relevance to a potential employer. The only thing you will do differently as part of your preparation if you are a job seeker is a self-discovery internalization exercise, which involves two things. First is a hard self-audit assessment. After all, who will understand what drives your senses of purpose and passion better than you? This step is also just as much an evaluation of the soft and hard skills you possess that will support that drive. The next logical and complementary step is to solicit as much honest feedback as you can by talking to your past peers, bosses, and anyone else who has knowledge of your former work experience. The objective is to get to the heart of who you are from both a hard skill and a soft skill perspective so you can ultimately align yourself with a role that is best suited to your personal sense of passion and purpose. (We will discuss this process further in chapter eleven.)

It can also be said that the preparation process is timeless—that is, it would be the same no matter what time frame you live (or lived) in, as we can see very easily as we look back through history. As I mentioned earlier, the only constant we have is that we are so often called on to adapt in order to keep going, and no one knew this better than the pioneers of this country—the settlers and entrepreneurs who looked for new markets. Sales professionals at heart used their own version of the P's to create sustained success in not just their chosen space but through the trials and tribulations of multiple vertical migrations, as they were eventually forced to adapt to changing environments. Take, for example, Pete, who lived in California during the Gold Rush—a classic boom and bust cycle if ever there was one. Starting in 1848, gold was being found in rivers, creeks, and underground mines; reports indicate that more than 90,000 people came to California in 1849 to find their fortunes, and by 1852 California's annual gold production exceeded $81 million. However, the gold rush would, for all intents and purposes, be over by 1864.

As prospective miners flooded California, Pete's parents were opportunistic and smart enough to offer them room-and-board services. These boarders—who came from the East over the California trails, from South American jungles, from Europe, and even from China—ultimately provided Pete with the big-picture education he would utilize for his own success, telling him vital information about the threats they faced, the things they would need, the things they hadn't known they would need, and so on. Though they had come from all over the globe from different cultures and spoke different languages, there were common purposes, obstacles, and needs among them.

Pete admired these miners for following their passions and dreams with courage and conviction, and understood that personal fulfillment was not the only thing that could be achieved by following one's purpose or passion. Through his conversations with these individuals, he realized that a person in pursuit of his purpose or passion would almost assuredly achieve professional effectiveness. Coupled with conviction and courage, this represented a powerful formula and framework for success.

However, Pete knew, thanks to his self-discovery internalization exercises, that he didn't enjoy doing manual labor himself; instead, he enjoyed philosophizing and thinking conceptually about his surroundings. He loved the tales the newcomers in his parents' boarding house told him, and he had a natural and insatiable appetite to learn, recognize, and understand the motivations and differences in people.

With his desire to provide services and solutions, he saw a big opportunity and realized he was interested in doing a different kind of prospecting. Instead of prospecting for gold, he was going to prospect for miners in need of support and a framework for success predicated upon a readiness template designed for putting into action a set of repetitive processes. Knowing what the miners' lives were like, he hoped to find a way to present them with products and services that would give them opportunities to create their own frameworks for success. His idea was to expand his services beyond just equipment and supply sales. He would offer a turnkey solution designed to help mitigate threats and barriers; however, these solutions would revolve around transportation services as opposed to general goods and tools. Although he would peddle some goods and products, often they would be bundled into the overall transportation solutions.

Pete chose the transportation vertical for a variety of reasons, and he would eventually go through his own version of the P's to ultimately settle upon the space within that vertical that suited his particular experience, talents, and passions the best. First, during its heyday, there was no easy way to get to California by ship or by trail. Those who tried faced death and disease all along the way. Shipwrecks, cholera, and typhoid were common obstacles. Still, people were so filled with the fever to find gold that they often did brave the trip by ship and then abandon their vessels upon arrival. Pete saw this happening, and realized he could carve out his own niche in the marketplace.

He also chose transportation as his focus due to his familiarity with and knowledge of the area and its landscape; he had grown up in Northern California and knew its people, including some of the Native American population. He also knew the terrain like the back of his hand. With this knowledge he hoped to create value for his clients by finding ways to improve their chances of finding gold, and their overall security.

First, however, he would need a foundation, and that would require preparation. It was time for Pete to take all that he had learned from the travelers he had met and combine that with his own understanding of mining and its methods, the local topography, and merchandising. He would have to find creative ways to leverage his relationships and turn his ideas into a platform upon which the miners could build their own frameworks for success.

So, he got a hold of some paper and writing utensils and began the process of listing the concerns and needs of miners in general. He then matched those concerns with some very specific solutions he wanted to provide. Those solutions were based on his knowledge, skills, and relationships, all of which he would utilize to provide a niche solution that revolved around transportation.

Next, he undertook learning about and understanding every piece of equipment the miners used as well as how and why they were used; for instance, he needed to know where and why to use a gold pan or a cradle. He then studied every type of mining technique as well as where, when, and why they were used: Why would a miner dig against a hillside? When did it pay to be downriver, and when was upriver the best location?

Pete also worked hard to understand the landscape as it related to the cost of goods in the open marketplace. He had to understand how water, erosion, and forces of nature deposited gold in specific areas, and he had to understand how to help others find and test those areas.

Last, he made it his business to know who was making deals, along with where the deals were being made and why. In other words, who was his competition? What kinds of services were other businesspeople offering to the miners? What industries and areas might they not have become aware of yet?

Pete understood that in order to engage his target profile (a later step in the Pyramid of P's), he first had to make sure he was an expert on the subject of mining. He understood that he would need to establish his credibility with first-time customers and create an atmosphere that fostered repeat business and favorable word of mouth. If he could establish himself as someone who could provide prospectors with a readiness template in a turnkey, fully customized way, he could not only differentiate himself from other storeowners, but he could become incredibly wealthy. Even more important, the interactions this business would produce would satisfy his inner purpose of helping others create their own frameworks for success.

Pete's habit of securing products, learning miner methodology and the miners' primary barriers to success, and in-depth competitor knowledge would be the ongoing activities that would form the foundation of the preparation portion of his readiness template. Mining technology would continuously evolve, and the miners would be forced to adapt. There was lots of trial and error. Surface mining and panning would eventually give way to sluice boxes and hydraulics from larger corporate entities once surface gold dried up. By the mid-1850s, the climate had changed enough that individual miners couldn't make much money anymore. Rather, larger employers with the capital to invest in larger-scale mining would come to dominate. Pete would eventually have to adapt to this new profile as well.

As part of his preparation, Pete had to understand more than the miners' assets and methods, the landscape and topography, and merchandizing. He had to understand the overall needs of his customers. He had a thirst for information and a natural curiosity about the driving forces behind migration, and he sought to internalize the miners' unique challenges and obstacles. He would use all of that knowledge to formulate his service-based solution.

Another part of Pete's preparation included lining up and leveraging his existing relationships with merchants, hotels, bars, restaurants, brothels, laundry services, suppliers, doctors, and ship captains—all of which would provide information for a fee. Some of that information would be valuable because it was timely, and some was valuable in a general sense. Pete had good instincts for the value of network marketing, partnering with others to provide services you don't possess and creating mutually beneficial business synergy. Everything would add to his ability to provide a valuable service to the mass migration of miners—which we'll learn more about in subsequent chapters.

Knowledge is power, and the foundation for improving our chances for success in opportunity creation is making the investment in preparation by gathering knowledge, internalizing it, evaluating it, and organizing it in such a way that it becomes useful whenever you want it. In its most basic form, preparation is simply in-depth and directed study—a deep dive into your targeted vertical, space, and company. It's making the investment and taking the time to research and to solicit any and all applicable information, customers, prospects, competitors, and your network. Ultimately you would then record, categorize, filter, and evaluate the data in order to strategically leverage it and incorporate it into your sales readiness template for sustained success.

There is a reason why sports teams create templates and why they gather intelligence on their competitors, the terrain, the game, the history, the trends, etc. This is the same thing armies do in preparation for war: They gather intelligence, and use that data to make decisions. In order to be successful at anything, you have to prepare; you must invest the time it takes to research, and you must be willing to become a subject-matter expert (SME).

A good sales professional will create a system that works best for him or her. It doesn't matter if you collect and store information and files in paper folders or digitally—whatever works for you, just make sure you do it. The same way a good student will prepare for a test by gathering information and studying, so will a professional salesperson, an organization needing to create the right business model and sales template, and that job seeker wanting his or her dream position do the same. The goal is to use the information to position you for maximum effectiveness and efficiency. That's true for athletes, it's true for armies, it's true for sales professionals, and it's true for anyone who wants something badly enough.

CHAPTER 6

PLANNING

O nce you have completed your preparation phase, you will have an enormous amount of information with which to work. You'll have the rundown on the company in which you're interested if you're a job seeker; if you're already a salesperson or if you're a company's decision maker, you will know your competition inside and out: who they are, where they are located, why they exist, how well they are doing, and the secrets of their success. You'll have a list of all the contacts you might need to know at these organizations, including, for example, hiring managers and/or fellow salespeople, and you'll have double-checked that their phone numbers, email addresses, and so on are correct. You'll have done all the networking and taken all the notes. Now, what do you do with it?

Preparation is great; it's the first important step to building your sales readiness template whether you're an individual or representing a business. It gives you a vast amount of information in the broadest context possible so that you might understand the universe in which your target company operates or the landscape of the territory you wish to enter. However, preparation means nothing if you don't first evaluate what you have gathered and then use what you have learned to create a plan and, more important, follow up on it.

Planning, the second half of the first level of Paul's Pyramid of P's, is the process of

1. Gathering all the pieces of information you learned during the preparation phase, whether it's on paper, in the cloud, or in your

head; evaluating it; and ultimately internalizing it. Study what you now know; learn it backward and forward until you are certain that there is nothing you don't know about the vertical, the space, and the company in which you are interested.

2. Getting a good sense of the end-game positioning for yourself and for your target. What is your objective, and what do you hope to achieve? Do you want to be hired for a job in a vertical that is outside of your direct experience? Do you want your company to enter a new market or simply perform better in the one it's currently in? Do you not only want to improve your numbers and exceed your quota but also find a way to ensure that the success is sustained? Having a clear objective and goal in mind can give you more focus and a greater sense of purpose when navigating the broad field of information through which you have to trek.

3. Looking for common threads of success. In your analysis of all the information you collected in the preparation stage, try to find the facts, messages, or themes that are consistent across the board in order to create as clear and as exact as possible a picture of what the vertical, the space, the company, and the job are. The planning stage begins the process of coming down from the thirty-thousand-foot level and narrowing down the sphere of concern to the ground level. The preparation gives us the proper context for formulating the plan that will include the day-to-day action steps necessary for success. It will help create the context for all the remaining levels of the P's in an effective and efficient way.

In creating this picture, you uncover what the vertical, space, company, or job in which you're interested is like or entails. For example, you interviewed four different salespeople working within the company in which you're interested, and you read a dozen web and print articles about the organization itself. And each of those sources told you that at this particular company, the sales cycle is six months to one year, the engagement level is likely to involve interactions with multiple buying influences, and the specific territory to which you will be assigned has struggled for years. Perhaps they did not convey this to you in the same way each time, but during your review and overview of the information you collected, these pieces of information should stick out to you as commonly occurring across the board. As a very basic example, recognizing them will not only give you a better understanding of what you will be doing every day and what type of engagement to expect but provide a window into the precise challenges you are likely to face in your territory.

The planning process is not limited to job seekers. The same model and process works the same way for an existing sales professional or business. Follow this model to improve your sales (as an existing salesperson), or as you enter this market (as an organization). It will also help you focus your planning as the stage progresses. As an organization it is vital to perform an internal sales audit upon yourself using the sales readiness template as a guide for measuring the capability and effectiveness for both your infrastructure and work flow processes.

Your plan will need to take into account your entire end-to-end sphere of activity. That end-to-end can be from sunup to sundown and include weekends. Or maybe it means just thirty hours a week. It really depends on the exact vertical, space, and job. There is no set boilerplate. It's the process of discovery, as we have been describing, that will determine the level of activity to meet your specific objectives as well as the expectations of the role or the business.

Regardless of the vertical, the space, the company, or the role, time management and efficiency are directly related to effectiveness for sales professionals in particular. In effect, it's going to be important to understand that being accountable to yourself for your activity and your time is priceless. But more than that, you have to understand the details of the role in order to create the proper level of timing and activity. A very basic example: You know that getting the position you want will mean traveling four days a week. Or maybe you'll be working remotely. Your action plan would have to accommodate this.

If you're an existing salesperson, perhaps the company you're investigating holds a certain sales volume expectation, and you'll need to know if your territory can support the same. The activity required to achieve or exceed expectations can vary greatly from vertical to vertical, space to space, and company to company. However, you can typically determine a formula for success. The activities you identify would simply be the ones that, based upon your research in the preparation stage, are the best determinatives of success. A simple example: Doing A + B = Y, you are expected to create ten Y's by the end of Q1. So you will then plan your activity in such a way that your ability to do A + B = Y is at the optimal level. In your planning phase, you will structure your activity on a day-to-day basis to ensure that it will. Another very basic example: You will plan to contact the necessary number of clients per day to produce that amount of sales. Every experienced sales professional has seen the proverbial 30/60/90-day action plan that is supposed to help you create a framework for success. But it's pretty much a joke in reality because far too often it's not based upon any in-depth preparation, planning, and research. In my opinion it's antiquated thinking. My insight and experience indicates that the truly important 30/60/90 day plan is not the one that starts on day one, but rather on day 90 before you ever begin. Modern day sales training too often forgets that it's the pre work that creates the structure and framework for success. The modern day best practice that emphasizes the need to create your action plan on day one of the job is a joke! The Pyramid is not a joke. The exercises and the steps you'll take in this process are based on actual in-depth research and high-level thought, not pie-in-the-sky 30/60/90-day plans churned out in thirty minutes. The planning process in the Pyramid is not your action plan. It is, rather, just a part of a far more valuable sales readiness template designed to ensure maximum and sustained success.

As the decision maker at an organization, your plan will take into account that you will be competing against a number of companies, each with its own particular differentiators and business models. For example, some will emphasize an aggressive price point while others will rely upon their ability to deliver a comprehensive suite of solutions. Some will have business models that rely upon outside, virtual sales forces to create opportunities while others have mixed approaches with a combination of internal and external sales professionals. You have to assume that each of these organizations designs its business model because it believes it's the best way to identify the profile target, develop relationships, and create opportunities. The key for you is to know and understand all of it and then account for all of them in your own plan. The key will be to plan and build the model for activity that will put you or your business in the best position for success. You can copy a competitor's model and simply find ways to do it better, you can do something completely different, or you can create a plan for yourself that is a combination of activity models. The key is to create an activity plan that makes efficient and effective use of time. Knowing these aspects can help you formulate action steps that can bring your own organization into line with these best practices and help you compete in the same marketplace.

Planning also includes a process of identifying what is or what will be in your own backyard. In this phase, you'll want to define your territory: What is its geography? Who are your existing clients, and how many prospects are there? Here you can use whatever information you've already gleaned from your target company; you can also use, for example, Hoover's, an industry-related listing, or even a simple Google search. This is the point where all of your research and preparation will pay off. If you made the proper investment during the preparation stage, you should have all the information you're going to need to help you plan for these things properly. Once you understand exactly who your existing and potential accounts are, you can plug them into an Excel sheet (or any other format with which you are comfortable) to categorize and prioritize them.

Another portion of the planning process has to do with ensuring you possess the basic tools to support your own success. These can be as simple as pens, paper, and a printer/scanner/fax machine but can also include laptops, Smartphone's, and tablets through which, along with Internet access, you can conduct your business from a mobile platform.

Examples of some of the tools you might use to support your planning activities can include but are not limited to the following:

- A **company car** to get you where you need to be. This might be essential, or it might not. The car's value is, in large part, dependent upon what the business model is and what the competition is doing. The key point: If it's a differentiator in creating sales opportunities, then it's something to value, and something to account for if you're a job seeker or business owner. An internal sales professional that doesn't meet clients face to face would have no use for a company car. An external sales professional that has to drive through a multistate territory and be responsible for taking clients out would find a company car extremely useful.

- **Marketing support** (PowerPoint templates, brochures, flyers, a WebEx or GoToMeeting account, etc.). Good sales professionals know that sales and marketing have to work together. You should be sharing tools (e.g., CRM) as well as the overall vision of the organization.

- An **expense account** to entertain clients and cover costs while on the road. If your role requires that you build relationships, and you can expect to be playing golf and going to dinner, then having this resource is invaluable. However, if your role doesn't require face-to-face interaction, and the competition is not engaging in any of this activity because it doesn't equate to sales creation, then having an expense account is of little use and value.

- **CRM software** to track the progress of opportunities and perform follow-up tasks. CRM is not only a tool to help you track the pipeline; it also serves as a platform for helping you act on a day-to-day basis.

- Access to **white papers** and network-related intelligence—the latest news and discoveries coming out of your chosen vertical.

- **Current information** about industry events, competitors, your territory, etc. This information can support you because it can give you real-time insight, which is imperative to proper planning. Old data may not only be useless, but may also be counterproductive.

- **Service, operational support, sales support, and technical support people.** These can all be instrumental in your success, and your planning activity has to account for how, when, and why to use them on an ongoing basis. As with all these examples, their value is very much dependent on the vertical, the space, the company, and the job. For example, some sales roles won't involve any of the support people listed, while for others it will be the norm.

- A **virtual assistant**, so you don't have to handle manual administrative tasks such as answering phones, creating reports and PowerPoint's, setting up meetings, and telemarketing, and you can instead focus on sales-related activities. They are listed as an outsourcing tool for the preparation stage, and they are just as valuable during the planning stage. They might give you an edge over the competition. Again, it will depend upon the business model and the environment, but removing administrative burdens and freeing up more time for you to focus on your strategic objectives is always a good thing. Having a virtual assistant could be a great tool to help support your planning activity and action plan.

- **Basic application software.** Word, Excel, Outlook, and PowerPoint. You will likely use them on a daily basis.

- **Call preparation sheets and planning sheets** (digital or analog). These should highlight technical and business questions and talking points that can guide the conversation. As an example, you might have a call-planning sheet for your next meeting, and you might have a larger one for the overall sales objective. If for example you are involved in a complex sale with multiple buying influencers, and the sales cycle is a long one, you might think about the Miller Heiman methodology and their Blue Sheet, Green Sheet, and Gold Sheet planning tools. If you are in a transactional environment, a quick cheat or even a napkin might do.

So far in the planning stage, we have filtered through the data you collected during preparation, gathered and internalized it, found all common threads within it, and set those as focal points around which to formulate your plan. We've laid out the tools you'll want to have at your disposal as you progress in this phase and indeed throughout the entire Pyramid of P's.

Now it's time to take all of those aspects and actually put them into creating a workable structure—a plan for the engagements you are likely to undertake as the job seeker looking to relate your transferable relevance during an interview, the individual salesperson looking to improve your performance, or the company owner willing to perform an internal sales audit because he or she wants to create a template worthy of expectations, and a framework designed for sustained success for all current and future employees. For a basic example, say you're a job seeker looking at an outside sales position. This might put you in the field on Monday through Friday from 9:00 a.m. to 4:00 p.m. Knowing this; you could schedule your follow-up and planning activities between 7:00 and 9:00 a.m. and again between 4:00 and 6:00 p.m. Then you can spend all day on Friday doing administration, more follow-up as necessary, and more planning.

Further, you'll want to set up a thirty-, sixty-, or ninety-day action plan that includes short- and longer-term goals as well as what specific steps you will take to accomplish them. Your thirty/sixty/ninety-day plan will not be the typical kind. Yours will be built upon real-time data because you made the investment in a high level of research during the preparation stage and you already have a strong understanding of your positioning in the market place.

Be as specific as possible here. The details will vary depending on the vertical, the space, the company, and the role. A very basic example, for illustrative purposes: How many phone calls will you make every day? How many emails will you send per week? What about face-to-face visits? Will you give any formal presentations? Understand the formula for success for whatever the vertical, space, company, and role are. Now, with that full micro- and macroscopic understanding, you can confidently and effectively create the action plan that will exceed sales expectations. By this point, it will be a pretty simple process to fill in your plan with the amount of work that will be guaranteed to create that volume for you in the set amount of time that you've given yourself to make it work.

Let's look at all this now in the historical perspective we began in chapter five, where Pete, an entrepreneur during the time of the Gold Rush in California, was going through the preparation stage of the Pyramid of P's. Looking at the words he put down on paper based on all the information he had collected, he felt pretty secure that he had a good grasp on the overall big picture. He had done all the necessary preparation and had all the information he needed to begin the work of extracting data to create a narrower focus for the various planning stages ahead. Pete knew he could prepare for anything, but that preparation wouldn't mean anything if he didn't have a plan for how to implement it.

As part of that planning, Pete knew and understood that he needed the infrastructure and resources for all the solutions he wanted to offer. His next step would be to begin obtaining supplies in a cost-effective way. Suppliers continued to come in, and they sold their goods to local merchants. Pete was smart enough to know that he could buy in bulk, so that was what he did.

During this time Pete also made the investment in contracting out for security to men he knew and trusted to protect his new warehouse. He invested in former soldiers for transportation security. The security positions required brave, dependable men of integrity—all attributes the American soldiers possessed in spades. He hired them on a contingency basis.

Though racism was a big issue in his place and time, Pete had befriended some of the Native American population in the area where he lived. This did not happen overnight; he had already spent years building up enough trust and credibility with the various tribes, many of which were situated near the rivers and hills that were currently being mined for gold. Now that he was planning to launch his own business, Pete called on these friends to work for him, providing guide services and survival skill instruction for those who came in to mine the mountains or pan the rivers.

However, as we all know, nothing comes for free, and his Native American friends demanded a guaranteed supply of food for their families in exchange for the work Pete was asking them to do. Because of his existing familial connections in the local agricultural community, Pete was able to agree to these terms without issue. The trade-off was a good one.

Once his employees, per se, were secured, Pete spent weeks combing the land and the rivers, observing the mining and panning operations that were already in place. He noted everything that was working well and what wasn't and began to see patterns among the various small "businesses." From these observations he began to internalize the formulas for success. He internalized where gold was more likely to be found and why, and what methods would be most efficient for extracting it. He understood which areas were more dangerous than others and what those dangers were. He knew which areas had Native American populations that would be less hostile, and he knew the reasons for any conflicts that did exist. In short, he became a subject-matter expert on any topic his future clients might want to know about were they to hire him for the services he'd provide.

In this way, Pete was being a good territory manager—one who knew how to prepare and how to plan. He understood that his clients would expect him to show them the path to success and help them understand it (a universal business necessity that still holds true today), and so he worked very hard to map out that path and make it a reality for his clients. Where could they go to find the most gold with the least threats of theft and violence? Which method of extraction would be the most effective and efficient? He had to be a subject-matter expert on all these topics and more—on anything his clients might need or want to know. Pete demonstrated his value as a consultant because he was able to effectively communicate some meaningful insight on situations and problems that his clients were not aware of.

As part of Pete's preparation, he also studied the travel patterns of those who were coming to California to find their fortunes in gold. What he discovered was that half came by sea and the other half via the California Trail. When they got to San Francisco, most headed to the place where everyone else already was: the American River. Those coming from the California Trail arrived in groups or makeshift small companies, some of which had organized and planned ahead for what they would need. They brought supplies, equipment, and food. They often had someone with at least a good basic knowledge of gold. Maybe somebody else in the group would have some technical and mechanical ability. Some groups would make sure they brought men who were good with guns for security, and if they were lucky they would bring doctors.

These small companies or groups of men all pretty much followed the same path. Wherever they were from, they boarded a train to Independence, Missouri, where they then hopped onto the California

Trail. The trail was fraught with danger, and many men died along the way. Fortunately, these groups understood the value of preparation and planning, and in so doing they created the foundation for a perfect profile to which Pete could offer his business's solutions. Some groups would need more of his services, and some would need less, and he would have to tailor his offerings accordingly. Pete made it his objective to know and understand who would make for an ideal profile, and he would also make it a point to know exactly why. It simply made good business sense to do so.

At the end of the day in the planning stage, sales professionals, job candidates, and sales-oriented businesses must internalize all of the information gathered during the preparation stage to become subject-matter experts as much as possible; we then must make optimal use of the infrastructure already in place and existing tools in order to position ourselves for success and, in the case of the job seeker, effectively relate our relevance to the industry, the vertical, and the space even if we have no hard-skill experience in them.

CHAPTER 7

PROSPECTING

The first level of the P's included preparation and planning—the activities and the things a sales professional, a business, or a job seeker would do in the process of creating his or her sales readiness templates during their off-peak time.

The second level of the P's includes prospecting, profiling, and presenting. Quite simply, these are the things a sales professional does on a daily basis to create and manage sales opportunities. The difference here is that while you could do your preparation and planning at any time, prospecting, profiling, and presenting must be done during a sales professional's peak time, meaning those hours in the day when you have the best chance for actual engagement. Peak times can vary depending on the vertical, the space, the job, the role, and the sales category.

Prospecting is at the heart of what sales professionals do. It's the act of engagement. Prospecting for sales professionals can, in simple terms, be defined as the act of searching for and engaging existing or potential clients to begin the process of creating opportunity. Success, effectiveness, and efficiency at this level of the P's are largely dependent upon the information you have at hand. At this point, you have made a sufficient level of investment in your preparation and planning efforts, and you have all the necessary data at hand. That data, in modern times, may be aggregated and accessed through an existing CRM such as Salesforce or leveraged through a database third-party provider such as Hoover's.

In more distant times, that data may simply have existed on paper or in your head. The platform for the act of prospecting is largely determined by what is deemed to be most effective for the vertical, the space, the company, or the role. That platform determination will have been decided upon during the filtering process at the preparation and planning stage

Regardless of the platform on which the data is domiciled, the point is you now have the information you need to help you make efficient and effective use of your prospecting-related time. You have a strong understanding of the population size and makeup that form the parameters of your territory. That makeup will likely include both clients and prospects. At this point you have filtered through all the data as well. For instance, if during your planning and preparation stages you know that the job in scope indicates outside sales works best and that your territory is largely made up of noncustomers, then you'll know your engagements will require that you primarily cold call in person by knocking on doors, make phone calls, leverage referral contacts, and send emails. In each and any instance at the prospecting stage, you are likely just asking for the time to have a conversation in the hope of getting additional meetings for deeper conversations. However, the vertical, the space, the company, and the role will in large part determine the art and the goal for the engagement. The type or category of the sales will also be determinative. Transactional and complex sales environments are completely different as they relate to the level of engagement and the overall objectives for prospecting. More on that later.

The act and concept of prospecting has not changed, but the technology and tools to support the efforts have, like everything else, evolved, and the workforce has had to adapt. For simplicity's sake in defining the act of prospecting, we will keep the examples here in the present. Regardless of the vertical, space, company, or role, the act of prospecting has common threads for any sales professional and business, and the same is true for any individuals seeking to transfer or migrate unmatched hard-skill prior experience to a new vertical or space.

The common threads for understanding the basic act of prospecting include:

1. Defining the territory. Every sales professional engaged in the act of prospecting will have a defined territory. Those territories might be defined explicitly or implicitly. In any case, have a prospecting list with a defined set of target parameters in advance. The parameters can be defined by geography, vertical, space, size, or a combination of all of those things. This is often described as your territory.
2. Prospecting requires support tools or platforms of some type to enhance the efforts.
3. The act of prospecting in any vertical, space, or format requires that you have the mindset that all engagements must be worthwhile for all involved.
4. Planning for prospecting and the act of prospecting require that a sales professional remains flexible.
5. The goal for prospecting in any vertical, space, or format is to engage an ideal target efficiently and effectively and then advance the sales opportunity to the next step.

To prospect, prior to making the effort to engage, a salesperson would have to create a call list with all the contact information and would have all the supporting tools in place as described in the planning stage. Some of the modern-day prospecting support tools include PowerPoint presentations; call preparation sheets, laptops, phones, application software, CRM, and cars. It's also common today to work in a team-oriented environment at the prospecting stage. Modern-day sales forces often will bring internal resources and subject-matter experts into prospecting engagements to enhance the experience. These internal resources can include, for example, a technical solutions specialist or a clinical specialist for a capital medical sale. Again, the vertical, the space, the type of sale, and the type of client determine those details—all of which would be determined during the preparation and planning stages.

The act of prospecting can be done in many different ways. The action steps for prospecting are dictated by the action plan you already put in place. Leave enough flexibility in the process of prospecting, as things always evolve in real time, day-to-day, week-to-week, and year-to-year. Your prospecting activity should change accordingly, to do whatever creates a positive reaction for your targets.

The following is a list that includes some basic prospecting tactics, the platforms from which it is done, and some modern-day prospecting tools that support those efforts:

1) **In person** (external activity). Fly or drive to existing clients or prospects. Meetings may be preset, or you might be going on a pure cold call with a door knock. You may do this activity alone or with a coworker (e.g., a manager or support specialist).

2) **By phone** (internal or external activity) or any other **mobile technology**. You can do this alone or sometimes as a joint call with your internal resources, such as technical specialists. The phone is simply one example of a platform. There are many others. Skype, Web-Ex, Go-to Meeting are also popular **communication applications** that provides flexibility in that they provide a way either to talk, type, and visualize to enhance your prospecting engagements through both desktop or mobile technology.

3) **By email** (internal or external activity). Email is simply a communication mode for delivery. The act of prospecting through email can be launched through multiple platforms that include both desktop and mobile technology.

4) Trade shows and **networking events** or any place where you are likely to get opportunities to meet and communicate with existing or prospective clients. The vertical, the space, the business, and the type of sale determine the platform of communication. Your method of prospecting will be different for B2B, B2C, wholesale, retail, transactional, complex, consultative, etc. But more on that later.

5) A **CRM tool** used to enter important sales-related data. Contacts, status comments, strategies, and activity can all be documented here and can help you understand how to make decisions efficiently on where and how to prospect for both existing and potential clients.

6) **Sales automation.** This is a modern-day sales-enhancement so-lution designed to improve efficiency for sales professionals by removing the tactical and administrative burden of prospecting. Some acts of prospecting are repetitive in nature and can thus be automated in the same way we mass-produce on assembly lines. For example: If you send the same emails out with the same mes-sage on an interval basis, then why not create a template and have the process automated? Why not send automatic emails to existing clients or potential ones, to remove the burden of hav-ing to take the time to do it yourself manually? The advantage is you'll have more time to concentrate on the strategic things that require a more complex and personal level of engagement.

Prospecting is the act of engagement, and sales automation can help you do that more efficiently by removing the time-con-suming administrative burden of anything that is repetitive. This is an area that continues to evolve in the modern day sales ecosys-tem. The technology continues to become increasingly smarter with analytical components, and is becoming more intuitive in nature. Sales automation can and will, in my opinion, do the same for sales-related opportunity creation as the assembly line did for manufacturing.

7) **Outsourcing.** This can include any number of support-related solutions. As previously stated, the tactic of outsourcing is mean-ingful for just about every level of the P's. The vertical, the space, the business, the role, and the sales category largely determine the type or the level of outsourcing. There are an endless num-ber of examples; one might be a virtual assistant who can make telemarketing calls for you to set up meetings. If you have a busi-ness, you may outsource to call centers for this task.

8) **Social selling.** This is a modern-day term that refers to some of the social platforms sales professionals and businesses use as pros-pecting platforms on which to engage existing or prospective cli-ents. These include but are not limited to LinkedIn, Facebook, Pinterest, and Twitter. We should also include mobile technology in this category, as there are an ever-increasing number of busi-ness-related applications to help us work from our tablets and

Smartphone's. Sales professionals and businesses are now getting access to information quickly, easily, and in real time. These mobile technology applications are designed in large part to support and enhance the prospecting engagement experience.

9) **The digital online marketplace**. The online digital ad-tech universe is an immense and expanding newer prospecting platform for sales professionals and businesses, a marketplace where we can offer goods and services in an ever-increasingly targeted way. (More on that in the profiling section.) As it relates to prospecting, the online space that is already in place, such as affiliate networks, online forums, e-commerce stores, and ad exchanges, is changing the way consumers and businesses are buying and selling goods. Sales professionals and businesses increasingly have to adapt to this new platform and reality. However, like all the platforms and supporting tools listed, the level of use and the value of this one are all dependent upon the vertical, the space, the job, the role, and the sales category.

As we have listed a number of modern-day platforms and support tools to help define what prospecting means, we have to remember that the foundational basics and the value in the act of prospecting has not changed throughout history. Prospecting is simply a preplanned act of engagement designed to create an opportunity. That was true a thousand years ago, and it will be true a thousand years from now. The value of prospecting is equal for any existing sales professionals or businesses. The appreciation and the ability to understand how, why, when, and where to prospect for any particular vertical, space, or role is of the same value for any individual seeking to communicate effectively and relate prior job-related relevance in his or her aspirations for cross-vertical migration.

Let's look, then, at what prospecting looked at before the turn of the twentieth century. Going back to Pete, our Gold Rush entrepreneur, remember that he'd already completed the planning and preparation phases, so he had all the pieces in place. All he had to do now was begin the process of prospecting for his targeted customer. Now, Pete was no fool. He knew he couldn't wait at the gate of the California Trail *and* sit at the docks at the same time. Instead, he started up a form of network marketing: He put the word out to his referral sources in town that he was looking for people to help him watch for new customers. In this way, you could say he was outsourcing by getting as many others to do as much for him as possible and finding ways to create mutually beneficial business synergy at the same time. Pete understood the value of a whole-sale approach to some aspects of his prospecting engagements. To put it simply, Pete was setting up an "I'll wash your back if you wash mine" situation that would benefit both his business and those who he hired on to help him out.

Next he looked at location, location, location! Even back then this was a bit of a magic formula for a successful salesperson. Though Pete's entrepreneurial ideas were original, they would mean nothing if he couldn't get them in front of the people who could use them most. And he had seen with other businesses around where he lived how being in the right place at the right time could work in his favor. So, whom did Pete contact? The laundry folks, the bartenders, the hotel owners, and the shop workers—anyone who might have contact with large groups of people who were coming to find gold in San Francisco. He also put word out to the security forces people hired to transport their gold back across the California Trail to the banks back East. Those security forces crossed paths with would-be miners on their way to California and could certainly stir up some interest in what Pete had to offer. And he made sure all of his referral sources were well educated in his product and its market to help them understand his ideal target profile.

As with anything else, nothing in business or in life is free. Pete paid a finder's fee to anyone who referred business his way—as long as it resulted in a successful transaction. Pete saw this as money well spent. His clients were required to pay up front, so he would use that working capital for referral fees. He also did plenty of client prospecting on his own. He made it a habit to greet and engage in conversation as many of the newcomers getting off the ships or coming by trail as possible. It was hard to do, but Pete did his best to balance his time as strategically as possible. Simply stated, he tried to make it a habit to be as available as possible.

CHAPTER 8

PROFILING

Information and knowledge are power. To this point the in-depth preparation, the study, and the planning has enabled a sales professional or a business to filter data efficiently, to allow for customized territory planning, and to synchronize a messaging platform to begin a targeted prospecting campaign. However, in order for our sales professional, our job seeker, or our business to move forward, each will first have to take a deeper dive into fully understanding unique client profiles. So before a sales professional can begin the act of prospecting, he or she must first understand what a typical client might look like. The act of profiling is simply taking all the information gathered during the preparation stage on the company, the vertical, the space, the competition, the discussions, etc. and determining who or where your most ideal customers are, who will be most likely to need your product or service, and why they would or would not need or want those products and services.

For an example, let's go back to our space sales alien in the year 3035. Let's assume he doesn't perform the necessary preparation and planning. But through luck, he somehow makes it through the Earth's atmosphere and doesn't smash into a mountain or drowns in the ocean. Instead, he lands in the Sahara Desert. After some conversations with snakes and lizards, he finds out that nobody there is in need of moon rocks.

However, our space sales alien by nature is not one to be deterred. And it just so happens that on his way to Earth, he stopped off at an electric heater distributor and decided to buy a bundle of heaters in the hope of adding them to his sales tally for the trip. He assumed there had to be a need for heaters on Earth, as he heard it could get pretty cold there.

Our unfortunate space sales alien again has fallen victim to his inability to prepare and plan properly. It appears that lizards and snakes have even less of an interest in or need for electric heaters than they do for moon rocks. The need for water seems to be a common theme among the animals in the Sahara, though. Too bad our poor space sales alien has none of that! He then, of course, doesn't have any sales either. With both products (moon rocks and heaters), he really had no idea who his ideal profile was or where he might find that person because he never made the investment up front in preparation and planning. The most artfully done presentation delivered from the latest and greatest platforms in the world won't make a difference if you don't understand your ideal profile.

Sales professionals and businesses need to understand their targets so they can make optimal use of their time. Everything in sales and creating sales readiness templates is about being as effective and efficient as possible.

Job candidates have to understand the need to profile so they can effectively relate the relevance of whatever process they used to determine client profiles on their previous jobs. Just knowing and understanding the need to identify the profile properly can give evidence of relatable value for whatever position to which a job seeker is hoping to migrate.

The value of profiling remains the same today as it was in the distant past. The process of profiling is simply leveraging information and filtering it in a way that effectively and efficiently aligns what is being offered with what is ultimately needed. The goal of profiling for sales professionals is simply to support their effort to be as efficient as possible and for improving their chances for successful opportunity creation. Technology continues to provide platforms and solutions that are designed to increasingly narrow and define the scope and demographic of the client profile so it is more readily accessible to those who seek to leverage it.

Profiling is still very often an offline, face-to-face, manual process. That is increasingly changing as the demand for greater speed and effectiveness has risen. Companies are paying huge sums of money to-day for help in identifying ideal profiles. The entire digital online space today is committed to leveraging and mining data and monetizing it in some way. Affiliate networks and exchanges exist in large part simply to match two demographically aligned services and solutions in order to fa-cilitate sales transactions between them. Organizations such as Hoover's have entire business models designed to help organizations and indi-viduals efficiently profile their ideal targets. The same is true for the thousands of lead-generation companies that exist today. Profiling is big business these days, and the trend indicates that it's going to get much bigger. The use of keywords and demographic profiling by micro target-ing, along with decision support software are in high demand within every sector of modern day society.

To profile properly, you must go into it knowing that the goal is sim-ply to know to whom to sell and why. You have to be able to answer those questions for your prospective targets as well as for yourself or your busi-ness. That was true a thousand years ago, and it will be true a thousand years from now. Profiling is a continuation of your research. Much of the relevant information used to define an ideal target profile was gathered during the preparation stage. Here a few best practice tips for profiling. It's a good idea to research on your own, as it's often the best way to in-ternalize it. You can, for example, start by going to company websites to study the business. From there you can track down existing and former employees to get an understanding for why their clients made the deci-sion to buy or not to buy. The basic take-away is to always take a deep dive at every turn.

In addition to having a deep understanding of the existing environ-ment, good sales professionals make it a habit to be aware constantly of changes in the market profile. History shows that things always evolve, and so will the needs of your ideal profile. Keep your eyes and ears open and always follow the information path. If, for example, your ideal target profile includes existing clients, then it would be a good idea to be diligent in conducting client overviews. It's important never to stop asking good questions. It's sometimes even more important to have the ability to offer valuable hard to spot insights to your clients, regardless of the vertical, space, company, or role. Collect data as you go as a best practice.

Also be sure always to record that information on paper or digitally. Organize it in such a way that it's meaningful and accessible to you. A good sales professional understands that knowing the ideal profile is pivotal in creating opportunities. He or she understands it is critical to have the tools and the knowledge to understand how to identify targets properly. He or she understands how to identify the buying habits and motivations in existing relationships and then, in turn, how to leverage that recorded history and incorporate that data as part of his or her sales readiness template.

All salespeople are different, and their means of tracking information should be whatever works best for them. The important thing is simply to make sure you have a system. Use call sheets or profile sheets (paper or digital) to record all engagements and interactions with clients and prospects. It will prove useful in helping you determine and define the ideal profile. These sheets should have the parameters that outline what the profile is. A good sales-professional understands that those parameters are likely to change and evolve over time. Once you truly know and understand who the profile client is, you can then incorporate those targets into your plan for sales engagement activity, such as prospecting and presenting.

Every profile has its own unique emphasis, requirements, and challenges. Each client or prospect has a unique culture, mission, vision, and strategic objective. Every target profile has a range of buying influencers, from singular to multiple, and it's important to understand the context of your particular vertical, space, and business. Regardless of whether the influencers are singular or multiple, a sales professional needs to recognize that each may have competing and separate issues from one another as it relates to decision trees and thought tracks.

A sales professional absolutely must know and understand how and when to ask good questions. The ideal goal for a good questions-based campaign should ultimately be to create mutually beneficial situations, and that cannot be achieved without understanding the target profile. The target profile, on the other hand, cannot be understood outside the context of having internalized how you, your specific solution, and your performance equation are perfectly aligned with the needs of the target. More on the performance equation later.

Good sales professionals come prepared with questions designed to guide and influence their audience and to determine, evaluate, and discover if the prospects they are talking to are indeed ideal profiles or not. They also come prepared to share valuable insight that their prospective clients may not be aware of. The vertical, the space, the job, and the role will be very determinative for prescribing the correct format for questioning.

There are many different formats and types of questions. For example, an open-ended question is designed to elicit a discussion whereas a closed-ended question is designed to elicit a yes or no response. A transactional format and a complex one are vastly different, and thus the art of asking good questions is largely contingent upon which one the professional is engaged upon. More on the formats and sales categories later.

One very important note to keep in mind: The more micro targeted we can be in identifying our ideal profiles, the more efficient our sales-related activity will be. That is true whether you're an existing sales professional or a business seeking to find more ways to create sales opportunities efficiently and effectively. It's also important for job seekers to understand the importance of profiling within the context of their existing experiences and how it might relate to a job of interest. For any job seeker hoping to make a cross-vertical migration, it will be important to know how to relate his or her relevance and effectively align prior profiling means and methods with whatever job he or she is interested in pursuing.

The overall point to understand here is that once the profile is defined, the sales professional will spend a lot less time engaging the wrong people at the wrong time and in the wrong places. He or she will instead—hopefully—spend a lot more time working on the strategic objective of sales-opportunity creation. Once we understand to whom we want to prospect and why, and have identified the ideal profile target, we can then begin the process and act of presenting our services and solutions in an effective and efficient way.

This was a challenge our old friend Pete faced during the California Gold Rush. Though he had spent weeks studying the terrain, visiting mining camps, exploring travel routes, searching for new areas to mine, and securing his relationships with his Native American contacts and his referral sources in town, he wasn't exactly sure of the size of his target market. However, he had done a thorough and broad-based big-picture study of the overall marketplace during his preparation stage. Based upon his business acumen, his collection of data, and his instincts, he was able to narrow his focus and plan of action to capture a very specific type of prospect. He would soon put that information to good use with actionable prospecting and profiling, and eventually would be able to present and articulate a clear value proposition.

Pete realized he couldn't be all things to all miners, and he couldn't hope to compete head to head with other businesses. However, he could carve out a strong niche for himself. Within that niche would be a profile containing some very distinct characteristics, including serving the needs of individuals or small groups of men that were primarily coming by ship. He wouldn't ignore the prospectors coming by land, but the people coming by ship fit his profile the best. These men would typically be novices and would need transportation aid, survival guidance, security, and training in gold mining—as opposed to many of the groups that were coming by way of the California Trail, who came with knowledge and expertise. Pete knew that those who came with ready-made, turnkey-style organizations would not need much more than supplies, and so he didn't have as much to offer them. And there were other businesses that had already monopolized the equipment supply chain. Pete was smart enough to know he would find his path to success in offering ancillary services. The framework and the formula for success were simply focusing on the things that most of the others were not.

Pete bought enough equipment from one of his competitors and kept it in his warehouse for stock so he could provide it when it was needed. But the real value of what he offered was a turnkey-solution-based service that would be paid for up front. He created a system by which he would receive a percentage of the gold found in exchange for providing transportation, survival guidance, mining training, and security. Those coming in by boat and in need of these services would make up the primary parameters for his ideal profile. His equipment and general supplies could not compete with the price monopoly of the other companies, so Pete found ways to bury and lump the cost into the overall cost of the services. The pricing for services was flexible and could be negotiated for a la carte offerings. Pete could differentiate himself by offering customized solutions: Buy what you need and no more.

CHAPTER 9

PRESENTING

It's not enough simply to know where to target, who to target, and why to target a prospect. Sales professionals and businesses must also be prepared for what to present, why to present, when to present, and how to present. If the act of prospecting is the initial step for engagement, the act of presenting is the most logical next step to follow. The act of presenting in the context of sales can most simply be described as a sales professional delivering a message to a targeted audience with the overall goal of increasing the likelihood of a successful sale.

Presentations are a mix of art and science. The science is the preparation that goes into perfecting both the platform from which it's delivered and the format for the atmosphere in which it will take place. The art is the delivery of the presentation. It's the stagecraft and the performance.

The act and the art of presentation have changed very little over the course of history. Everyone has heard of Shakespeare's "friends, Romans, countrymen, lend me your ears" speech, delivered by Marc Antony. Many others may remember an equally significant modern-day presentation by the late, great Steve Jobs when he wowed everyone in a packed auditorium by unveiling the iPhone. In each case, there was a predefined audience, and the goals were to deliver a message and advance the steps in a sale. In the case of Marc Antony, that sale was holding Brutus and Cassius responsible for Julius Caesar's death, and in the case of Steve Jobs, it was to advance the sale of iPhones and Apple products.

In both cases, they used the most advanced technological platforms of the day. The Globe Theatre in Renaissance England, where Shakespeare's play was performed, was designed to carry the human voice over the largest possible area. Jobs had the television and the Internet, which were designed to carry his message to the largest area possible. In the modern day, that means the whole world. The technology, and the associated presentation tools and platforms, have evolved over time. Those platforms have ranged from the bullhorn to the microphone to amplifiers, radio, TV, and WebEx. However, as it relates to the fundamentals of sales and for this book, the act of presenting and the value of presentation have not changed and are not likely ever to change.

The format of a presentation includes more than just the platform from which the message is delivered. It's important to be a master of the platform from which you are to deliver your presentation, but it's just as important to be cognizant of the type of presentation you are expected to give. The type of presentation is also a category within the presentation format. Presentation types are varied. The methodologies and platforms with which people present themselves, their services, their products, or their solutions are largely dependent upon the era, the vertical, the space, the job, and the sales category. The format for presenting can range from a one-sided "sit and listen" style event to one that is more open and designed for live interaction with lots of give and take. The format can also vary in length, style, and substance. For example, the presentation may be as simple as an off-the-cuff, two-minute elevator speech delivered informally to just one person. It can just as likely be a formal setting in front of a large group in a grand auditorium, or perhaps a smaller, panel-style presentation and whiteboard for some key decision makers in a conference room. Regardless of the format, the size, or the complexity, the goal remains the same for presentations: to relate a message designed to illicit a favorable response as you work through the sales process.

At this point, we can assume that the sales professional, business entity, or job seeker that is doing research has made the proper level of investment in preparation and planning. We assume he or she has put a great activity plan in place, has defined and understands the ideal profile, and has begun to prospect intelligently through the existing client or prospective account base in his or her quest for opportunity creation. The sales professional must know how to get to the essence of what needs to be communicated and presented, and has mastered the platforms and formats most associated with his or her vertical, space, job, and sales category.

The job seeker at this stage is reviewing his or her own history and has effectively filtered through the information gathered during the preparation stage to come up with the common threads that will help relate his or her relevance for a chosen role. Those common threads will be a mixture of the science of the presentation and the art. For the sake of this book and the profession of sales, it's my opinion that presenting is presenting. It was the same a thousand years ago, and it will be the same for our space sales alien one thousand years from now.

As stated already, the only things that change are the platform from which presentations are delivered and the tools used to support you in delivering them. They didn't have WebEx in ancient Rome, and a thousand years from now our space sales alien might be able to deliver his presentation telepathically through the universe. However, for the sake of simplicity, let's stay in the present and point out some of the common threads of presentation. We have already defined our target profile; thus, we know whom we need to present to and why. Regardless of the era, vertical, space, job, role, or sales category, a sales professional has to understand what to present, when to present, and how to present. It is within the "what," the "when," and the "how" that we can find these common threads.

What to Present

The message is incredibly important. It's not enough to be the master of the platform and the format. The sales professional has to understand exactly what message he or she is going to convey that will have the most effective impact on the ideal profile. If the goal for presentation is to advance the likelihood of success in the sales creation process, then saying the right things to the right people matters a great deal. A primary key to understanding *what* to *present* starts with knowing your value proposition and knowing your differentiators. Those differentiators and value proposition will be clearly defined through the performance equation. More on that later.

The value proposition and the differentiators at this point are understood. The sales professional and the business have made the investment at the preparation and planning stages. The process of identifying the ideal profile ensured that the value proposition and the differentiators had to be understood and that your solution is aligned with your prospective audience. Part of that process also meant knowing your competition and how you are positioned against them. More on positioning later.

Knowing yourself, your business, your competition, and your audience before ever setting foot in front of them will ensure that you will know what to present. There are a few best practices that go along with the common threads that should be pointed out here. Each of the common threads and best practices is designed to ensure that the presentation will be at an optimal and effective level. They are described here through the lens of the modern day, but the premise for this book is that it was the same a thousand years ago and will be the same a thousand years from now.

A good best practice for verifying that your message is on target is to do a pre-discovery call. Another best practice would include setting the expectations for the audience. The pre-discovery call is simply gathering intelligence prior to the presentation through asking good questions of the key stakeholders who are likely to be part of the decision process. That pre-discovery-phase interaction can also be used to set expectations beforehand. An audience likes to know what they are in store for.

Have multiple PowerPoint's (or other platform support material, such as brochures) for the same client but for different groups. For example, a job in the medical vertical might require the ability to present to more than one type of audience: clinical, bio med, technical, and administration all may have a need for your solution and will participate in the decision process. However, each may perceive the solution in a different way. The point here is your solution may provide value to your target as a whole, but your message during a presentation might have to be customized for separate audiences within the same company.

What to present includes more than being able to understand what to present. Good sales professionals have to recognize and understand that the platform and the format often dictate what is to be presented as well, so flexibility is a key component of the science and art of presentation. A good salesperson should have scripted presentations for short-cycle engagements and should incorporate the ability to be flexible, and to learn how to think on his or her feet and respond to objections and questions off the cuff for those elevator-speech moments. The guy in the elevator is probably not prepared to listen to you for an hour as you break out your laptop and shove a PowerPoint in his face. So learn how to give the same message with equal effectiveness in both long and short forms.

When to Present

Knowing when it makes the most sense to present can be key. Prior to making the arrangements for a presentation, good sales professionals or businesses should know exactly when the decision makers would be most available.

Knowing and understanding the stage of the sales cycle in which the presentation is being given is another key. Timing can be everything, and it's important to know that. A good sales professional needs to understand the timeframe for the decision process within the given sales cycle. There are things to be cognizant of as you filter through your thought process and make timing decisions.

These include the following question: Is there a budget process in place? If there is, what is the budget cycle? A sales professional has to know and understand the context of timing as it relates to effectiveness. It might not make sense to give a presentation to a group of decision makers if that decision can't be made for another two years. Is there a board or a panel involved in the decision process? This could be the case with budgetary timing; a salesperson might need to know if the need for board approval affects the timing. Presentations are about impact, and knowing when to present is one of the keys to achieving your goal for advancing to the next step in the sales creation process.

The timing for when to present has to include more than just being aware of the prospect and the stage of the sales cycle. It must also take into account what the competition is doing. A good sales professional should know and understand when or if the competition is presenting and should also determine the importance of the order. Going last or going first may make all the difference in the world, and making the adjustment in your favor is a key best practice to keep in mind. As with all things related to the professional world of sales, much of the decision process for timing can depend upon the vertical, the space, the job, the role, and the sales category.

How to Present
The science and the art of presentation would not be complete with knowing only what and when to present. It's just as essential to know how to present. Think of the platform (auditorium, classroom, boardroom, elevator, phone, TV, radio, WebEx) as the stage. Think of the format (keynote speech at a college stadium, a corporate event at a large hotel, a one-on-one in an office, a panel presentation in front of a board, a business presentation in a conference room) as the guiding principal for what type of interaction is going to take place. The *how* is going to be the performance. It's going to be the art. And the art of anything often begins with some self-awareness.

There are a number of things a good sales professional should be aware of when it comes time to present a message, regardless of platform or format. These include things like how you walk and talk, and how fast or slow your words come out of your mouth. It's also going to be about your nonverbal communication style—your posture or how much you fidget. Are your hands in your pockets? Do you come across as confident or nervous?

A good sales professional a thousand years ago, today, or a thousand years from now will still need to perfect the art of communicating with style and substance if he or she hopes to elicit a favorable response from his or her presentations. As it relates to the profession of sales, that desired response is for a next-step advancement in the sales process. And *how* you present is often just as critical to success in making that advancement as *what* and *when*.

There are a number of common threads that are timeless and paramount in helping to ensure presentation success. Some of these include

1. **Practice, practice, practice.** The vast majority of the human beings on this planet are scared to death to speak in public. Scared human beings act nervous, can't think straight, and often make poor decisions. Those are all the ingredients for a bad presentation event. Therefore, the best way to mitigate risk is the time-honored tradition of practicing. It doesn't matter if you practice in front of your coworkers, your family, the living room wall, or your dog. Just make sure you do it.

2. **Be prepared for surprises.** Be familiar with all the platforms and all the support tools you might use to present your solutions. The vertical, the space, the job, the role, and the sales category will often determine that platform and the format, but in the real world of professional sales, last-minute changes and surprises are common occurrences. For example, let's assume you are a sales professional in a consultative sale. The common format for presentation is most often an informal discussion with a small group of professionals, and the interaction is typically a back-and-forth question and answer session. When you arrive, you find that the key decision makers have changed their minds as to the format and are asking you to set up a formal PowerPoint and create a WebEx for some folks who want to listen in off premises. In this instance, you'd better hope you know how to format the PowerPoint, know how to connect to the audio-visual equipment in the room properly, how to sign up for a WebEx through an existing account, and how to drop that WebEx into Outlook and send an invite out to those folks who are off premises. If you do not come into that meeting prepared for these types of contingencies, it can prove fatal to your existing sales opportunity.

3. **Who do I bring with me?** This is a must-answer question. Again, not every vertical, space, or job will require the assistance of others, but some might. You have to be prepared to present alone or in a group setting with internal support people. For example,

in the healthcare enterprise software application business, it is typical for both a technical solutions specialist and a clinical specialist to participate in a presentation. For some roles it might be typical to do joint presentations with other vendors that offer complementary products or services. Or in the case of a transactional retail sales category, the sales professional would most likely expect to be doing relatively short, one-on-one presentations with an audience size of one or two. The range is extensive. The primary point here is to know and understand the context of your particular situation and act accordingly.

4. **Know and have the support tools you need.** Some of the modern-day tools can include laptops, audio-visual equipment, marketing materials, and USB sticks to save and distribute PowerPoint's, company trinkets, company white papers, and brochures. The potential support tools are too numerous to list here, but as with just about everything else in the world of professional sales, these items will differ depending on the vertical, space, job, and sales category.

5. **Collect contacts.** This is a must, regardless of the vertical, space, job, or sales category. A typical best practice can include having a sign-in sheet for everyone who comes to the presentation or meeting. It's always a good practice to have a document (paper or digital) that leaves room for feedback. Those contacts may form the basis for future opportunities, and the feedback may serve as the foundation for perfecting the science and art of your presentation.

My final point for this section is that the science and the art of presentation are not boilerplate in the world of professional sales. The presentation is, however, a vital component of the sales readiness template for the sales professional or business. A primary goal for presenting a solution is to have impact and advance the sale through the process.

It's just as important for job seekers truly to have internalized the means and the methods of their prior or existing efforts in prospecting, profiling, and presenting in order to relate effectively their relevance for future jobs of choice as they attempt migrations outside their existing verticals and spaces.

The vertical, the space, the job, the role, and the type of sale as they relate to both the art and the science most often determine the degrees of difficulty and complexity. Those sale types can include transactional, complex, consultative, relationship, farming, hunting, B2B, B2C, wholesale, retail, inside, or outside. Much more on the sales categories later.

In our historical example, once Pete got in front of these target profile prospects, it was time to present them with a value proposition. Pete did his presentations verbally, and he utilized printed notices that gave descriptions of all the services he offered. His value proposition was rooted in what he began to call "the performance equation": performance = process + product + pricing. From a marketing perspective, that value proposition was perfectly aligned with Pete's unique sales differentiators for the goods and services he was offering. Pete's process was built for speed, ease, continuity, reliability, and effectiveness. His customers were simply looking for a process designed to increase the likelihood of success. In addition to having a valued process, he also offered a diversified set of product solutions for his identified target base, and the price point for which he offered those services and products was perceived as reasonable from both ROI and opportunity cost perspectives.

Now that we understand the act of engagement through prospecting, have identified the ideal profile, and have perfected the art and the science of presentation, we must then understand how to create the essence of the message for our target audiences.

CHAPTER 10

THE PERFORMANCE EQUATION: PERFORMANCE = PROCESS + PRODUCT + PRICING

I f the second level of the P's are at the heart of what a sales professional does on a daily basis, then this third level of the P's is at the heart of what is communicated and ultimately serves to become the primary driver for success. Here, it's much less about what you do and more about what you understand. Like every other level of the P's, the depth and the investment you made at the preparation and planning stages will determine your ability to capture the essence of the performance equation. Capturing that essence is key to identifying and communicating the differentiators for the process, product, and price, and gets you to the heart of your true positioning in the marketplace.

For sales professionals, the ability to recognize, understand, internalize, and effectively communicate the performance equation is pivotal in driving success.

For a business, an internal sales audit and evaluation of the sales readiness template serves as the framework for the overall business model. And just like the individual, the business needs to create a system in which a common recognition, understanding, and internalization of the performance equation is communicated in a common language across the continuum of the organization to ensure sustainability and portability of success.

And finally, **a job seeker** has to recognize, understand, and internalize the performance equation for his or her existing and prospective jobs, and must demonstrate an ability to communicate and relate the transferable relevance between the two as he or she attempts to cross a vertical, space, and job.

Therefore, in this section, it's worth exploring and understanding what the performance equation means and giving some brief examples of what differentiation might look like as it relates to a process, a product, and a price.

What Is the Performance Equation?

We are now past the point in the pyramid where we have clearly identified the ideal profile, and we have reached the point of engagement and presentation. But before we open our mouths or put pen to paper, we had better make sure we have recognized, understood, and internalized exactly what needs to be communicated and why.

I believe that just about any value proposition is a function of the above equation. The target profile in the context of the sales process has a needs-fulfillment expectation. Most decisions come as results of deliberation among competing alternatives. Businesses and people make choices because they somehow are able to identify the differentiators that gave evidence for whatever was most meaningful to their basic issues or strategic objectives. This equation is designed to shine a light on those differentiators.

By definition, *performance* is simply an accomplishment of a given task. And as it relates to our sales professionals and businesses, a primary given task is to create sales opportunities.

The given task for our job seeker is to relate previous job-related experience for a migration into a separate vertical, space, job, or role that can provide an optimal level of performance. The job seeker not only has to articulate the performance equation for his or her existing job but must also be able to define and communicate the same for the job he or she is targeting if he or she hopes to communicate, align, and transfer his or her relevance successfully.

Therefore, it can be said that one of our primary objectives for going through the process of performing an internal sales audit, and creating a sales readiness template from preparation to positioning is to get to the essence of what is most valuable about what we have to offer. The key to working through the Pyramid of P's is that it provides a path from which you can recognize, understand, internalize, and ultimately communicate and present to a predetermined audience whatever message and differentiators are most likely to have the most favorable impact resulting in the creation of a successful sale. That is the primary objective for both an existing business seeking to create the most effective and efficient business model possible for its salespeople and a sales professional looking to perform at the highest level possible given the context of his or her vertical, space, job, or role.

Everyone values performance on some level. We appreciate performance in the cars we drive, admire performance in athletics, hold performance in the classroom in high esteem, value the performance of companies we buy from or partner with, and are beholden to and in awe of the performances on the battlefield by our men and women in uniform.

Job seekers and sales professionals yearn to be aligned with businesses, products, or services that rank high on the performance equation within their competitive landscapes. It's within the performance equation that we can see the framework for success. In fact the real and perceived senses of performance are often the driving factors behind customers' decisions to buy or not. The ability to perform is formed by all its associated processes, products, and pricing differentiators, and often serves as the basis for what is called *value proposition*. The totality of the sales readiness template and the performance equation as outlined through the Pyramid of P's serves as the ultimate framework for success for sales professionals, businesses, and job seekers.

The performance equation is the third level of the pyramid, and in many ways we can view it as the most important of all the levels to master. This is really the area in which all of our efforts, which began with preparation and have taken us through every level of the Pyramid, culminate into the true essence of the message we hope to relate to our audience. It's going to show up in the things we say and hopefully be supported by a common message in our marketing materials, internal support, and service infrastructure. When it comes time to present from any platform within any format, it's imperative to understand exactly what we need to say in order to have the optimal level of impact on driving sales opportunities through the funnel. It's not enough to have become the masters of the sales readiness template or a particular business model. It's not enough to have become the subject-matter expert (SME) for a particular vertical, space, or job if we can't somehow use that information, skill, and knowledge to come up with an effective message and set of differentiators and value points that give evidence of true performance in the eyes of our target profile customer.

The essences of those three P words—*process, product,* and *pricing*—are what define a value proposition and give evidence of performance. If, for example, you're an existing sales professional, you likely want to be working at a place from which you can perform. If you have an existing business, you likely want it to be a place that performs. And if you're a job seeker, you likely want to find a place to work that performs. A client will value and pay for performance, a sales professional hopes to achieve performance, and a job seeker hopes to find performance in his or her quest for a job of choice.

Every business on the planet that exists today and has ever existed or will exist can be broken down into a process, a product, and a price. The significance of that statement is that the equation does not apply to just a sales organization but really to any type of business or entity. It could apply just as equally to a business as to the military. For that reason, this third level of the P's is unique—the relatable relevance to prior experience doesn't necessarily have to be rooted in sales or a hard-skill match.

The primary common thread for the performance equation is that it doesn't matter what hard-skill experience you have or from what vertical, space, job, or role you come. It's highly likely that whatever entity it is, it most certainly has a particular process, product, and price point from which you could communicate its particular differentiators. The Pyramid of P's as a communication template is particularly useful in helping anyone do so.

For example, there may be a situation where a military veteran is looking to make the transition to the civilian workforce and is interested in a sales profession. If that veteran is willing to make the investment in going through the rigorous process of creating a readiness template, he or she can relate his or her work-related relevance just as easily as anyone else who may have come from a sales-related background. More on that later.

In each of the process, product, and price categories, a business has a real and perceived difference (a differentiator) in comparison to its competitors. Each of these points of difference has some degree or level of both real and perceived value in the open marketplace. Performance is the key to needs satisfaction, and that satisfaction has marketplace value. In most cases, that is why the term *value proposition* comes into play.

The bottom line is that scoring high on the performance equation will position sales professionals and businesses well for success against the competition. What does it mean to score high? In the simplest of terms, the more differentiators you have for your process, your product, and your price in comparison to your competition, the higher you score in the performance equation. Understanding where you rank on the performance equation and why will give you the ultimate insight into exactly how you or your business is positioned in the overall marketplace.

Let's take a brief look at what a process, a product, and a price are as they relate to the professional world of sales.

Process

In a broad definition, *process* can mean simply any series or number of steps taken to reach a goal. For the purposes of this book, we will define, measure, and evaluate *process* within the context of the sales landscape.

Every business or entity has a way of doing things in terms of its process. Every business or entity has a set of services and solutions and some type of support system or infrastructure in place for how it interacts with end-user clients. Each of those process-related variables will have characteristics that, when measured against alternative competitor solutions, can be positive or negative differentiators. It's the job of every sales professional and business to recognize, understand, and ultimately internalize these differentiators.

Process, within the context of the sales landscape, typically revolves around the customer experience from end to end. That begins typically with the initial interaction or start of the sales cycle between client and customer, and continues through the entire life of the relationship in terms of the support given. The sales cycle and the life of the interaction between client and customer will vary greatly depending on the vertical, space, job, and solution service or product. Results and expectations matter. Within that timeframe of the sales cycle, and within the lifetime of the interaction, there are a number of expectations and experiences that count as differentiators.

The bottom line is that a service and support reputation, along with proof of results in meeting or exceeding someone's process expectations, can mean the difference in having a competitive advantage or not. The number of scenarios and combinations are just too limitless to detail in writing.

But in general, a good example of differentiators could be simply having a process or system that is built for speed, ease, and continuity—one that is likely to result in the customer having a good experience and wanting to come back. The primary point is that a sales professional, a business, and a job seeker have to understand and evaluate the worth of speed, ease, and continuity within the context of their particular verticals, spaces, jobs, and roles. Each has to determine if there is open-market value for those things. He or she has to understand how much speed might be of value, and then must be able to measure that speed in comparison to the competition or alternative solutions.

All of them must be able to ask themselves, "Is my solution and service faster or slower than the others, and how important is that in relation to success?" Communicating that as a differentiator may be the difference between winning a deal and losing one. That is a basic example, but it is one in which these concepts would have to be understood. The number of differentiators are too many to list, and their number and the complexity will be determined by the vertical, space, job, role, product, service, and solution.

The following are just a few examples we could evaluate, consider, and utilize as positive or negative process differentiators.

1) **Speed:** Speed or the lack of it in all areas of process may or may not be king.
2) **Ease of use:** How easy or difficult is it to interact with the company? Do they answer the phone? Do they call or email back in

a timely manner? Are policies and procedures clear and easy to understand? Or are they murky and complex?

3) **Customer service and quality of the service:** Do they meet expectations? Do they have the right number of service people in place to manage client expectations? Are they open 24/7/365? Do others consider them the gold standard for service? Or do they sacrifice service strategically in order to devote a greater portion of their resources to another area—perhaps product and price?

4) **Customer support and the quality of the support:** Are the support people courteous, knowledgeable, and friendly? Does the company have the right number of support people in place to manage support expectations? How do they troubleshoot? Are they open 24/7/365?

5) **Quality of the goods or services produced:** How are the products made? Of what are they made? What's the reputation for the quality of those products and the process with which they are made?

6) **How are the products or services produced and delivered?** Will the ways they are produced make a difference in the minds of the client profile? How about the manner in which they are delivered?

7) **Do they outsource any or all of their customer service and support?** Does that make a difference to the client?

8) **What is the company's reputation for meeting or exceeding expectations?** Do they overpromise and underperform?

9) **Flexibility?** How flexible can they be in their support, their service, and their speed? Do they make exceptions to guidelines? Do others consider them customer friendly or rigid?

10) **What is the business model?** There are many characteristics we must evaluate for differentiation, but understanding the existing overall business model and the strategic objectives that are the basis for it is a must. Not every business model requires that a business have a top-tier process, product, and price all at once. Some may want to sacrifice one aspect of the performance

equation to concentrate on another because it gives them a strategic advantage—do they sacrifice the process in order to gain a separate advantage in pricing or product? You need to find out and understand why.

To put this in the historical perspective we've been following over the last several chapters, let's go back to our Pete story. Pete's process was one built for speed, ease, continuity, reliability, and effectiveness. His customers were simply looking for a process designed to increase the likelihood of success. This meant they needed processes and services. They needed more than just the right tools. They also needed the training for using the methods and tools that would give them maximum effectiveness.

Many of Pete's customers came from urban settings and needed in-depth guidance for survival. They would need to know how to hunt wild game, how to prepare it, what plants to use for sickness, and what kind of water to drink. Pete's Native American guides provided all of this. These customers needed a process that was built for speed and ease and could provide peace of mind. Miners wanted to feel secure in transporting themselves, their goods, and their gold to and from their claims. These customers needed the peace of mind that comes with having a service, and a process they could rely upon for securing their gains.

Pete's contractual security forces were military veterans from the Mexican-American War. His customers valued the peace of mind that came with a service that provided people who were not out to con them or steal from them. Pete prided himself on his ability to provide reliable, credible men and the peace of mind that came with them. People had enough to worry about out there with the bad intentions of their fellow miners. They needed a service and process they could trust. Pete's veterans fit this bill. Therefore, he provided a set of solutions and services that had as its foundation a process that was repetitive, could be relied upon, and was credible. It would eventually gain a widespread reputation. That reputation would help strengthen and build value, and contribute to the overall framework for economic success.

Product

In the context of the sales profession, we can generally classify a product as a solution in the form of a tangible product or a service of some kind. The number of products and services that exist in the world today are like the stars in the universe, and even trying to categorize them would be too onerous for any one book. What is important to understand is that just as there are characteristics we can recognize, compare, and evaluate under the process section, the same is true for products. Some examples of characteristics to consider include the following:

1) **Diversity:** How diversified is the product or solution set? Is the product or solution designed to meet the needs for just about any prospective client within a broad-based target profile? Does it matter? A diversified solution for a product or service might mean multiple products and solutions designed to meet the needs of a whole range of separate client profiles.

2) **Niche:** Is the product or solution designed to meet the needs of a very narrow and specific target profile in a very limited way? Does it matter in the context of the vertical?

3) **Quality of the product or solution:** Is the quality high, medium, or low? It's important to understand your vertical, space, and profile here. A business might be selling what are considered low-quality goods, but this isn't a bad thing as long as it is selling to customers who want them, and the company recognizes and understands how to present the differentiators from any of its competing alternatives.

4) **Type of product or solution:** Do the products or solutions represent new technology, or are they more of the legacy or aging variety? Is the solution innovative in terms of improving an existing solution or product? Or is the solution revolutionary, state of the art, and new in nature?

5) **Outsourcing or turnkey:** How much of the product or solution is outsourced? How much is designed, created, controlled, and delivered in house end to end? How much do these things matter in the context of your particular vertical and space?

One example: Bankers and brokers are both in the business of lending money. The product for both is "lending money." But their business models are quite different, and their characteristics may become differentiators depending on the target profile. We can classify the products of bankers and brokers by the process in which their loans are offered.

A bank has depositors and a broker doesn't. The bank utilizes those deposits to lend money to customers. A broker on the other hand does not have those same bank deposits to use for lending, and thus has to borrow money to lend money. A bank that controls its own portfolio and has its own money to lend can offer its clients flexibility in terms of underwriting and approval guidelines. Basically it's the bank's money, and it can do what it wants with it. If the bank feels like making a loan approval outside of lending guidelines, it's the bank's decision. It doesn't have to rely on any outsourced partnership for approval to do so.

If that same bank has to outsource its lending capacity to a separate financial institution, it would not enjoy the same flexibility because it would no longer be in control of the funds it wants to lend out to the public. Basically it would in effect be acting as a broker, and it's not really the bank's money, so at the end of the day it can't do what it wants with it. It can't make the exception and go outside of approval guidelines for loans. That bank acting as broker would be constricted to following the guidelines of the outsourcing bank.

The ability to control or not control the money might make a huge difference to the client profile with a challenged credit history. Common sense says the bank with the ability to make exceptions to lending policy would be the better option for that client. In the world of competing alternatives, the prospects decision may be dependent on the bank's control and flexibility even though the broker might be offering a lower price point or a quicker approval timeframe.

That's just one example in which outsourcing might matter as a differentiator. The lines between a banker and a broker are blurry at best. The value of outsourcing within the context of the lending business may or may not make a difference depending on the organizations designated ideal profile. Value really is sometimes just all in the eye of the beholder. The key for the sales professional is be the one that understands how to create clarity within those blurred lines, and to also offer meaningful product related insight for the end user. It may mean nothing in the context of another vertical. The key is to know and understand the differentiators for your vertical, space, job, and role.

6) **Flexibility:** How flexible can the product or solution be in terms of how it is both delivered and utilized?

7) **Plans and strategies:** What new products and services are in the pipeline? What does the road map look like? What is likely to change in the business model or strategic objectives? And how might that affect or not affect existing product and service solutions? What percentage of the budget does the organization typically devote to R & D? A business, a sales professional, or a job seeker needs to take an interest in all these things.

8) **Infrastructure:** This is the people, the facility, the equipment, and the technology that support the products and services. The extent to how existing and future product solutions are supported from an internal infrastructure standpoint may be an important differentiator. The type of infrastructure in place today and what plans there are for tomorrow in terms of how solutions and products will be supported can be enormous differentiators.

Looking at our historical example, Pete had a mixed and diversified product line that included a combination of tangible goods, survival guidance, training, and security. His tangible products included goods such as wagons, mules, pickaxes, shovels, pans, and food. The less tangible product line included the guidance for the movement of those goods and for finding pre-scouted, targeted spots to mine. The product line included survival guidance and security forces for peace of mind.

The real value in the product line was diversity. His product differentiator was that it was diversified enough to be able to meet the needs of just about any of his prospected target clients and at the same time was designed for flexibility to offer customization. The product and services had an a la carte-style list. The hard services had a cost, but depending on the totality of the services chosen, the percentage of the gold find would be proportionate to the totality of the services signed up for. In essence, the more Pete's services were to be involved in the operations of his clients, the higher the percentage of the findings they would owe.

Pricing

This is usually the first thing anyone thinks of when it comes to the decision to buy or not to buy something. How much does the product or service cost? In a sea of competing alternatives, price is certainly an obvious differentiator. That is indeed important. However, there is more to pricing than simply the cost of things.

For example, sometimes the higher price makes more sense. Sometimes the decision not to purchase can result in an opportunity cost. And sometimes making the choice to buy something makes sense from an ROI standpoint—meaning it just may pay to pay.

Just as there are characteristics we must evaluate for the process and the product, there are characteristics we must consider and evaluate for the pricing differentiators. The vertical, the space, the solution, the business model, and the overall strategic objective often dictate the price point and emphasis.

For example, if the product or solution is considered a commodity, then the price point often becomes the most significant driving factor in the decision for the end user. An example of a commodity might be coffee, oil, or raw materials. A commodity is most typically identified when it's a solution or product that in and of itself may vary only slightly in terms of quality, meaning there are not really many differentiators in the product itself or even the process, so the only thing to be evaluated is price.

On the other hand, in other product categories, the price point matters very little or perhaps an equal amount in relation to the product and process differentiators in the performance equation. If the product or solution is considered or classified as a niche, premium product, solution, then perhaps the price point to be considered is not as much of a priority. An example might be the high-end automobile space. The price point differentiation might not rank very high on the performance equation when making a choice between a Ferrari and a Lamborghini.

There are additional characteristics for price point evaluation that go beyond the solution category and the business model. These can include things such as opportunity cost, ROI, and outsourcing.

Opportunity Cost

Most of us think of cost as a tangible thing, meaning I make the decision to spend capital, and then it's gone. However, in the world of commerce sometimes it's the decision *not* to spend the money that is the true cost. For example, making a choice to go with the lower price saves money from a tactical standpoint in the short term, but perhaps that short-term thinking will cost the business from a strategic standpoint over the long term. For a deeper-dive example, consider the electronic medical record (EMR) space in the healthcare IT vertical. A hospital can decide to purchase an EMR from a vendor at a lower cost in comparison to others because they are hoping to save money in the short term in order to use the extra dollars saved to purchase new patient monitors. That might seem like a good idea. However, in doing so perhaps they have given up on a greater reward over the long term. Perhaps that EMR product solution is limited in terms of which departments can utilize it, and perhaps it does not have the capacity to allow for the growth that might happen five years from now. Or perhaps the price point was cheaper, but the process in which the solution is implemented, delivered, and supported turns out to be more costly in the long run to support the infrastructure. Five or ten years from the time of purchase, the hospital might decide the entire system has to be scrapped because it no longer can support its strategic objectives.

The more expensive EMR they initially bypassed turns out to be well equipped to allow for that strategic growth, and its ability to offer the solution in every department in the hospital is a differentiator that has an impact directly on the long-term bottom line. So in the end the short-term tactical decision for savings on the price point came at the expense of product and process differentiators, and the long-term cost was in the end much higher. There are countless white papers out there for any number of verticals, spaces, and products that can describe this scenario as well. In the end, that decision not to go with the higher price-point alternative turns out to be a huge opportunity cost.

ROI

This is simply a return on investment. Every business makes the decision to invest in its business model, and every end user in the open marketplace makes a choice to buy or not to buy. Sometimes that decision to buy is rooted in an expectation for a return on the money spent. It simply means you make the decision to spend the money today because it will help you achieve a tactical or strategic goal that will make some type of profit that exceeds the amount of what you spend. Automation tools are a good example of a common investment that companies are eager to make as a means of capturing a desired ROI.

The ability to offer the end user an attractive ROI can often help to make the case for why a higher price point today makes sense in relation to any competing alternatives that perhaps don't offer that same level of return. It's similar to opportunity cost in many ways. It's also true to say that not every solution offers an ROI, and the value of being able to do so is like just about everything else in the sales profession in that it's dependent upon the vertical, space, job, role, and solution.

Outsourcing

Outsourcing is a characteristic that should be evaluated for all three P's in the performance equation, especially for pricing. If a business has to outsource for anything, there is a cost associated with it. That cost is typically passed on to the end-user customer. Therefore, an ability to offer a turnkey product or solution often can create a powerful differentiator in the marketplace.

Let's go back to our example of comparing a bank that lends money and a broker that does the same. The bank, on one hand, has a portfolio and money collected from depositors. It has the ability to lend that money to the public and is in control of the entire process from end to end. In doing so, it not only controls what type of lending products it wants to offer and in what manner it processes the delivery of it, it is also in much more control of the price point. Because a bank can operate as a turnkey solution for lending, it can offer more flexibility for its product, its process, and its price. Every business has a cost of goods sold and a sales price. The amount in between is the margin for profit. A bank, by design, has the ability to offer its own funds and act as a portfolio lender. It often has the ability to offer a lower price point and do it with flexibility because it doesn't have to pay a premium for having to outsource for those funds.

A broker, by design of its business model, does not have the luxury of having a pool of deposits on hand to lend to the public. Instead, it is dependant upon borrowing those funds or in some cases acting in a correspondent capacity when lending those funds. In both instances, its cost of goods sold is likely higher, and the ability to offer a lower price point with flexibility may be greatly diminished in the open marketplace. On the other hand, the advantage of being a broker is the reduction in risk that comes with using other people's money. Implementing a business model that offers a swifter process, and better customer experience may also offset the negative effect of having a higher price point for the broker.

Therefore, even though the bank has an inherent price point advantage up front, that doesn't automatically mean the bank has the winning formula versus the broker.

So, just like product or process, understanding the points of differentiation for the pricing characteristics is the key to success in capturing an impactful performance and value message. Just like the process and product categories, the pricing evaluation is just as dependant upon any number of variables and combinations, including, which vertical, space, job, role, and solution are in scope.

Performance = process + product + pricing. That's the performance equation. So regardless if you're a business, a sales professional, or a job seeker making a cross-vertical migration, you will want to be sure to align yourself with an entity that gives you an ability to communicate and present the essence of performance in ways that will be meaningful to the ideal profile. If you can do that successfully, you will be successful in your end-goal task for sales creation regardless of the vertical, space, job, role, or solution.

Here is an example of what the essence of a performance equation message might look like for a given solution:

"I have a process that is built for speed, ease, continuity, and reliability end to end and a product line that is diversified enough to meet the needs of just about any end user within my ideal target space. We offer it at a price point that is perceived as reasonable and acceptable in the minds of our clients. Some companies and competing alternatives can offer differentiators for perhaps one or two aspects of those P's, but very few can do so for all three. We know we offer a solution and a product that can provide meaningful differentiators for each of those P's; thus, we are confident that what we really offer is expertise, security, credibility, and ultimately the proof of performance."

The key at this point is to understand the full context of where you are, what you do, and why you do it. The performance equation brings to the surface and helps us truly understand the apex for what we truly want to recognize and understand as sales professionals, businesses, and job seekers. We want to understand the true essence of how we are or will be positioned in the marketplace. To be the masters of our true positioning is, in the end, the truest essence of what we seek to understand, as it is what will ensure we are performing at the highest form possible as it relates to achieving the end task of sales creation effectively and efficiently.

That recognition, understanding, and internalization of our true position is the final piece that in the end highlights the value for our adherence to the Pyramid of P's as either a sales readiness template or a communication template.

Looking at it from a historical perspective, our old friend Pete had some pricing that was certainly attractive, most notably from an opportunity cost perspective. His hard, tangible goods were not cheaper than what they could be bought for at someone else's store. However, he designed his offering so the premium paid for those goods would be baked into the overall product solution selection. In reality, Pete's investment in preparation and planning to define his ideal profile really paid off when it came to price perceptions. The net result was that the perception of value outweighed the concern for cost.

The cost for products and services were important to the client. However, as Pete's business reputation grew, the cost for services became increasingly more than just an afterthought. The value of the services was the priority, and presenting those services in an impactful way helped to ensure a strong impression that the price was worth the service in return. Simply put, it was just good business and worth the money to secure the services Pete was offering, and to do otherwise might result in a much bigger opportunity cost. In effect, he designed his services to do the one thing the miners valued more than anything else: to improve their chances of success. For an inexperienced miner of the like that fit Pete's profile, the choice to go it alone often resulted in a huge opportunity cost. Pete was worth the price. The ROI for a miner was a tangible one.

Therefore, Pete's value proposition was a very strong one. He had a process built for speed, ease, continuity, effectiveness, and security. He had the kind of process that customers found credible, and they would come to trust the experience. It resulted in not just repeat long-term business but referral business as well.

Pete offered a product line encompassing a combination of tangible assets and service solutions. His product line was diversified enough to satisfy the needs of just about any miner. It was a full-service turnkey solution that was also flexible enough to provide a la carte, customized offerings. Pete had an ideal target profile, but at the same time there wasn't any miner currently working or anyone en route who couldn't find some value in his diversified product line.

In addition, his pricing was competitive enough to be attractive to any existing or prospective client, especially from opportunity cost and ROI perspectives, and it was uniquely valuable from a business model standpoint in that the joint-venture portion was based on a proportionate scale in relation to the services rendered. As an example, if you contracted for the full suite of solutions, the shared percentage of the gold extracted was in a sliding scale comparison. Therefore, if Pete had a process built for speed, ease, continuity, security, and effectiveness along with a product line diversified enough and flexible enough to meet the needs of just about any miner and finally a price point that was competitive, then he had what equaled performance.

CHAPTER 11

POSITIONING

S o, what is positioning? The word can mean a great many things. We have all heard of a GPS, or global positioning system, which can indicate our location—an exact longitude and latitude for where we are in the universe. Typically, most of us think of location in the physical aspect. However, as it relates to this book and to the Pyramid of P's, we will review what positioning means within the confines of the sales profession.

Positioning is the apex of the Pyramid. It sits atop all the other P's because everything that precedes it in the sales readiness and communication template contributes to the context of who you are as a business or professional and what you offer to the marketplace, including why and how you offer it, as well as when you *should* offer it. Finally, it lets you know exactly to whom you should be offering it.

When you understand the full context of your positioning, your efforts begin to act like the point of a spear as it relates to the efficiency and effectiveness for all your actions. It's not just your actions that have become sharpened; your mind has been sharpened as well. At this point in the Pyramid, you also have the highest possible level of understanding and the most concise and clear picture of exactly how to carry out all of your tactical and strategic objectives for sales opportunity creation.

No level of training, product knowledge, action plans, or utilization of the most artfully honed methodology application would translate into very many sales without a thorough understanding of positioning in the marketplace.

Our poor misguided space sales alien proved that in his failed attempt to sell moon rocks and electric heaters to the animals of the Sahara. He had the know-how and the ability to fly a rocket through space, but he never had a clue as to how he should have positioned his solutions and products as they related to his target territory on Earth.

Making the investment and taking the time to self-audit, and to adhere to a repetitive, process-based platform and operating system like the Pyramid of P's is the kind of framework for success that can ensure sustainability because it's comprehensively designed to create a highly visible path laced with certainty.

Good news! Let's assume that in the year 3035, we have the ability to go back in time and do things over again. So our space sales alien decides to make it a new day, and instead of jumping into his spaceship at a moment's notice, he develops a whole new paradigm and pauses before acting impulsively by just jumping into his rocket. This time, he makes a decision to create the conditions for a more certain path to success. That path and framework for success will include a commitment and an adherence to a sales readiness template. That template will be the Pyramid of P's.

The product will still be moon rocks. Our astronaut, with a new-found attitude and a strong work ethic, begins the methodical internalization process, and invests into the deep dive of preparation, research and study. This time, he gathers, categorizes, and internalizes everything he can find out about the Earth's atmosphere, terrain, landscape, and inhabitants. He even includes the exact coordinates of the mountains and oceans. He learns about the dangers of animals and cannibals. He learns about the inhabitants' likes and dislikes. He learns there are differences between the animals, the fish, and the plants, and that geography and culture can make a difference as it relates to needs and expectations.

He studies the competition. He studies the other alien-based competitors; their business models; their value propositions; and their *products, processes, pricing*, and their reputations for *performance*. He learns about their experiences, their successes, and their failures. He will eventually have enough quality information to help him narrow his focus down into a *plan* of action that will include identifying and *presenting* to the ideal *profile* for his moon rock inventory.

Our space sales alien understands the context of who would most likely buy, why, and where he would most likely find them. He studies all the modes of communication on the planet Earth and gains an understanding of the presentation platforms and the various formats with which his target profile prefers to engage most often. He recognizes and internalizes the real and perceived differentiators for the process, the product, and the price point he can offer. He practices and masters presenting the essence of the value proposition that gives evidence of the inherent proof of performance that his differentiators can bring to light in the eyes of his target profile. He knows exactly who his clients are, where they will be, and when they most likely will be available to hear his message and presentation.

The target that makes the most sense is the human species. Unlike plants and animals, humans have brains designed not just for learning but also for curiosity. Moon rocks will interest them. People from a state called Iowa are known to be naturally curious from a cultural standpoint, are highly educated, and have a reputation of being friendly to outsiders. Iowa is also flat, so there are no mountains to crash into, and it is landlocked. Therefore, he has no worries about drowning in any oceans. There are no records of any alien or competitor companies in Iowa at the time; thus, we can expect to hear very little objection to the space sales alien's differentiators and value points for the moon rocks. Iowa is considered pretty much virgin territory—a fantastic upside. In fact many of the recent news articles have shown there is some discussion throughout the small towns of Iowa about a built-up demand for moon rock inventory among the area's inhabitants.

At this point our space sales alien finally feels confident enough to set foot inside his spaceship. This time he is perfectly positioned to proceed with focus and clarity. No wasted efforts on this trip. No unwarranted sidetrack stops to the electric heater distributor. The framework for success is in place. The discipline and adherence to the fundamentals are about to pay off. The likelihood of success is looking very good. Our space sales alien fires up the rockets, and off he goes to a very successful do-over.

At this point we know that our space sales alien works for a company that has a business model with a strong infrastructure in place that can support its sales professionals and their objectives. We know that the business took the time to perform an internal sales audit to make sure that their infrastructure did indeed have a sales template that was ready and able to support its sales objectives. We know that it's a business that values having a repetitive, process-based operating system and framework designed for flexibility and portability in place. He works for a company that knows the framework and sales readiness template is what serves its interest and will serve the interests of all its sales professionals not only today but in the future as well. We also now know that our space sales alien has bought in to that system, and the sales readiness template will be the platform for creating his own optimal framework for success in achieving his long-term and sustainable sales goals.

At this point it's evident that he indeed understands the power that comes with information gathering, categorizing, and internalizing as a means to prepare for all things sales related. He has understood how to filter through the mountains of data in order to pull the common threads. He knows that these threads will serve as the framework and plan for his interactions and engagements as he prospects, profiles, and presents his way through his days, weeks, and year. The adherence to the sales readiness template will help our space sales alien recognize, internalize, and communicate all the differentiators within the performance equation as they relate to his process, his product, and his pricing points. And finally, our space sales alien will reach the apex of his success in his ability not only to act with precision but, just as important, to have the highest possible level of understanding with exactitude of his overall positioning for himself, his company, the vertical, the space, the job, and the role.

It is within those same common threads and the fundamentals of all the P's that our space sales alien can use the Pyramid as not just a sales readiness template but also a communication template. He knows with certainty that he can now and forever relate, communicate, and transfer his relevance for any future job of choice regardless of the vertical, the space, the job, or the role.

It's very important to note that no part of the P's is mutually exclusive, and none can be truly effective without the sum of them. The preparation, planning, prospecting, profiling, and presentation of the differentiators for a process, a product, and a price all revolve around and are integral parts of the overall positioning. They work together in tandem. The bottom line is that when we adhere to a sales readiness template like the Pyramid of P's correctly, it serves as the ultimate effective and efficient directive vehicle for all the actionable efforts of a business and a sales professional. It also does the same for the job seeker when used as a communication template for vertical migration efforts in relating and transferring job-related relevance while in transition.

In looking one last time at our historical example, we can see that preparation was indeed the foundation for Pete's success. Without it, he may never have concluded that competing head-on with other entrepreneurs of the time for the same services would have been a disastrous and losing proposition. It was that process that led him down a discovery profile path that resulted in creating an incredibly successful niche-service offering in the gold mining transportation vertical and all the ancillary services built along with it. That step-by-step process is what eventually led to a unique and winning position in the marketplace.

If preparation is the foundation to any success, then **positioning** is the pinnacle that puts it into context and gives it visibility, strength, and standing. The in-depth understanding of who you are and where you are in a market space is invaluable to any business. His value proposition and his understanding of how to implement it could not have been possible without developing an understanding of his positioning in the marketplace. The positioning is definitely the pinnacle of the pyramid, but the key to the effectiveness of the P's is that they are designed to work in tandem. Basically, it all has to work together or it will not work to maximum effectiveness and efficiency.

Pete eventually became an extremely successful salesman and entrepreneur, due in large part to the framework for success he developed along with his adherence to the readiness template he created, which was designed for actionable and repetitive processes. For Pete, information was the key to understanding that his unique **positioning** within the marketplace could not have been a success without the heavy preparation and planning he started with. Without that initial **preparation** and **planning**, he never could have successfully implemented the steps that revolved around the **prospecting** and **profiling** of targets. Without that

foundation, he never could have effectively **presented** his **value proposition** in such a creative and meaningful way to those who would be most
likely open to hearing its message. Without that foundation, he never
could have identified all the differentiating aspects of his value proposition along the continuum of the **performance equation**, which came to
include the **process**, the **product**, and the **pricing**.

PART III: RELATE YOUR RELEVANCE

CHAPTER 12

HISTORY OF THE P'S & THE CONCEPT OF TRANSFERABLE RELEVANCE

As I've said before, the Pyramid of P's, acting as the basis for the fundamentals of sales, was the same a thousand years ago as it is today, and it will remain the same for the next thousand years and even the thousand years after that. No matter what the time period, the science remains the same; only the landscape and the technology change, forcing salespeople, businesses, and job seekers to change right along with them if they want to stay in the game. To explicate this idea and give some further examples of the practical uses of the Pyramid of P's, over the next few chapters we'll go back to our story about Pete and see how he—and many who came after him—continued to use the Pyramid as they made decisions to migrate to different verticals.

Pete's business was a big success. But by 1855 the landscape had changed dramatically. The surface gold had pretty much been dug up, the migration of new miners had slowed, and the largest corporations with the ability and the capital to mine the area in massive and techno-logical ways meant the target profile for Pete's solution had waned. His cycle of opportunity was coming to an end, and he recognized it. The question for Pete would be what to do next.

By this time in Pete's life, he was a subject-matter expert in all things related to mining, and his skills, as a master salesman and entrepreneur were evident. The question he asked himself and that would eventually be asked of him was, "What was valuable and relevant specifically about his set of skills?" Pete would eventually have a eureka moment. But first things first. He believed in preparation, and he believed in planning. He understood that before he could make a new choice and change what he was going to do for a living, he had to understand what the specific elements and aspects of his work life have been if he had any hope of making them relevant for anything that was purposeful. He had to think beyond just the obvious hard skills he possessed.

Pete's first step was to do a self audit, and to ask himself what he enjoyed most about his role in providing mining services and solutions, and **WHY.** He first and foremost loved creating frameworks for success for himself and for others. He was a curious person by nature, and he could never hear enough travel stories from his customers who came from the California Trail and the others who came by boat overseas. In those early days of 1848, at his parents' small hotel, Pete would stay up until all hours of the night listening to travel stories. The modes of transportation—ocean vessels, reverse steamships, wagons, trains, and horses—were fascinating to him, and those stories gave rise to Pete's understanding of the value of transporting goods. They also became the foundation for his success in sales and marketing.

After a long time of thinking about it, Pete decided he was most intrigued by the steamships that traveled the inland waterways transporting goods and people. Many of the miners who came to California had spent time aboard steamships during their great migrations west. That was it! Pete loved the value in transporting goods. He loved helping people go where they wanted to go, getting the goods they needed, and ensuring those people and goods got to the end-destination point in a way they expected. These elements were the essence of his **"why"** for wanting to pursue a life in transportation sales.

It was really what he loved most about his mining experiences too— the intrigue of helping solve the conceptual puzzle of how to navigate a landscape filled with so many life-threatening barriers. He loved assembling the assets, the people, and the necessary relationships to create a set of services that could accomplish the transportation needs and expectations for so many. Pete's sense of purpose could be satisfied by the simple fact that he loved creating that framework for success. His sense of passion revolved around anything that involved the transport of goods and people.

So, when the need for his framework had waned by the mid-1850s, Pete thought, *Steamships!* He had heard and learned all about them from the people coming west. Pete thought about it and decided it was time to go east.

Steamships

Pete decided he was going to find a job involving steamships, and find a way to provide services and solutions for helping to transport goods, services, and people. He packed his belongings and, armed with the knowledge of steamships passed on to him by those who had come west and from the preparation and study he had done on his own, he headed out on the California Trail going east.

Pete carried with him his journal about steamship history. In that journal were descriptions of how steamships were used, what kinds there were, where they could be found, etc. He thought the basic knowledge would be enough to find work, but he knew more than just the basics. He knew the history of it all as well. He knew that steamships were newer technology in the early 1800s. The steam engines that powered the paddlewheels of boats were revolutionary. The powerful steam engine allowed goods, services, and people to move against the river current, which, on rivers such as the Mississippi, could simply be too strong for manpower propulsion, thus transport and commerce was restricted to one way.

The Louisiana Purchase and the boom of the cotton industry in the South had given rise to a huge need to move cotton northward. The steamboat became a pivotal piece of technology in moving that cotton against the current, up the mighty Mississippi. Those boats carried more than just cotton, though. Business included rice, tobacco, timber, and of course people.

By that time, the West had already grown expansively with people and commerce. Those populations needed a way to travel and transport goods. The steamboat was the perfect piece of technology, and Pete wanted to be a part of that framework for success somehow. He had never actually seen one of the boats, but he paid attention to the descriptions, the uses, and the differentiators. He knew how long they were, what they were made of, how some were built for passenger comfort and luxury and some were built with multiple boilers for speed. Pete had heard about the famous Natchez steamers. These were grand steamboats that were mostly built in Ohio and were used for the transport of goods and people. Pete hoped he could somehow find his way to the Mississippi River and perhaps even meet the famous Captain Leathers, for whom the Natchez steamers were built.

Pete didn't get a chance to meet the great and famous Leathers because he never made it that far south. Instead, in 1855, the then-twenty-four-year-old stopped in the crossroads city of St. Louis, a two-pronged point in a great supply chain. Supplies and people going west to the California Trail passed through St. Louis, as did goods (including bales of cotton, cottonseed, sugar, molasses, and poultry) and people coming north on the Mississippi River. To Pete, this again looked like an incredible opportunity, with people coming and going from multiple directions, just as he had seen in the California Gold Rush. In addition, St. Louis also had location, location, location. This seemed like a good place for Pete to be. Surely he would again find a way to conceptualize the landscape, and discover points of opportunity to create frameworks for success for somebody.

Pete idolized steamboat pilots for their skill and knowledge. They had to know and understand river currents and how, when, and why they could change. He had to be familiar with all the ports and the details associated with each one. It took meticulous study and preparation.

He also had to know about what threatened steamboat operations. Boiler explosions were a big problem and made working on a steamboat very dangerous. Inspection agencies didn't exist in the 1850s, and workers, merchants, and passengers pursued their transactions at their own risk. Pete met some former steamboat workers, and some of them were badly scarred from boiler explosions. They also warned him of the gamblers who could rob a man of just about everything but his skin.

On May 30, 1852, the Steamboat Act was passed. This act gave enforcement powers to the Department of the Treasury and created the federal maritime Steamboat Inspection Service. The law required inspection and testing of the hydraulic boilers, and licenses were issued to operate them. In retrospect, according to most reports, this act proved to be pretty useless, but it was a start.

Pete, true to his nature, knew he didn't want to work with his hands for a living, and he had no more mechanical aptitude for hydraulic boiler systems than he had for hydraulic mining. But he saw an opportunity from the same place he had seen his mining opportunities. He wanted to provide services, and he wanted to create frameworks for success in the transportation services vertical. He figured steamboat transport services were, at their core, no different from services provided by the mining transport business. His success in this realm would be, for the most part, contingent upon the same basic set of principles, ideas, and repetitive processes that had made him successful in the mining business.

Pete heard the stories of miners who worked themselves to the bone on the ships for very little pay. And he thought it sounded pretty boring to have to master the work skills to operate a boiler or a furnace and learn how cylinders and pistons worked. The idea of being awakened in the middle of the night to fix such things was absolutely frightening to Pete. The days and nights on a ship—sweeping and mopping decks, doing laundry, or being a cook—sounded very mundane.

However, Pete could identify with one person onboard, and that was the dock superintendent, who acted as the chief broker on behalf of the ship's owners. The superintendent was in charge of making sure the provisions and supplies were purchased as cheaply and as efficiently as possible. They were the chief buyers in charge of handling the sales people.

When the steamboats came into port to get support, the supply store representatives would line up. Pete wanted to work on behalf of those suppliers. He felt his time as an entrepreneur, providing targeted supplies and services, could serve him well in this capacity. The supplier representatives had to understand their customers, their differences based on their destinations, the types of ships, and the relationships that needed to be developed to help give him an edge over his competition's supplier reps. Bad cargo, damaged cargo, or the wrong cargo could be a problem. The supplier that provided the best **process**, the right **product**, and at the right **prices** would have an edge in the **value proposition** game. Pete knew that if he were to have any success in sales on these docks, he would have to understand how to position and sell to these chief buyers.

The key for Pete would be to find the right supplier—one that would be positioned for the best framework for success. He wanted to supply the steamships with the optimal framework for their success and do the same for himself and his employer.

Suppliers, buyers, and men who worked on ships needed to understand the intricacies of loading and packing freight properly. That took experience. Space was valuable because it equaled money and could also equal safety. For instance, it was valuable to know that deadweight was best placed in the center of the ship's hold to act as a steadying mechanism, while cured provisions were packed at the very front or the very back to safeguard them from heat damage. For the passengers boarding these ships, such arrangements would be safer than capsizing. Buyers and owners alike valued anyone that could differentiate himself by offering unique insight related to anything having to do with safety and dollars. Pete wanted to be that guy and he knew it would take some work to get there.

The Rise of the Rivers

Pete knew that as he'd begun his venture as an entrepreneur in gold mining, he would do the same for the steamship business. He knew it all began with preparation. Pete had learned a lot about the famed Mississippi from those travelers who had arrived in California. It flowed all the way from Northern Minnesota down to the Gulf of Mexico, cutting right through the heart of America. It became—and still is today—an important entity of commerce in the United States. The great river highway made it possible for the rapid growth in the Midwest and upper Midwest and acted as the platform for the huge migration west. The enormous source of timber along the Mississippi created a huge boom. All that expansion out west required wood.

The economic transportation history along the Mississippi River was transformed, like most verticals, by technological innovation. The transportation modes on rivers evolved from Indian canoes to keelboats and flatboats and eventually to the steam engine. The ability to go bidirectional at will was a game changer for the flow of goods and people. The steamboat would eventually be supplanted by diesel engines. However, for the purposes of this book we will remain in the steamboat age to illustrate the commonality of transferable relevance from vertical to vertical as technology continuously creates change, forces adaptation, and creates an atmosphere for opportunity for those who understand how to adapt and transfer their relevance to the destination careers of their choice, rooted in passion and purpose. No matter how much technology changes the game, you can always find a way to do what you love to do—as long as you're willing to put in the work to understand how and why.

Though the West was beginning to expand, it was still generally a wilderness in the 1850s. So for the settlers and people migrating there, the waterways were like our present-day freeways. They were quite simply faster, safer, and a lot more comfortable than a stagecoach on a bumpy road. The steamship was a great innovation. We were to that point still reliant in many ways on horses pulling wagons and carriages. However, wagons and carriages could transport only so much and only so fast. Until the steamship, large transports of goods in inland America could really go only with the current. The expansion of our country was hastened and made easier by the steamship because of its ability to carry huge amounts of raw material at great speeds in areas where such services hadn't existed. Rail services did exist in the 1850s on a large scale, but they could not support the vast areas of our country that were exploding with populations.

Prior to the steamship, larger sailing vessels could go upstream, but it could take weeks to wait for the exact winds and exact currents to do it. It was also a challenge to get in and out of harbors, and to avoid sandbars and collisions with other boats. The steam-powered ship could be more agile and eventually became the dominant transportation source on water. It replaced manual oars and even sails on rivers.

Pete needs a job

When Pete arrived in St. Louis, his plan was to go to New Orleans and perhaps find a job working on the Natchez. However, St Louis was much to his liking. Its crossroads atmosphere and the opportunities it presented to men of conceptualizing and entrepreneurial natures were perfect for him.

Pete knew he didn't want to be a steward, a deckhand, a cabin boy, or a watchman, or even the dock superintendent. Those were all more or less labor-related. He also knew he didn't have the direct hard skills needed to become a pilot, a captain, or an engineer. He did know the basic differences between the types of boats, what they carried, and why. He also knew some things about the competition for transportation in general. The railroads were a competing option for moving goods, services, and people. The wagon and horse and keelboat rafts were also competing options. He had learned all about these things from his miner friends. Many of the men who had come west were former steamboat, railway, and raft workers.

Pete was most intrigued by the commerce associated with the steamships. His conceptualizing nature, his communication skills, his success in offering transport-related services in the gold field, and his passion for those things had him perfectly aligned to offer value on behalf of a supply company. The trick would be to find out which one would even listen to him and give him serious consideration. He had no steamship or hard-skill experience in any of the services associated with waterway transportation and commerce.

William "Mr. B." Ready

Pete met Mr. B. one morning at one of the docks. Mr. B. owned a wholesale cargo company that was, like so many other businesses of that time, growing because of demand. As a wholesale goods organization, they simply contracted with local producers of goods, purchased those goods in bulk, and made arrangements for transport to end destinations for retail and wholesale organizations that were in need of those goods.

Pete, understanding that Mr. B.'s business was growing, asked if he could have a job as a sales representative. The company needed men who knew and understood how to contract and negotiate with not just the dock superintendents, but also the end users for business-related goods. The sales professional had to be able to handle the full sale and delivery cycle, from producer to transport to end user, efficiently and effectively. Mr. B.'s primary mode of delivery to his end users was steamship, and he needed men who understood the commerce of steamship cargo delivery as much as he needed men who could broker transactions for goods and services.

Mr. B. asked Pete about his steamboat experience. Had he ever worked on or with one? Pete replied no but said he had been in the mining business out west, in California. He had worked as a sales and supply agent for men looking to mine for gold.

Mr. B laughed and said, "Well, I'm sure you were good at what you did, but gold mining has nothing to do with the business of steamboat transportation. I need a man with business acumen and experience—a man who understands river transportation and the complexities of the steamboat cargo landscape. It appears you don't have that kind of related experience. You seem like a fine young man, and it looks like you were successful in the gold business. You might want to return to it."

Pete patiently listened to what he said and agreed sadly. He went back to his hotel feeling a little deflated. St. Louis looked like a great place to find some work but might not have been the kind of place that could use a man like Pete. He didn't have any direct experience with anything out there on the big rivers. He didn't have relationships. He didn't know the way of the land, and he had never worked directly with any of the relevant technology.

Pete asked himself, "What do I have to offer?" He went to sleep that night with all of these lingering thoughts and doubts.

Transferable Relevance

Pete woke up in the middle of the night with a different thought. He replayed the conversation in his mind over and over. Mr. B. didn't even want to consider him because he couldn't see any value in someone who didn't have the exact hard-skill experience with steamship technology and commerce. The more Pete thought about it, the more he thought, *So what?* How could he not have seen it? How could he not have responded to that rejection?

He needed a second chance at a conversation. He was confident he could create an image of value. When Pete really thought about the job description, it was clear he was extremely qualified for this role, and he believed he could offer a very high level of value.

He found Mr. B. the next day. Pete made his approach and asked Mr. B if he could perhaps have fifteen minutes of his time. Mr. B. liked Pete and asked him to have a seat.

"What can I do for you, Pete? Would you like me to help you find a job as a steamboat worker?" Mr. B. asked. "I have some great contacts. I think I can help you."

"No, sir," Pete answered. "I have no desire or passion to work with my hands or in any type of technical capacity. I want to work for your company. I'm the perfect man for the job, and I'm relevant in every way."

Mr. B., looking amused, laughed. "Pete, I admire your tenacity, but—"

Pete cut him off. "Sorry, sir. All I want to do is ask you some questions and then make a case for why you need a man like me. You will say yes."

Mr. B., a patient man, said, "Sure, kid. Ask me anything you want."

The Job Profile

Pete had brought with him the job profile description Mr. B. had published in the newspaper. Mr. B. needed a man who knew how to buy from local retailers, collect those goods, negotiate with dock superintendents, and strategically sell them as a supplier in bulk to purchasers at end-destination sites along the river. The steamships would be the transportation vehicles for those goods. Mr. B. needed a man with steamboat knowledge and experience. The man chosen for the job would need to have established relationships with steamship personnel and the end users at destination spots along the river. The man would need to build credibility with those buyers to ensure he would win the contracts on behalf of Mr. William Ready. The candidate needed to understand both the retail and wholesale commerce landscapes along the river. He would need to know how to collect and ensure delivery of the wholesale and retail goods.

Pete knew he needed to be an expert in all things related to the boats, the rivers, the people, and the towns along the mighty Mississippi. His role would be to purchase goods from retailers such as farmers, producers, lumber mills and sawmills, cotton companies, etc. He would then arrange for those goods to be transported to destination buyers. His employer would also have him act as an agent to secure transport for human cargo. Safe and on-time travel could be sold at a premium. Pete could provide that. He had spent time developing relationships with the dock superintendents in charge of overseeing the loading of the boats, and making sure cargo was going where it was supposed to go.

Pete knew all of those things. Now he just needed a way to communicate that knowledge in an effective way to Mr. B.

The P's

"Mr. B," Pete asked, "Do you believe in preparation and planning?"

Mr. B. said, "Yes, of course I do. They are the foundation for everything, in my opinion."

"Well, I am glad we agree on that. Let me explain to you what I understand about the steamboat business as a display of the amount of **preparation** I have done in readying myself for this kind of opportunity."

Pete went on to explain to Mr. B. that steamboats ran on what was called a packet, meaning they had regularly scheduled runs between destinations. It was still preferable to travel by railroad, which still required lots of stops and travel to other railways because they were not yet interconnected on a grand scale. Passengers forced to travel between railroads were often hassled by thieves and con men.

"Mr. B.," said Pete, "I know how to contract with the steamship companies that will be transporting your goods. The destination cities are growing, and the demand is huge in those cities. It's a good time to be a supplier if you know how to compete for the services. The steamships link the North and South as never before, and both need each other. The South needs the North's manufacturing goods, and the North needs the South for things like cotton. There is fierce competition between the boat companies to secure lucrative cabin passenger business as well. Mr. B., I know this. I studied the market, and I can make deals to reduce freight costs."

Pete went on, "Mr. B., I understand what it means to **prepare** and **plan.** Before I ever got here, I took a step back, thought about the things I've learned, and put pen to paper. I began writing down everything I could think of that was of importance to the steamship business. It was, in effect, a big-picture overview and needs analysis."

Pete read out this list:

- Steamboats make money by charging passengers fares and shippers for carrying cargo.
- The different kinds of docks
- The different kinds of ships (propeller, side wheeler, steam wheeler)
- The different stewards, relationships, and preferences for each

- The ships' destination points
- To know if the boilers are tagged and inspected
- Histories of the captains
- Understanding of packing and packaging
- Understanding of safety
- The dangers of following land routes along the river. Flatboat men have a reputation for being wild frontiersman, and the area is still a very violent place.
- Understanding how to contract properly with end users in destination areas to receive their goods
- Understanding the differences in terms of expectations and needs as related to the types of passengers who are most likely to be aboard
- Understanding the different concerns based upon what cargo would be aboard
- Which ships carry what type of features for loading and holding coal

Loading coal was a huge production that took a lot of men and a lot of time. Men brought coal up the wharf in wheelbarrows. The men loading the coal worked in gangs and were paid by the hour. It could be important for Pete to know which gangs were more effective and efficient in comparison to others. It would be important to know which wharfs those gangs would most likely occupy. His employer might find that type of logistical intelligence valuable.

"In short, Mr. B.," Pete continued, "I already understand that you can't do too much preparation. I am a man who knows how to take that preparation and put a **plan** together to work it! I know that information is power. I understand that without any hard-skill experience to show, I have to invest as much time as possible in making sure I understand everything that will be relevant and valuable to you or any prospective employer and customers. I studied the various **processes,** the **products,** and all the associated **pricing** that goes along with them. I knew that getting a job as a captain of a ship would be impossible, as it's something that requires a very specific skill set. Captains have not just the hard skills but the soft skills as well. They have courage, good judgment, and the ability to lead men. These are things I could align myself with, but the years of working a ship, the education in engineering, and the pure mastery of the currents and weather are the hard skills I do not possess.

"However, Mr. B., I think I have plenty of relevance for that job description you wrote. I can take all of that preparation and use it to put together an effective plan that will ensure a fast start. Mr. B., all of that preparation gave me the insight to understand the exact **profile** of not just your ideal suppliers but also your ideal end-destination customers. When it comes time to interact, negotiate, and display the value of your services, I am confident that my **presentations** will be top notch, sir. Let me give you some examples of what that would look like. I want you to picture me as your employee and allow me to paint you a picture."

Presentation

"The orders for goods are made to the suppliers prior to arrival. So, transactions are done in advance. Not so at the dock. Therefore I will make my presentations at the dock for both future business and my repeat business by earning credibility as a subject-matter expert and by demonstrating great service and reliability. The docks will be my platform for presentation, and the format will typically be a series of open, one-on-one or small-group engagements. Our customers will know we understand what they need, why they need it, and when they need it."

Performance = Process + Product + Pricing

"Mr. B., I firmly believe that repetitive **processes** work. A repetitive process is by its own definition an act upon which one can rely. I believe in that as a course of my own personal work habits, but it also has real value in the eyes of the client. In my opinion, a customer, whether in the mining business or the steamboat business, hopes to have an interaction with a company that provides him or her with a process built for speed, ease, and continuity. The fulfillment of that expectation is what creates repeat business and builds lasting reputations. In fact I know that in the business I ran in the gold fields, that repetitive process my customers relied upon became the true linchpin of my value proposition.

"Mr. B., I believe a process, a product, and a price can equal performance if there are enough differentiating aspects to them. I know I provided those differentiators in the gold fields, and I know your company offers the same in these waterways. Mr. B., I am the man who can communicate that value proposition. I know you have a process built for speed, ease, and continuity. I know you have a diversified product and solution offerings to meet the needs of just about any destination organization that becomes aware of it, and I know your price is competitively in line with the marketplace. Your company performs, Mr. B. I want to help it perform even better."

Positioning

"In fact, Mr. B., I have sought out your company in particular because, based upon all of the things I just described, I believe it is in the best position to win. Therefore that puts me in the best position to win. So I have one question for you, Mr. William B. Ready. Have I given you enough evidence today to give you a chance to help us both win?"

Up to that time, Mr. B. had retained as much of a deadpan look as he could. Then came a wry smile. He said, "Pete, I think they had a lot more than just gold out there in those rivers of California. I think they must have been God-given pools of knowledge. I have to admit; in all of my years I have never seen a man present himself in a more professional and convincing light than the way you have just done.

"I never gave too much thought to hiring anyone outside of the business because I didn't see how he or she could possibly succeed. And for the most part, I think that is still the case. I still think that what you refer to as hard-skill matching is an important predictor of success. You have indeed proven me wrong and shown me it is not absolute. I believe you, Pete. I do think the lessons and actions you took as an entrepreneur out west in servicing the needs of those miners have what you called transferable relevance to this business. In fact, I now think it has basic transferable relevance to anything commerce and sales related. However, I am convinced that it's an uncommon event to know and understand those foundational steps you described for me as your P's. I do not think most men would take the time for true introspection and devote as much time as you have to preparation and knowledge. In fact, I am confident it's rare.

"I don't believe you or anyone else could possibly transfer right into a job as a salesman with a company in an industry in which they have no experience. Except in your case, and for those other rare cases out there, I do accept it and believe it. You're hired, Pete! I'll have a contract for your services drawn up by our people at the office. We can discuss terms of pay tomorrow morning over breakfast, and I will expect you can begin working here as early as next Monday."

Pete just smiled, held out his hand, and said, "Thanks, Mr. B.! You won't regret it."

Mr. B. replied, "I don't think I will."

Pete, as suspected, went on to prove himself worthy of the presentation he had given and the trust Mr. B. bestowed upon him. He excelled and enjoyed his job for some years to come. He also learned anyone can transfer his or her relevance as long as he or she is willing to do the work to understand why it's relevant, and hopefully the reasons are rooted in a real sense of passion and purpose.

CHAPTER 13

THE WAR IS OVER & TIME TO PASS THE P'S

There are some things that just don't have transferable relevance. Nothing in life prepares a human being for the fear of and death by war. The military does its best to give some preparation through boot camp. It attempts to provide a framework for success in its planning for the customized battle stage of the day. The military does its best to provide a presentation of battle reality in simulations and repetitive processes, and to educate its men on the profile of their target to maximize their effectiveness—in other words, they train their soldiers to know their enemy.

The military does its best to provide and arm its men with the knowledge and framework of strategic and tactical processes, the latest and greatest products, and the goal of having to pay and offer the lowest price possible. All of this in the hope and belief that with that process and that product at that price, the value proposition of the American soldier offers the world the finest fighting force on every level. They do this in the hope that ultimately the culmination, the performance equation, can result in the optimal level of commitment to winning, to differentiate themselves from the others on that stage of war, see their targets, and achieve their ultimate goals, which is simply to survive and ensure the human beings with them survive. The military teaches that there is a higher purpose than oneself.

However, the truth is there is no such thing as transferable relevance from your prior work as a civilian when you're a soldier in boot camp. Nothing can prepare you for the reality of war.

Pete went to war in 1865—that god-awful War Between the States, which cost the lives of 600,000 men. A grand percentage of zero was how much Pete wanted to talk about the war. He had three kids and his wife, Sarah, waiting at home. They missed him; he knew that for sure. There may be nothing relevant or transferable about going to war, but there sure was something transferable and relevant about what soldiers came home with. Pete came home with a high sense of appreciation—of the simple smell of grass, the wind on his face, the laughter of his children, and the feel of Sarah's hand on his back.

Life was now gravy. The world around him may not have quickly seen, understood, or appreciated the value Pete brought home with him. But his years in the military and on the battlefield strengthened his foundational value rooted in a work ethic and an unshakable attitude. He had heightened sense of duty, discipline, and focus for doing things and doing things right. He was poised to be of use at a higher level than he had ever been. All he needed was to know what to do and to simply be given a chance. It was time to go to work again. His family needed him.

Pete was less interested in the fast-lane life of travel that the steamship business required. His main focus now was to be close to home, yet his passion was still rooted in all things related to the transportation of goods and people. The war was over, and the country was expanding. Pete remembered well the stagecoach travel from his days out west. Cities like Chicago were filling up fast. Education for his children, a home for his wife, and the opportunity to live a peaceful life were what Pete wanted most. His old job with Mr. B. was still available to him, but Pete had different priorities now. Mr. B. understood; he was sad not to see him return to his old stomping grounds, but he was happy for whatever made Pete happy. Mr. B., as always, wished him well.

Pete and his family moved to Chicago. At that time, there were thousands of carriage companies operating throughout the United States. Pete began asking some of his contacts around town for help in finding a job. He didn't have much luck right away. Employers, as he had expected, wanted men with direct carriage experience of some kind. He had been through this before. For some reason, a lot of these companies were not too keen on hiring soldiers who hadn't had any relevant experience. Pete thought, *I guess the last several years of fighting on a bloody battlefield don't count much in the eyes of these prospective employers.*

Pete had a lot of friends in the same boat. Some had lost limbs, and some were just lost. For the ones who didn't have families or businesses to return to, finding work was difficult in the big city. The answer was always the same: If you don't have direct experience, we don't need you.

Pete felt differently about that thought track, of course, because he had heard it before. He'd gone from the gold mines to the steamships on the rivers and had a great deal of success at both. Those were two distinct businesses that on their faces, or in the measurement of the hard skills required to perform them, were vastly different. Pete understood that the common thread between the two was rooted in providing services and solutions for the transport of goods and people. The value of both those services was rooted within a common and basic framework, and in the eyes of the target customer the differentiators were the same. Pete knew, maybe more than most, that if given the opportunity to have a conversation with anyone holding a job string, he could make a strong case for his value.

The year was 1866. Pete ran into Eric, a friend from the war. Eric had a small family and was from the San Francisco area. He had missed out on the gold rush; he had been young at the height of the boom, and he had spent those years instead working with horses on a ranch. Eric loved horses; they were his true passion. He knew everything there was to know about them, and from his days working on a ranch through his days in the war, others had relied upon him as a subject-matter expert.

Part of that ranch work had involved buying and selling horse stock for his family and for others. He had supplied stock for people passing by, for mining companies, and even for the U.S. cavalry. He and Pete had the same rank in their outfit, but Eric had been unofficially in charge of the horses. It had become his responsibility not only because he wanted to get the pick of the bunch but also because he wanted to be in charge of their overall care and maintenance. The unit had relied on those horses to ensure that people and supplies were transported effectively and efficiently. Lives had depended on it.

After the war, Eric was feeling down. His wife was from Chicago and had no interest in pursuing a life out west. Eric didn't want to let her down. They were starting a family, and it was up to him to create a safe framework for all of them. He had to find a job.

He told Pete he just didn't know what to do, who to ask, how to ask, and what he was qualified to do. There were not many ranches in downtown Chicago in the 1860s. They had some slaughterhouses for pigs and cows on the south side. Eric spent his time asking for jobs in banks, general stores, and a bunch of other places. He wasn't having any luck. He got the same answer every place he went. Owners wanted men with experience. Eric had only known horses and soldiering. The war was over, and there wasn't much need for a ranch hand in Chicago.

Pete listened patiently and then laughed out loud. Eric, looking perplexed and a little angry with a flushed red face, asked, "What's so funny?"

Pete replied, "I'm not laughing at you! Eric, you are one of the most valuable people I've ever known. I've walked in your shoes, and I understand the anxiety you're feeling right now. I think I can help you. First thing I want you to do is agree to have an open mind, to listen, and to answer some questions. Can you do that for me?"

Eric, feeling less threatened and a little more hopeful, said, "Sure I can."

"So you say you know how to do only one thing because that's all you have ever done. Correct?"

Eric replied yes.

"And you say nobody wants to hire you because you just don't have the experience or the know-how to match the needs of the role you are applying for, correct?"

Eric replied, "Yes, that's right."

"Have you given any thought to working for one of those carriage companies?"

Eric replied, "I did ask for a job in one of those plants that makes them. They told me just like everyone else I've talked to—no experience, no job!"

Pete said, "Well, maybe you haven't asked for the right kind of job, and you just haven't told your work story in a way so they can see what I see. I know how valuable you are. It's your job to let them know it."

Eric said, "That sounds great, but how does my story about working on a ranch or soldiering have anything to do with the carriage business in Chicago?"

"Maybe it doesn't on the surface of things, but if you dig deep down into the foundational fundamentals, I think you have a whole lot of transferable relevance to the carriage business. Eric, if there is anything I've learned in making some of the job transitions I have made, it is to recognize, understand, and internalize what you are truly passionate about and how you can best find a purpose for it."

Eric replied, "That sounds great, but how do I know what that is?"

"I think the best way to do that is to think about it and talk through it. You like horses, right?"

"Like them? I love them!"

Pete said, "What do you know about horses?"

"I know just about everything, I think."

"Can you name some different kinds of horses?"

Eric replied, "Sure I can. There are Appaloosa, Mustangs, quarter horses, thoroughbreds, Arabians, Clydesdales, Belgians, Shetlands, draft horses, American saddle breeds…"

"Wow! That's a lot of horses just to rattle off the top of your head. Are there differences between those horses?"

Eric laughed. "Of course. They are all different. Horses are bred for lots of different tasks and lots of different environments."

"What do you mean?"

"Well, for instance, a quarter horse can go superfast for super-short distances, and this is why cattle drivers prefer them. They can be light on their feet and can easily outmaneuver cattle. A thoroughbred is no longer bred to be exceptionally fast. Those fancy types bred them originally in England. The rich guys like those horses mostly to show them off and for how fancy they are. You won't see any of those horses around here that I know of.

"The Morgan horses are not as big as quarter horses but have good temperaments. They can work cattle and be used for riding and are basically all-purpose horses. Then you have the Percheron horse that came out of France. You see a lot of these pulling carriages around the city, along with the Morgan's.

"Then you've got those crazy, wild Mustangs. Now, I love all horses, but most of the ranchers I knew hated Mustangs. They didn't like those wild horses grazing on the land they set aside for their cattle. Lots of those horses were slaughtered. I didn't like that much and didn't participate in the killing.

"Besides those horses, mules are always in high demand for heavy work on a ranch and on the open trail for their sturdiness."

"Wow!" exclaimed Pete. "That's a lot of information about horses. I had no idea there were so many different kinds. Eric, did anyone tell you to get out and learn all of that information when you worked on the ranch?"

Eric replied, "No. I did that all on my own."

"Why did you do it?"

"Well, first I was just curious to know all I could about horses, but also I like to learn, and I liked being the guy others relied on so they could make good decisions."

Pete said, "Ah! That's great. Now I think it's clear. Horses and all things related to horses are a passion of yours, right?"

Eric replied, "Yes, I guess that's right."

"Eric, would it be fair to say there is more to it than just passion? That you became that subject-matter expert because you got a great deal of satisfaction in providing others with advice that could ultimately have an impact because of the action taken based on it?"

"Yes, that is true. I never really thought about it like that."

"Let's back up for just a moment. You said you read everything you could get your hands on that had to do with horses."

Eric replied, "Yes, that's right. I always sent away for books. I studied and watched for differences in the horses that came my way. I guess I just wanted to know everything I possibly could. I wanted to know the sizes, colors, speeds, what they were bred for, why they were used, and what they were good at."

Pete explained, "Eric, you did the most important and valuable thing anyone could do. You engaged in the act of **preparation,** which is the bottom pillar and foundation for everything done well. Without preparation, a good job is not possible. So beyond just the simple fact that you prepared yourself to become a subject-matter expert, you must have had some use in mind for all that information. You must have had something beyond just curiosity."

Eric, said, "Well, I guess that's what I had a passion for."

"Yes, I know you were passionate about horses and giving advice. However, I think you must have had some use for that information beyond passion and curiosity."

"I'm not sure what you mean."

Pete said, "Let me just ask you this: If someone asked you for all the information you knew about horses, what are some of the things he might be able to do with all of that information?"

"I would tell him to use the knowledge to help people understand how to make good decisions when it comes to horses. We had people from all walks of life and all places coming through, and many of them had different objectives. Some were making their way to the gold fields, some were coming out to ranch, others to farm, some for adventure, and even some I suspect were just outlaws on the run. These people were short, tall, skinny, chubby, old, and young. I guess I just enjoyed being the one they could rely on for help in making good choices."

Pete replied, "Okay, that makes complete sense to me. So you didn't just invest in preparation. You made the choice to use that information because you had a **plan** in mind. You see, Eric? That is what I was trying to get at when I asked you how you would tell someone to use your knowledge. You may not have fully realized it, but as you were gathering knowledge, you were also **planning** for how to use it all along.

"If there is one thing I have learned, it's that it's not enough just to collect information. There is real value in finding ways to use it or in helping others use it for an end destination or goal. Those goals are as varied as all the people who came to your ranch. They all had different needs and requirements, and you made the arrangements to be a source upon which they could rely. In other words, you made plans for using that information.

"The use of information to accomplish end-destination goals requires a measure of **planning** on the part of the person or entity holding that information. You **prepared** and you **planned,** Eric. You knew people were going to come your way, and you knew they would all be coming for different reasons and have different needs. So when these passersby came, did they come to you first?"

Eric replied, "No, they went to the owner. He sent them to me."

"And who ultimately benefited?"

"All of us. I enjoyed being the go-to guy, my boss enjoyed the business and repeat business that came from it, and the people passing by enjoyed the results of getting good advice."

"So it sounds like you had satisfied customers, right?" Pete asked. "It makes perfect sense. You invested in the **preparation,** and you made the choice to **plan** for the use of that information to benefit all the stakeholders involved."

Prospecting

"Eric," Pete said, "did you give any priority or put in some thought as to what you would do each day as it relates to whom you would engage with and why? Did you have to go out and find customer prospects? There has to be some method or thought process for making your choices for interaction. Did all your customers come to you? Did you have to go off the ranch and find customers?"

Eric replied, "No, I didn't have to leave my ranch to find prospects. The customers came to us. For the most part, I just needed to be available at the right time and in the right place."

Profiling

"Eric," Pete said, "you mentioned all the different types of people who came through the ranch and all their different needs. It sounds like you not only studied and prepared for knowing your horses, but you studied your target as well. I think we can say you did some serious **profiling.**"

Eric responded, "Well, when you put it like that, I guess I did. I thought it was important to understand the differences in people. I couldn't be much use to anyone if all I understood was one side of the equation. I hadn't thought about why I put so much time into learning what those customers wanted."

Presentation

Pete said, "When it came time to have those discussions with the passer-by targets, did you have to check your books before answering people's questions?"

Eric laughed and exclaimed, "Check my books? Heck no! I know my stuff like I know my own hands. I simply listened to what they told me, and that helped me understand what they wanted. It was my habit to dig a little bit deeper, to find out why they thought they wanted the things they wanted. It wasn't difficult for me to give opinions and help them make choices. I just understood how to see all sides of the equation, and I could lay it out for them."

"So, we could say you knew how to give a great **presentation.**"

"You make it sound like I was a politician on a soapbox. It was more about me just laying out the options I thought best fit with what you called their profile."

Pete replied, "I know, Eric. I didn't mean it in a negative way. What I'm guessing is that you laid out your whole message in a clear and concise way, rooted in the security of having a foundation of knowledge and aware that your audience ranged from sometimes a single person to perhaps a small crowd."

"Yes, Pete, you're exactly right."

"Eric, when you were out at the ranch, were there other ranches where these people could go to buy horses?"

"Yes, sir. There were lots of ranches to choose from."

"Do you think they chose your ranch over the others most of the time?"

Eric replied, "I can't say for certain, but my boss was pretty happy with our traffic. I used to hear him brag that we were the best choice in the territory and had more repeat customers than anyone. He used to say to others I was the one man he couldn't do without. I used to smile at that." He grinned. "I was damn proud of it."

"Eric, have you given much thought to why the passersby so often stayed to listen to your presentations and bought from you?"

"Well, I thought maybe they really liked our horses, and they liked me."

Pete replied, "You're exactly right, Eric. However, it was more than just that, I suspect. You said there were other horse ranches to choose from, right?"

"Yeah, that is right."

"Do you think they had good horses and good horsemen?"

Eric replied, "Yes. I know for a fact they did."

"Okay, then let's you and I try to understand the value offering and the differentiators in your presentation."

Product

Pete stated, "Your product was horses. What made your horses better than any of the others on those other ranches?"

Eric replied, "I don't think any one ranch had better horses than the rest, but we probably had more to choose from than most of them."

Pete asked, "So, then part of your value proposition was that you had a product line diversified enough to be able to meet the needs of just about any passerby coming through, correct?"

"Yes, that would be true."

Pete went on to say, "And it's also probably safe to say that some of the other ranches were diverse, some were niche, and some were neither."

"Yes, that would be the case."

"So there were differences and similarities, correct?"

Eric replied, "Yes. When you put it like that, I can tell you what type and how many horses all the other ranchers had."

"Then you knew how your product line was positioned against your competitors' product lines."

Eric replied, "Yes, it is fair to put it that way."

Process

Pete went on to say, "The next piece of your value proposition probably hinged on a process. Do you think you made the buying interaction an easy one?"

Eric replied, "I enjoyed it, and I'm sure the customers did too."

"Part of your **process** was the boss simply turning it over to you, and you were the turnkey for the transaction, so the customers basically had to deal with just one person."

Eric laughed. "Well, yes, but you could say it was two people because the money went into the hands of the boss."

"Okay, let's say it's two people," Pete said. "But your boss was there to greet them and then to thank them with a smile and say goodbye. The entire **process** in between was all you, and that sounds like a process built for speed, ease, and continuity. Sounds like a process people wouldn't mind coming back to or telling their friends about. Do you think the process was the same at those other ranches?"

Eric replied, "Most places could be a bit trickier in that their deals involved several people."

"Do you think at any of those other ranches they had a guy like you, who put as much time in as you in terms of the broad range of **preparation,** the **planning** that followed, and all that detailed customer profiling?"

"I must have been doing some things that fit together in some kind of puzzle or grand design of which I wasn't even aware. And that design was somehow the key to making it all work so well. I can't say for sure what the others did or didn't do, but I was often told that I had a good reputation for being the go-to guy in the territory."

Pete replied, "I'm not surprised at all. In my opinion that knowledge transfer to the customer and ability to customize a solution was a huge differentiating factor in the **process** portion of the overall **value proposition** you were out there providing. So your **process** was not only built for speed, ease, and continuity, but designed for a high level of customization to truly fit the needs of the **prospective profiles.**"

Pricing

Pete asked, "How about the cost? How was your **pricing** compared to the other ranches'?"

Eric replied, "The pricing was pretty consistent all the way around compared to the others. Horse sales can vary, and negotiations were really based on each individual situation, as a horse, its type, and the buyer's situation and motivations can vary dramatically from transaction to transaction. Overall, though, I prided myself on making sure my customers got fair deals and got exactly what they came looking for."

"So, your value proposition basically revolved around a number of differentiating factors rooted within a process built for speed, ease, continuity, and customization; a product line diversified enough to meet the needs of almost any prospect or passerby; and a pricing model that was perceived to be in line across the board."

Performance

"Eric," Pete asked, "Do you think a horse should perform in the way that it's advertised?"

Eric replied, "Yes, of course."

"How about a business? Should a business perform as it's advertised?"

"Yes, absolutely."

Pete then said, "It sounds to me like you had the makings of the performance equation: **performance = process + product + pricing**. Does that sound about right?"

Eric said, "Yes, sir, it does! I know my boss loved the performance outcome for sure. I never thought about all of these things the way you have laid out the puzzle pieces, the performance equation, and all the rest. This is an amazing way to view the history of my work and my life. I had no idea how much I really did on a daily basis and how all the things I was doing were somehow making such impacts on what I was trying to do and what my boss was hoping to accomplish."

Positioning and the Formula for Success

Pete said to Eric, "It sounds like you were set up and **positioned** just perfectly for a formula for success."

Eric asked, "By **positioning** you mean we were simply in a better position to win than the other ranches?"

Pete replied, "In effect you were. However, none of it would have been possible if you had not taken time to build a foundation, rooted in preparation, with all of your studying, and to plan in anticipation for when these things would come your way. There was also your ability to formulate a profile, recognize and understand their differences, and your advantage of what you had to offer. Furthermore, your ability to present your solutions in such an effective and customized way that they could resonate with your prospects was amazing. Your ability to differentiate your ranch and its solutions on the performance equation was the key and a major part of the formula for success. And finally, the realization that the power of it all working together resulted in the highest and most optimal level of positioning. Wow, Eric. What an amazing formula for success you had!"

Eric was almost in shock. "My God, I had no idea I had so much value."

Pete laughed and replied, "I always knew you had it. There was a reason you were the horse guy in our outfit. We knew we could count on you. Our lives depended on it. To me you were the most valuable man in the unit!"

The Self-Audit begins

Eric said, "This is a lot of information to digest."

Pete replied, "It is. I think you may have been asking for the wrong jobs at those banks, stores, and carriage companies. Although I think those carriage companies deserve a closer look from the both of us. You and I both have some **transferable relevance** to offer those guys. Eric, we have had different experiences and have different passions. However, our foundational levels of skills are equally transferable for job profiles that are rooted in commerce. I think both our passions can be satisfied and our purposes fulfilled, and both of us are suited for similar roles.

"On the one hand, my purpose is rooted in my love of communicating service solutions for the transportation of goods, services, and people. I'm going more for a direct sales role. The kind that expects me to sign up vendor relationships in need of our transportation and delivery services. I do know that some of those same companies want technical sales support specialists. From what I've heard, it's a role in which that technical support specialist would participate in the sales creation process with the direct sales representative, but more as a technical subject matter expert. I like horses, but I don't love them. My real passion is offering transportation related solutions that have meaningful impact on my customers and produce positive results for my superiors.

"On the other hand, you have a passion for horses. But you are just as passionate about offering a customized solution that leads to a result and action for others, in much the same way I am. We have worked separate jobs and have very different backgrounds, but our foundations are actually the same in terms of how we just described those puzzle pieces and formulas. Walking through all those P words was the same exercise I discovered when I made my transition from the mining business to the steamship business before the war. I realized then that the details of the specific job type or its product didn't matter so much; the underlying repetitive processes used to create sales opportunities were the common threads of what made me successful. I learned I could find those common threads embedded at a deeper level than what first appears obvious to most. I simply had to stop, recognize, understand, and internalize my foundational value, and then I had to be sure to match it up with a target job profile that could fulfill my passions and sense of purpose."

Eric said, "Yes, that makes so much sense to me. Now what?"

"You mentioned to me earlier that this was a lot to digest. It is my suggestion to sleep on it, so we can begin to **internalize** it. Once that **self-audit** is complete, then our next step is going to be to communicate our foundational value and transferable relevance to the targets that best fulfill our needs. Communicating it is the key to gaining success."

Eric said he was going to go home and think about it some more. "You know what, Pete? All the time we served together and have known each other, it never occurred to me that our basic and foundational values and sets of experiences were so similar. Who would've thought a steamship guy on a river and a horse rancher from out west would have so much in common and an equal level of what you call **transferable relevance** for jobs in the carriage business in this huge, bustling city? Not only is there a deep common thread in foundational value, but we both have alignments rooted in a common purpose, yet from different passion points."

Pete replied, "You're a quick study, Eric, to have learned all of that and have the ability to articulate and conceptualize it already."

Pete and Eric did sleep on it, and they found a way to communicate their transferable relevance effectively. Their equal common purpose was to settle down and raise a family in a stable environment but with a variation of viewpoint. They both took a great deal of pride and satisfaction in representing a solution and service they believed in, and had great pride in providing opinions that ultimately led others to take action. The only real divergence was that Pete's passion was more rooted in transportation-related services. He loved the variables in the constant innovation for the way goods and services were transported and delivered. Eric's passion was more deeply rooted in his love and appreciation of horses. He loved to recognize and understand their differences, and was fascinated by the variety of what they could do.

Eric agreed with Pete. "You're right—we do have similar foundational values, and we do have those values rooted deep within a sense of passion. I don't know everything I need to know about the carriage business, but I think I'm going to go home and begin the preparation. I don't think I can communicate my relevance until I do some basic research and understand the business better. I know they use horses, and I'm pretty confident that knowing and understanding horses and their particular breed differentiators can give some meaningful and obvious value to a sales related position. I now know I'm passionate about communicating a horse-related service and solution. I think I just need to start the process of becoming a subject-matter expert in the different types of carriages, what they're used for, why they are used, and who wants them and why. It isn't going to happen overnight; it's going to be a process and take some time."

For the first time since coming home from that god-awful war, Eric had a sense of direction. The fog was lifting, and confidence was beginning to seep in. Finally, he thought, he could fulfill his purpose and be passionate about it.

Pete was smiling the whole time. "You got it, Eric! You are exactly right. I'm a little ahead of you in the preparation and planning stages because of all the homework I've been doing. But I know you understand exactly what you have to do, and you will catch up quickly. There are a thousand carriage companies in Chicago to choose from. Knowing what we know and understand about the performance equation and the overall formula for success, I think we are going to have the pick of the lot."

Pete and Eric were not the only ones moving to the city. After the Civil War, thousands did the same, to be part of a new way of life. There were new technologies and new ways of living; it was a different world. The way Pete saw it, public transportation and the demand for it was evolving. The rise of the rivers and the rails had changed everything. But at that time, in cities like Chicago, the carriage still ruled the roost. The carriage business in that period of American life was right at the heart of transportation, and Pete simply loved everything about transportation and logistics. Eric felt passion every bit as much but more from the angle of working with horses and providing direction and advice for all the different ways they could best be used. A technical sales support position was a perfect job for Eric.

Preparation: The cycle begins again

The two men agreed to meet every week as they readied themselves for their objectives. Pete was ahead of Eric in preparation. He already knew a lot at that point.

Pete knew that Chicago had a huge demand for transportation by carriage both from private enterprise and from public transportation perspectives. Much of the transportation was horse-drawn. Chicago was famous for its public horse-drawn omnibus, which could carry twenty to thirty people and charged just a few cents per ride. The private providers charged more but also offered customization and privacy.

The city of Chicago was filled with horses and horse-drawn transportation vehicles. There were drawn delivery wagons, fire trucks, grocery peddlers, cabs, and countless private carriages. All of these vehicles were different in purpose, size, and shape. Pete and Eric would be targeting those private carriage companies to find out which ones seemed positioned the best from a value proposition and performance standpoint and which would be open to on boarding two men with no direct hard-skill experience in carriages. Eric was already excited because he knew this vertical was the perfect platform for his particular expertise. Pete felt the same way but more out of a sense of satisfaction of working through the complexities of transportation and all the client interaction it would entail.

Companies working with horse-drawn vehicles had to select their horses. They needed good horsemen like Eric to determine what age would be best, what style of horse would be best, which breed had the proper temperament to handle a crowded city street, and which ones were right for the Chicago climate and its changing weather. A man that could provide expert insight into those matters as a **technical sales support specialist** would be invaluable during the sales process. The carriages were valuable and ranged in class, style, and luxury, but the horses were the carriage company's most important assets. Pete knew they would be competing against the public omnibus for the business of transporting people.

Carriage styles ranged from two wheels to four wheels, to ones built for speed, comfort and leisure, or stability. As Chicago was growing, the need to travel farther distances became greater. Horseracing and harness racing became ever more prevalent in cities like Chicago as well. People simply wanted diversion from their busy lives. Leisure activities like pleasure rides on fancy carriages became a way for the rich to show off. Creating a way for these people to escape the hustle and bustle of the city for afternoon picnics became big business.

Pete had learned that carriages were becoming affordable enough for even farmers and the normal working class to afford, and they could be bought through catalogs like Sears. He was fascinated by this and couldn't wait to become a part of that kind of marketing.

Pete knew he needed to know everything possible about the parts and all the bits and pieces that made up the ever-expanding types of carriages. He studied how the horses were connected to the carriages, how to steer the carriages, which were harder to pull than others, and what the highest and best uses were for the varying styles.

Every one of these carriages had a practical purpose and an aesthetic purpose, and he knew the customer population would need someone who knew and understood all the variances involved, and could present them intelligently. That might be something of value for a prospective hiring manager to consider.

Pete and Eric both understood that in addition to the private solutions, people in Chicago and most companies didn't own horses, since they were difficult to care for, feed, and house. A major city like Chicago had an endless demand for moving freight from one place to the next, and horse-drawn vehicles would be doing that moving. All kinds of goods needed to be moved, including coal, oil, machines, food, and all sorts of general supplies. Pete and Eric also thought about finding possible work in the booming buggy-whip business. There was big money in whips, but in the end they determined the carriage business as a vertical appeared to be a better long-term fit. And besides, the whip business didn't fit into their sense of passion or purpose. It fit only into their desire to make a good living. For these two veterans, that wasn't enough. Each wanted purpose and passion out of life.

Some companies owned huge fleets of horses and carriages to deliver their goods all around the city. Monroe Meadows was one such company. After weeks of meeting, studying, preparing, planning, and internalizing their message and profiling the ideal targets to work for, the company Eric and Pete thought could provide them with an optimal fit for their transferable relevance, which was rooted deep within their individual passions, and ultimately satisfy their distinctive sense of purpose, was Monroe Meadows. That would be the target, and it turned out to be the place where they made their communication worthwhile. It became their home until both of their deaths many years later. Pete's role was to handle the sales and marketing aspects of delivery services. He was in charge of prospecting, profiling, presenting, and ultimately signing and securing vendor relationships for services in much the same way he had with miners and on the rivers. He excelled at the nuance of making it happen. Eric was in charge of the wholesale division of the department of horses and carriages—two of Monroe Meadows major assets. The company would rely on him for advice on choice, maintenance, and deployment of those assets. But in addition to his responsibility for maintaining those assets, he also was the designated technical sales support specialist. His official title was "Technical Sales Support Specialist

& Inventory Manager." Part of his job was to accompany Pete on most of the largest and more important prospecting engagements. His technical expertise and his amazing insights proved to be an invaluable compliment to Pete's efforts in the field. Both, of course were rewarded handsomely with commission.

Pete passed away in 1918 and Eric in 1920. Pete left behind his wife, Sarah, and seven adult children. Their postwar life was lived with as much happiness as could be expected. Pete had lived a life of appreciation and those that knew him would miss him.

CHAPTER 14

JUMPING OFF THE PYRAMID
NOT EVERYONE WANTS TO BE A SALESMAN

Pete lived long enough to have a whole crop of kids and grandchildren. Surviving the war gave him that extra zest for life sometimes common among combat veterans. Pete didn't take many things for granted. He lived well into his eighties—long enough to watch his favorite grandson, Paul, also march off to war in Europe in early 1917.

Paul idolized his war hero grandfather, who had gone to war more than fifty years earlier to decide the fate of the United States. He loved it when his dad and just about anyone else in the family would make references to his likeness to his grandpa, not just in looks but in personality and temperament as well.

When Paul was growing up, his dad, Phil, was a hardworking man who chose to work with his hands in construction. Phil was mechanically inclined. He could fix anything, and he loved doing so. He had a knack for just looking at things and instantly knowing how they worked and how to fix them.

Phil also had the gift of gab, and most people thought he was a natural born salesman like his father, Pete. However, Grandpa Pete used to laugh at that saying—*natural born salesman.* He believed there were about as many natural born salesmen as there were unicorns. In other words, there was no such thing. He believed that just about everything had a science and a process to it, and he especially believed that as it related to sales. He used to tell Phil that anything done well could come only as a result of hard work and practice. Phil respected and loved his father as much as anyone could love a dad. Many in the family thought it might be a disappointment to Pete that Phil never followed his footsteps and worked at Monroe Meadows in a sales-and-marketing position. The store was doing very well in Chicago. A good man with a strong level of business acumen and a love and desire for creating, managing, and closing opportunities on behalf of an organization that had as strong a value proposition as Monroe Meadows would have been positioned well to have a great deal of success. However, passion is a pretty important ingredient for success as well.

What a lot of the family couldn't understand was that Pete could not have been more pleased with this son and the life he had chosen for himself. Many in the family never understood that Phil was doing what he loved precisely because he had Pete for a dad. Pete taught his children well. Phil knew from an early age that your basic foundational strengths rooted within a passion were best directed and optimized when matched with a fitting purpose.

Phil never had a desire or passion to create conceptual frameworks for others. He never really enjoyed or had the patience needed to formulate or paint pictures of sales-related solutions for others. What Phil really loved to do was build real and tangible frameworks—the kind in which people lived and worked. He loved building things, but he was every bit as smart as his dad or any other successful businessman. He could talk the keys off of a typewriter when he felt like it. That was why people thought he would be destined to follow in his dad's footsteps.

If people had taken the time really to listen to and observe Phil, they would have seen his true passion lay in a different direction. Phil loved learning how things worked. He enjoyed having things in his hands; he loved tools and gadgets and could tell you everything you would ever need to know about them. Phil certainly had the preparation and foundation from which to build a successful career in sales or business, especially revolving around the tool or construction trades. However, he didn't possess the passion for solutions and service consultation or the conceptual-framework painting most often associated with a salesman's interactions. He had all the preparation and planning in place. All he had to do was take the next step and begin understanding how and who to profile, how to formulate a presentation, and ultimately create sales opportunities. However, that simply was not what interested him.

Phil Makes A Jump

Phil made the decision to jump off his dad's Pyramid at that point and focus his energies on building tangible frameworks for people and businesses. He was more interested in building pyramids people could touch and feel, not the conceptual platform upon which his father operated.

Phil learned from his father both the meaning and the technique of internalizing true foundational value. He learned the benefit of directing those values toward a sense of purpose and passion. Phil's passion was using his brain not for the conceptual but for the technical. His father had never loved the nuts and bolts of things like Phil did. Pete knew that about his son from an early age. They had talked about those subtle differences his whole life.

The P's aren't designed to be used the exact same way by everyone. The sales-audit exercise to recognize, understand, and internalize your foundational value is universal, and the P's can be applicable to a range of verticals outside of sales. The discovery, the recognition, and the application of our passions and purposes should be goals for all. Not everyone wants to take that next step into a career in sales. You can still use the pyramid to transfer and relate your relevance. However, if during your self-audit, you get to the point in the pyramid in which you discover that the prospecting, the profiling, and the presenting of a performance equation are not the things that excite you, then it's time to jump off the pyramid. That was the deeper and truest lesson Pete hoped to pass down to his family. He didn't want clones; he just wanted happiness and fulfillment for the people he cared about. It never mattered if those frameworks were conceptual or tangible. At the end of the day, he simply hoped that whatever they pursued and accomplished would be successful and fulfilling.

Paul (Pete's Grandson). A new war but the same Self-Audit

Paul grew up spending a lot of time with his Grandpa Pete. His two favorite things in life were playing baseball and listening to his grandpa tell stories about his life in the California mining hills and his days living and working along the river in the steamboat business. Paul was endlessly interested in hearing stories about the Civil War, but Grandpa never much liked talking about the subject. Paul learned most of his Civil War stories from reading his grandpa's journal and from Grandpa's war buddies.

Paul idolized his grandpa, who seemed to be able to accomplish anything he wanted to do in life. Paul used to wonder how Grandpa knew how to do everything seemingly so easily. How could he go from mining to steamboats, come home from the war, and get into the carriage business at Monroe Meadows?

What Paul learned from his days spent with his hero was that there was no magic secret to success. Grandpa insisted that Paul could do anything he wanted to do and that a person's path to true success and happiness would be found at a foundational level rooted within a passion and matched with a purpose. The ability to do what he called "transfer your relevance" was simply a process, a formula that, if followed, would guarantee a framework for success and happiness if one was disciplined enough to invest the time and work through all the steps. For as long as Paul could remember, Grandpa was always referring to a process that began with an introspective approach to understanding oneself. It was something he called a "Self-Audit". That Self Audit would then followed by a step-by-step set of actions that had at its foundation preparation and planning, and ended in something he called positioning.

Grandpa insisted that all of these action steps had to work together to be effective. He used to say, "You will understand when you get older and you're out there in the world working." He said none of it would make real sense to Paul until he had a job.

Paul used to ask, "Well then, what's the use of learning all of it?"

Grandpa Pete would laugh. "There is going to come a day when you want to make a change in what you do for a living. When that day comes, if you don't understand how to transfer your relevance, that change is probably not going to happen. You're going to want to transfer it, and you're going to have to understand how to speak to the matching value points so you get what you want."

"Well, Grandpa, what do I want?"

Grandpa laughed again and said, "Paul, hopefully you're going to understand what you love. You're going to have a passion for it, and that is going to help you fulfill a very high sense of purpose in your life."

As a kid, Paul never really knew what to make of such talk. The years went by, and he eventually finished school and had long since given up on the idea of playing center field for the Chicago Cubs. He was old enough now to begin getting a sense of himself. That long-awaited self-awareness his grandpa had spoken about kicked in. Paul was an idea guy. He loved all things philosophical and conceptual. He loved the give-and-take in any debate. He was a big fan of history, but he enjoyed more than just the stories. He loved history because of the patterns, the cause and effect of actions taken and not taken, and human beings' repetitive processes that resulted in repeated failures and successes. He understood that much could be gained through the patterns of history and the observations of things that surround you in the present.

War was raging in Europe at the time. Paul was idealistic, as were most of the youth in America. He was moved by the words of Woodrow Wilson. He believed in the rhetoric that this would be the war to end all wars and would make the world safe for democracy. Paul was set on volunteering even before the draft. His number had not yet been called, and there was the possibility it wouldn't. Not everyone his age would fight in the far-off foreign war.

When Grandpa found out about Paul's ideals and his passion for signing up, he did something he rarely ever did. He talked about the Civil War. Pete loved his grandson, and, like most other human beings who have participated in war, he knew firsthand how very unglamorous and ugly the reality of war was. The last thing he wanted was to have anyone he cared about suffer through it.

So he did what he needed to do. He sat his grandson down. In the most simple and direct way, Grandpa told him never to go to war if he didn't have to.

Grandpa said, "I know how it sounds. You're passionate about helping others, and you want to do your part for getting a shot at the Kaiser. You think that to do anything else but rush off to war is somehow a coward's way out. I can't say that everyone feels like I do about war, but I have to let you know how I saw it, how I lived through it, and what I think I learned about it."

He told Paul that the world was full of good things and bad things, and that history was full of misrepresentations of causes. This whole thing about the war to end all wars sounded like a bunch of bull-crap to Pete. "You know enough about history to know that the idea of human beings never again rising up against each other in armed conflict defies any logic," he said to Paul. "The war I fought in between the states was fought for two noble purposes: to preserve the union and, more important, to free the slaves. I was happy and anxious to fight for both. Like you, I felt causes in my bones. I am sure you are feeling that way right now.

"Not all wars are for bad reasons, and this one over there in Europe might be for a good cause. However, what I found out is that the reality of battle can quickly erase the motivation that comes from higher ideals, and in its place you're motivated simply to stay alive and to keep the man next to you alive. You spend most of the time in the field either bored out of your mind or interrupted by the terror, confusion, and noise of battle."

Paul listened to his idol without interruption. Grandpa went on to describe his experience in the Civil War in detail, and Paul knew it wasn't easy for him relive those moments. Paul marveled at the fact that those battles took place more than fifty years ago, yet it seemed so fresh in his grandfather's mind.

Paul thought, *It must be true, what he always said.* His grandfather had always said you can leave the war, but it may never leave you for all the days of your life.

Pete said his peace, and then he left it in the hands of God. Paul believed every word his grandfather told him, and much of it made perfect sense. However, there was no stopping the young man's passions or the absolute confidence in his own invincibility, a sense typical of the young. Young men never think they are going to die.

Paul thanked his grandpa and said, "Look on the bright side. I just may find some relevance to transfer when it's all said and done."

Grandpa Pete laughed out loud with pride, knowing that all he'd been trying to instill in his grandson over the years had taken some root. "I pray to God that the transferable relevance you find on your journey will indeed be rooted in your true sense of passion and ultimately a worthy purpose."

Paul replied, "It's in God's hands. He has a destiny for me to possess, and this may just be my River Jordan to cross."

Paul left as a boy in 1917 and returned a man in 1918. Time somehow leaped forward, and aging had set in—maybe not in terms of age, skin, or body, but in spirit. It was obvious just from looking at his eyes. They had seen a lot. His grandpa had told him he would someday hope those eyes could forget all they had seen.

Paul's relief and exhilaration at returning home alive were diminished in large part because in his absence his hero had made his peaceful passing into the afterlife. Grandpa Pete was buried at Mt. Carmel Cemetery in Hillside, Illinois. Visiting his grandfather was Paul's first order of business. Standing at his hero's grave, he said, "You were right, Grandpa, about everything."

Paul knew his grandpa would be overwhelmed with joy at his safe return. Much like his hero grandpa, Paul now had a higher and more acute sense of life. He would honor his grandfather by making sure to live his life with the appreciation life deserves. Take nothing for granted and live without fear.

Paul wasn't sure what he was going to do in his first weeks at home. He would need some time to decompress so he could free his mind to think about what he might want to do for a living. Millions of other soldiers were coming home at the same time. Everyone needed a job and it was going to be tough to find one. He had never had a real job before going to war. Paul had served with distinction and was awarded two combat medals for bravery. He had been a medic and worked in the ambulance corps; he had helped men survive and was responsible for transporting people and goods to and from the battlefield.

Paul was a good athlete, with a knack for stamina and running distances. He was huskily built, with powerful hands and forearms, yet he possessed the graceful running gait of a dancer. He was strong, quick on his feet, and did what he had to do and more in those moments when it was hard to do so. A lot of good soldiers did the same all around him. Some lived and some died. For the most part, it all seemed so random.

Paul did what he could to make sure as many of the men would live as possible. Speed and strength were good things to possess from a hard-skill standpoint, but to be truly effective a good soldier in the ambulance corps needed to evaluate and profile not just the wounded but also the terrain. Understanding the terrain, the conditions, and the paths to safety meant life or death. Knowing and understanding how to prioritize the soldiers' needs and exactly how and where to take them were the key differentiators in the process.

Knowing and understanding his product line, including medicines and bandages, was also key to life, and being anything other than a subject-matter expert meant there would be a heavy price to pay. Death was an opportunity cost that could not be gotten back. Paul knew that his ability to be **prepared,** to have a **plan,** and to **profile** a battlefield for **prospects** in need would hinge on how well he could **present** and deliver a service rooted in a repetitive **process** built for speed and ease, that having the knowledge of and applicable uses of his **product** made the ultimate **price**—death—a lower probability. Paul's ability to do all of that **positioned** him well as a soldier of service.

The men in his company relied on him, and Paul took that seriously. However, he couldn't provide his services all by himself. He relied on a number of other people to accomplish his goals. Paul gained an appreciation for not just the transportation of people to and from the battlefield but also the value of distribution of goods, which he was responsible for in many instances. He really enjoyed the strategy of logistics and had an appreciation for the fact that life and death often hung in the balance, hinging on the proper delivery of things. That simple truth gave him a heightened sense of passion and purpose during his time in the war.

Grandpa's box

About a month after returning home, Paul turned to the box of things his grandpa had left him. One of those things was his favorite clock. Paul had always loved the sound of that clock, and many nights he had enjoyed falling asleep at Grandpa's house to the simple tick-tock. Somehow it always made him feel safe.

When Paul pulled out the box, he found a large envelope underneath it. On the cover was written, "Paul, inside of this box is the key to your framework for success. Find your passion, find your voice, and transfer your relevance to a place that serves your highest sense of purpose. Love always, Grandpa."

Paul opened the envelope. Inside was a large diagram of a pyramid. At the very top was a simple title: "Pyramid of P's." The Pyramid was broken up into categories or platforms, labeled from base to top with the following words:

- **PREPARATION**
- **PLANNING**
- **PROSPECT**
- **PROFILE**
- **PRESENT**
- **PROCESS**
- **PRODUCT**
- **PRICING**
- **POSITIONING**

There were some side areas with clues. Grandpa had drawn an arrow from the preparation and planning section, indicating that these two blocks were related to something he called "**off-peak time.**" Then he had drawn arrows grouping prospecting, profiling, and presenting with a caption that read, "**What you do every day.**" He had then grouped the next three P's,—process, product, and pricing—and he placed an equal sign next to them with a caption that read "**Performance**. These represent **The Performance Equation.** That is **what you offer every day.**"

The final P at the very top was positioning, and it was larger and more prominent than the others. There was an arrow pointing to it with a caption that read "**the key to context.**"

Paul placed it in a frame and put it next to his clock. Paul stared at the document for hours while he contemplated its meaning. This actually helped take his mind off other things and helped him to decompress some. The P words began to play like a recurring dream he had. They were words his grandpa had used repeatedly for as long as Paul could remember. One day his grandpa might be giving an example of preparation; on another day, it might be profiling; another might be process, and so forth. Never before had Paul seen them displayed in this kind of format or context.

His grandpa had always told him that when he got older, he would understand. Paul thought, *He was right about that.* At that moment, Paul felt for the first time that it was all coming into focus. The P words had always made sense to him, at least in terms of how they were used individually and within whatever context his grandpa was speaking. But now he understood that he could never relate to transferable relevance because he'd never had a job, and in his youth he hadn't thought long and hard about what he wanted to do—besides maybe play for the Chicago Cubs and rush off to war to make the world safe for democracy. He was older now, not much more in years but more from experiences, which were more than just the horrors of the battlefield. They also included the wisdom and pride that came with having a sense of duty, a real job, and all the associated responsibility that went with them.

Paul had been a medic in an ambulance corps, and he moved and transported goods and people. He did his job very well. The day his grandpa had told him would come had arrived—the day when he would have to undertake the **self-audit** exercise of introspection. One day, Grandpa Pete had said, the exercise would help him to pursue a purpose rooted in passion built upon a set of foundational value points, with all the necessary transferable relevance to build his ultimate framework for success for a career in sales if that's where his passions stood. His grandpa had been training him his whole life, but he did not fully grasp the depth and scope of it all until this moment. Paul had goose bumps. What a gift his remarkable grandfather had left him. Such a valuable template, designed to position him far and above most people, irrespective of any level of direct experience, for whatever role in life he would ultimately choose. The Pyramid of P's was the key template for building the ultimate framework for success.

Paul did exactly what his grandfather had told him to do. He went through the exercise of examining his life and experiences and searched for the common threads, for the things he loved doing most. Paul knew he was a conceptual thinker like his grandfather. He had been born with self-awareness. He had a love of breaking down complex thoughts, ideas, and philosophies and debating them with ease, and he had no difficulty relating and communicating concepts to others.

In addition, Paul was passionate about the patterns and lessons of history, as the results could often easily be determined by simply examining the repetitive processes that created those decision patterns. To keep turning left is to eventually go in a circle. That was a simple way of understanding the concept. If one's turning was left to chance, one could end up anywhere. That's a basic example and a reason for creating a sales readiness template for yourself like the Pyramid of P's.

Paul understood that one of the keys to success was to know where he was going. If his path included providing solutions to others, the key to success would also include knowing where his customers were going, what they wanted, and why. Paul loved repetitive processes, and he loved to provide others with paths for success. He simply enjoyed being part of others' success. Even when he used to play baseball, he was in some ways a de facto coach. He was a better teacher than a player, and he loved that role. He was perfectly suited to be an advocate for value and performance. And with that revelation, Paul knew he was meant to be a salesman. The next step would be to understand what kind of sales job and in which vertical was he best suited.

Paul felt it was almost divine intervention that he somehow had landed in the ambulance corps. Looking back, he realized it was within this unit that he began to understand what he wanted to do with his life. He didn't really know it back then. The importance of moving both goods and people, and the logistical thought patterns that he had mastered on the battlefield, had positioned him so strategically in helping his brothers in arms. This was what Paul loved and what he was good at. The common soft-skill threads for becoming a sales professional were his conceptualizing nature, his ability to paint easy-to-understand pictures of complex ideas, his love of and appreciation for repetitive processes, and his knack for efficiently planning for action. All had served him well on and off the battlefield. The labor of love to become a standout and perfectionist in the craft of delivering goods would forever define his passion for anything and everything related to that transportation vertical. His experiences in World War I would forever shape the lens through which he would view the world.

Now it was simply a matter of doing some external homework. He had to think about what industry or vertical would match up with his unique set of foundational skills and provide the optimal outlet for his passions and sense of purpose. The one common thread he could do without was his expertise with death. He had seen enough death for a lifetime and was in no hurry to find a job that would remind him of it on a daily basis. Therefore the civilian ambulance service was not an optimal fit.

Paul again thought about his grandpa. Pete had worked his way from the gold mines of California to the steamships of the Mississippi to the horse-and-carriage business in Chicago working for a premier department store. Paul thought that no job on its surface had any commonality with the others, yet his grandpa had had crossover success in all three. Paul thought that if his grandfather could deliver transferable relevance for three distinctly different verticals while adapting to different technology, so could he.

CHAPTER 15

THE RISE OF THE RAILS &
THE COMMUNICATION TEMPLATE

P aul did what his grandfather had always told him to do when trying
to understand a complex problem: He stepped back and looked
at the big picture. Paul thought about all the changes in the ways
things had been done throughout history. Innovation always evolved;
some people evolved with it, and some didn't. His grandpa knew how
to do it because he was able to recognize that widgets change, but the
solution often remains the same. Therefore, the commonality of the solution was the key to communicating and transferring the relevance.

So the answer came to him pretty quickly: He would find his job in
the railroad industry. Paul didn't want to build or drive trains; he wanted
to be part of the solutions they delivered for people. He had always had
an appreciation for railroads while growing up. His grandpa had always
talked about them and how they had impacted his work in his mining
days. Grandpa Pete had always marveled at the fact that the country had
been joined together by the transcontinental railroad, which connected
the country from sea to shining sea right at the end of the Civil War. He
had supported President Lincoln's vision and decision to pursue that
goal during that fragile part of the nation's existence.

In Paul's time, the railroads were not a new technology; they had
been transporting goods and services for many years. And as the web of
rails spread, one could see the ebb of competing services, such as the
steamship, horses and buggies, and wagons. The railroads were simply
taking over, and wherever they went, people were sure to follow. In turn,

wherever people went, commerce would surely follow. Thus, people needed a speedy and reliable way to get goods and services from one place to another. Fortunately, after World War I, the last of the so-called Wild Bunch had already passed into legend, and much of the West was tame and safe for the delivery of goods, services, and people.

From what his grandpa had taught him, Paul knew he couldn't just go out and ask for a job at a railroad company. He had to take that first P shown on the Pyramid and do some preparation. He had to build his knowledge base as much as he could. If he expected to have any chance of getting a job without direct experience, he knew he'd better do the things he was sure nobody else would be doing.

Paul made the decision to set aside time for research. He was good at it. For him, it was more like a history exercise because it involved studying the evolution of the railroad and its various uses over time. That information gave him some insight as to where the industry would be going in the future as well.

Chicago was a perfect place to be for someone like Paul, who loved business and strategy that revolved around the transportation and logistics verticals. The city was a crossroads and a gateway to the West. Paul was looking forward to starting a life that involved offering solutions to would-be users. He wanted to be a middleman, to represent a railroad that was hungry to sign up new companies needing fast and reliable services to transport their goods to destination points quickly and safely.

At the end of World War I, the railroads were still the fastest and easiest way to move goods, services, and people from places to all destinations in the United States. The manufacturers in the East needed a way to ship their products, and the farmers in the Midwest needed a way to send food to all four corners of the country. Given this, it was up to Paul to understand how railroads targeted and **profiled prospects,** how they **presented** their solutions to those targets, and how they offered **value propositions** and performance rooted within **processes.** He needed to know how a particular type of railroad car would be best suited for food, gadgets, or people.

He needed to understand how to **price** for services as well, and when and why to discount. **Positioning,** like all market-related offerings, was the key. Paul had to be aware that there were different laws and fares from state to state. Railroads were notorious for price fixing, and Paul could remember his grandpa telling him about a guy called T. Rex the Trust Buster, who tried to break up monopolies to make things fairer and force more competition. The railroad business had a bad reputation for being not just unfair but also completely disorganized. The federal government, led by Woodrow Wilson, had come in and done a takeover in an attempt to improve cohesiveness across the broad spectrum of this vertical. By 1920, it was for the most part back in the hands of the private sector, and there were some newer rules of the road in place that would make it a less complex and more transparent business.

This was the time when Paul was attempting to make his entrance into the railroad business. He studied the new regulations. He knew the preparation he put in now would be key for him in presenting himself as a subject-matter expert in the same way he could as a medic.

Paul heard the railroads were an extremely tough business in which to be profitable. This did not deter him; on the contrary, it motivated him. In a tough position like that, he hoped, the services of someone with his process-oriented approach, rooted in his grandpa's template of P's, would set him apart and make him a valuable commodity.

Paul's first several attempts at having conversations for sales positions with the railroad companies didn't go well. It seemed that no railroad he spoke with was interested in hiring someone with any railroad experience. They all wanted men with mechanical backgrounds like iron workers or builders, or people with direct railroad experience. Some were willing to forgo the direct hard-skill experience, but those employers demanded at least a minimal level of experience in the logistics and transportation business. They certainly were not interested in a background with no private-world job experience and only a high school diploma.

Paul got the same lip service everywhere he went. They all appreciated his status as a veteran, but without the hard-skill match with experience in the railroad business or logistics; they just couldn't see where he would fit. They certainly didn't see how it would be possible for a person like Paul to be given an administrative or sales-related position. Paul knew what they were thinking: *What does this war veteran know about creating value in the transportation and railroad commerce business?*

Railroads were in the business of making profits by delivering goods and people to desired destinations. Paul knew these prospective employers thought there were many more qualified applicants to review and that he did not know a thing about creating value or working in the railroad space.

Paul agonized over the rejections. He had put in the work. He had followed his grandpa's instructions. He had gone through the self-audit and internalization process, recognizing, understanding, and internalizing his foundational value. He knew he wanted to be a sales professional. He knew what he was good at and was very confident as to why. Paul had put in the time and research to study his chosen vertical. He had the knowledge.

"Why," he asked himself, "can nobody else see it?" What was he missing? Paul sat at home and again stared at the Pyramid his grandpa had left him.

The P's serving as a Communication Template

It finally came to him: the final piece. His grandpa had told him there would come a day when he would have to do more than just understand the P's on the Pyramid. He would have to learn how to communicate them as well.

"That's it!" Paul yelled. He had to have a conversation that could relate and effectively communicate his transferable relevance in a way that matched up to the profile of a position he was looking for and would make sense to whomever he was presenting it. Paul had made the mistake of just asking for a job to get in with a good railroad company. He had neglected to be more precise and to make sure that what he presented about himself would make him valuable in the eyes of the person to whom he was presenting.

The Pyramid of P's is more than a readiness template for workers in sales. It is also a communication template that organizes the talk tracks needed to communicate one's transferable relevance. You have to learn how to communicate the relevant aspects of your work history. Those aspects have to be more than just relevant; they also have to be valuable and useful to the hiring manager. It takes a lot of practice to get it right.

Paul was missing one of the most valuable points his grandpa had tried to teach him. It wouldn't matter much how extensively he prepared and planned and digested information if he couldn't also intelligently engage others in a way that made the connection with his relevance. It was actually a lot easier said than done. If everyone could do it simply, then everyone would do it. Paul would need to communicate his transferable relevance with what his grandpa had termed *profile centricity*. That was just a fancy way of saying that his relevance needed to match up with the profile in as many ways as possible. The hard-skill portion of the matching was the easiest to see. It was the subtle and softer skill matching that was less obvious. Those soft skills included culture, passions, purpose, work ethic, attitude, and other less obvious relatable experiences. Without the obvious hard-skill match, the burden would fall upon Paul to make a strong case for a soft-skill match and draw as many common threads as possible for the hard-skill portion of the profile. This would not be an easy task.

The transcontinental railroad was completed in 1869, after Lincoln had died. Paul understood that it did more than just bind the nation from sea to sea; it meant it would be just as easy to enjoy goods and services in California as it was in New York City. People and goods would travel back and forth across the whole nation, and the great melting pot would truly emerge. Paul loved history, and he knew that with the influx of immigrants the need to transport goods and services to the four corners of this great country would be going on into the foreseeable future. In other words this was a vertical that would continue to be lucrative for a long time. Paul also knew that Chicago was a crossroads, and he was in the perfect place at the perfect time.

After some more introspection and a series of repeated rejections, Paul knew what he had to do. Showing up and asking for a job—any job—wasn't enough. He needed to be precise with his targets, and he needed to be precise in his presentation of himself. How could he have missed this point?

Paul got to work on his presentation. He sat in front of his grandpa's Pyramid of P's, and one by one he pulled out the P layers and went through the exercise of putting pen to paper until he was able to internalize his transferable relevance from preparation to positioning. He practiced and would not put it to use in a real job-seeking scenario until he was completely satisfied that he could answer every question, every objection, and was sure he was prepared for every contingency. He practiced with his friends, with family members, and with anyone he knew who might be able to hold a relevant conversation revolving around railroads, commerce, and sales.

It was the first Monday of May 1920, four months since Paul had returned home from Europe. He had wallowed in jobs and staggered through rejection after rejection from the railroad companies. Today he felt he was, for the first time, truly ready for a good conversation. Today he would speak the language of transferable relevance. This young man with no tangible private-sector experience, this young war veteran who had served his country so bravely as a medic in the ambulance corps, would stand up and have his foundational value recognized. Today this young man would forge ahead with confidence and present himself to those who would listen. He would not only enter this conversation as a match for a sales-related role but would also be the most prepared and able-bodied candidate to whom they would ever have spoken.

A Helping Hand

Paul's grandpa had told him about the Rocket Ocean Railroad, which had been famous since way back in the 1850s. It had gone through some tough times before and during the war, and the government had taken it over, but the plan was to return it to private hands at some point in the future. Paul knew this made the landscape a little less competitive, as the men looking for the most lucrative jobs would be looking at the private-enterprise railroads, not the government-owned ones. He also surmised that these other men would be loaded with hard-skill experience in the railroad business, which he did not yet have. Paul had done his homework on the Rocket Ocean Railroad, though, and he felt it was still positioned well to supply services for transport in the future. Paul was anxious to be the best sales person they ever had.

Paul wanted an appointment, but he needed a referral. It wasn't efficient just to show up at a downtown Chicago office and ask for a job; he needed a helping hand to get in. Creating a sales readiness template, the same as a communication template, the self-audit exercise Paul's grandfather put together, the Pyramid of P's, could all be done as a solo act. However, the truth is finding a job requires a little help from others in order to get in the door. For assistance, Paul looked to the rock of the family: his dad, Phil, who happened to have played a part in the building of the company's downtown office, and he got his son an appointment to meet with a man of influence. That man's name was Mr. Rail Boxman.

Paul showed up fifteen minutes early for his 9:00 a.m. appointment, wearing his Sunday best. Boxman was there, drinking his morning coffee, reading a newspaper, and having a conversation with another candidate for the job Paul desired. Paul shook hands with Boxman, who asked him to have some patience so he could finish his conversation with the other gentleman. Mr. Boxman told the man he was impressed with everything he had heard and thought it was likely he would be a fine fit. The man excused himself, thanked Boxman, gave a slightly condescending nod to Paul, and confidently walked out of the room.

Boxman told Paul that the other man was from a competitor railroad and was highly regarded because of his success in building relationships with key targets throughout the Midwest. He went on to say, "But some of those targets are the same ones we are hoping to secure and protect as our customers at this railroad. In any case let's talk about you. I know your father well, and I promised him we could at least have a conversation for a possible position here at Rocket Ocean Railroad."

Paul thanked Mr. Boxman and said he appreciated his taking the time to meet with him. "I know how busy you are," Paul added. "So I'll get right to the point. I'm here to speak with you about the open sales position. I want to help Rocket Ocean Railroad develop new business."

Boxman was surprised. "Your father told me you don't have any private-enterprise experience. But I have some openings at one of our loading docks. I need a man who will show up every day willing to work. And your father told me you are a veteran—I want to do my part in helping returning veterans as much as possible. I'd also like to thank you for your service to our country. The world is a much better place for having you boys do the things you do."

Paul thanked him sincerely for the sentiment. "And you're right about two things," he continued. "I will show up every day, and every day you'll get a 110% effort. The only problem is that job is not a match for my skill set."

"Well, I appreciate your confidence," said Mr. Boxman, "but I have to tell you the docks position is a good ground-floor opportunity. It's a good way to get an understanding of the real-world business from the ground up. A man who works on the docks and takes responsibility for the inventory we load for transport can learn a lot about the railroad business. It's where some of our most effective sales professionals got their starts. Our best people either started at the bottom or came to us from one of our competitors."

Paul shook his head. "Mr. Boxman, I didn't come here today to waste your time. I know how busy you must be. So I'm going to thank you for the offer of the docks job and then ask you to have a discussion with me while keeping an open mind. At the end of that conversation, if you still feel the same, I'll thank you for your time and trouble you no more."

Rail Boxman leaned back in his chair, hands folded across his belly. He gave a deep sigh, paused, and said, "Okay, Paul. I can do that for you."

"Mr. Boxman," Paul began, "I have the experience, the knowledge, and the desire to be an exact match for the role of sales agent."

"I thought we already covered that," Mr. Boxman interrupted. "I thought you don't have any railroad experience or even any private-enterprise experience."

Preparation

"You're right, I don't. Mr. Boxman, you mentioned that a job on the docks is an ideal place to start in this business because it would give me the ground-floor preparation and foundation I would need to be successful."

"Yes, that is exactly right."

"So you're a big believer in the value of **preparation.**"

"Of course I am. Knowledge is power. A man can't be effective at anything he does unless he is the master of his universe. If a man is going to represent something of value, I think, he needs to be a subject-matter expert. It's just good business to have men others can rely on for professional direction."

Paul replied, "Mr. Boxman, I couldn't agree with you more. And I know what it means to prepare. I learned a lot about it in the military. I learned how to shoot, about formations and tactics, et cetera. But I also did the kind of work that shows my thought process and action steps in preparation are identical to the kind of preparation that makes men successful in the sales side of the railroad business. I wasn't running railroads, filling boxcars, or creating new business relationships with supply vendors. Those are all very specific and tactical in nature. I was, however, doing things that were relatable in a conceptual way as opposed to a tangible, hard-skill matching way. Looking at it in a broader context, I understood that becoming the subject-matter expert for all things related to the transportation of goods and services meant the difference between life and death. Do you know the saying 'keeps the trains running on time'?"

Boxman laughed. "I've heard it a time or two, of course."

Paul replied, "Well, Mr. Boxman, I was that guy in my ambulance corp. I was the medic who kept the stretchers and the supplies running on time. I never went to school for it, and I never had any plans on using my medical training to go on to become a doctor. Still, I had to know at least a moderate level of what drugs did what, what different wound treatments were, and when to use them. I had to know in an instant how to prioritize people. I had to know at just a glance who had the best chance of surviving and where I could help someone the most. I studied the effects of movements based upon the topography of the terrain on the battlefield. Adjustments had to be made depending on if it was muddy, rocky, slick, or frozen. Not understanding the conditions meant my 'train' wouldn't run on time, metaphorically speaking, and when that happened, men died.

"I also had to be a master of battlefield tactics. I had to be able to see a battlefield in seconds, and I had to understand the enemy's tactics. My soldiers were my customers and the Germans my competitors. My soldiers needed for me to be the master of my universe. They expected that my train would run on time not just sometimes but every time. I made that happen because for every moment of every day that I was not engaged in the act of treating my customers, I was preparing to understand everything about what we were offering, what the open landscape offered, and what our enemy competition was doing at all times. I had to know how long it took a man to die and how long it took me to get that man to a destination where he wouldn't.

"I also applied the same science of preparation and repetitive processes to the transport of goods. Part of my job was to know and understand exactly what our customers needed and when, and how much inventory was necessary. If I weren't supplying our men with needed inventory, then our enemy, the competition, would certainly be unloading theirs as effectively as possible in the form of bullets, gas, and so on.

"Mr. Boxman, I understand the value of preparation. I know there are a lot of other good men you are considering for this position—men with whole laundry lists of hard-skill-match experience from working in the railroad business. I doubt any of them understand and have internalized the depths of preparation I have applied to things for which I have a passion and a sense of purpose. I am prepared for the basics. I already know who your customers are. I know whom you want as your new customers. I understand your entire web of railways. I know where they go and why. I know the freight you carry, and I know where it goes and why. I know the types of railway engines and the differences in the boxcars. I know what should be packed into those cars and why. I understand a good deal about the industry from its history. I know the evolution and what it's done and, most important, what it will do for this country.

"I understand the history of this railroad and its troubles. That preparation also makes me confident of how this company is poised for the future. I understand and have studied pricing; I've studied the regulations and what they mean to the normal course of business. Mr. Boxman, I'm the most prepared person you have ever met who doesn't work for you today. I simply applied the science of preparation from my time in the war to the preparation I needed in order to have this conversation with you."

Mr. Boxman was stunned, impressed—but not quite sure how to feel about Paul just yet. "How does that preparation help me gain business tomorrow?"

Paul smiled. He knew he had Mr. Boxman's attention. If someone asks questions during a presentation, it's a good sign that you're creating an impact.

Planning

Paul replied, "Mr. Boxman, that is a legitimate concern. I come to you without any ready-made book of business and contacts. But do you believe in **planning?**"

Mr. Boxman nodded. "You have to have a plan. The best idea in the world never gets you anywhere unless you have a plan."

"I agree. When I was a medic, I didn't just gather information for preparation's sake. I had to put it to good use. I planned for everything I did in advance and used the information I gathered in preparation to give me a big-picture view of the work field. This allowed me to understand where and how to plan for the things that would make me most effective. Information is indeed power, but not if you don't put it to good use.

"I studied the terrain every day as well as the weather, which could make such a big difference. I made it my business to pay attention, and I put my knowledge of the terrain and the weather into how I implemented courses of action. I knew what I wanted and needed to do on a day-to-day, hour-by-hour basis. I knew and understood everything I needed to know about the transportation of the goods arriving to help my guys. I knew how to plan for the use of those goods effectively, and I knew how to plan for effective and efficient transportation of my guys from the battlefield. To do anything less would have cost lives. Planning was the fuel, Mr. Boxman, that made my machine run."

Prospecting

Paul reminded Mr. Boxman that he already knew where Rock Island's trains went, why they went there, and what they delivered. "I know and understand the same for other rail lines that compete for the contracts to carry and deliver the goods," he went on. "I know that if your employees are not out there understanding how, why, and who to **prospect,** then you suffer what my grandpa used to call opportunity cost—a term a man like me, working as a medic on an open battlefield, knows all too well. If I were slow, if I took a wrong turn, if I made the wrong choices in terms of wound priority, or if I applied the wrong medicine or the wrong amount, men paid the highest form of opportunity cost. They wouldn't pay with the loss of a sale. They would pay with their lives.

"I had to treat my guys in some ways the same as you treat prospects who need you to transport goods and services to others. Those prospects are the ones who manufacture or sell the goods that fit into your line's boxcars. Which of those prospects prefer that the trains have diesel engines? What are the specific demands of the end-destination towns? Your employees need to understand these aspects, many of which are very specific. If one of your guys doesn't understand that, he is going to spend too much time chasing the wrong business. Mr. Boxman, I'm not quite sure that all of your salesmen, freight loaders, your engineers, your porters, your clerical folks, and your union mechanics are going to know all of that and understand how to apply that knowledge to proper prospecting. But I know they should."

Profile

What Paul had just described to Mr. Boxman was the value that prospecting on an ongoing basis can bring as it helps create the kind of understanding that leads to identifying the very best targets amongst the existing and prospective customer base. "People in the army know all about hitting their targets," he continued. "I was competing against other target searchers from the other side every day. In a sense it was my job to treat my guys like prospects. There was a battlefield, and it was filled with chaos. All in an instant, Mr. Boxman, I had to size up that battlefield in motion and in real time and make decisions during my prospecting. Those decisions revolved around a profile I developed over time—a culmination of all I had prepared and planned for in my goal to be as effective and efficient as I could.

"Mr. Boxman, your battlefield is the landscape of competing railway services and competing transportation verticals like boats, horse carriages, et cetera. Your men have to profile so they can save time and money and ultimately make the railroad money. I had to prospect and profile to find the men I could keep alive. Your men prospect to find relationships they can keep alive and ongoing as well. In a business sense, profiling is the key to effective prospecting—knowing and understanding your best targets and why they are your best targets, and doing it before and better than your competition. The narrower the target profile becomes, the more likely my efforts will be effective in creating sales related success.

"I was doing the same thing on the battlefield, Mr. Boxman. I had the same mindset. The stakes were a little different, and the competition was a bit rougher. Out there on the battlefield, it became a zero-sum game. Over here in the business battlefield, I get to come back tomorrow and have another go at it if I get beat."

Presenting

Mr. Boxman held up his hand, indicating it was his turn to speak. "Knowing and understanding what you do after you have prepared, you put your plan in place, you take the action steps to move forward with your prospecting, and you narrow those targets down through some appropriate profiling. You'd better know what you're going to do when you get the chance to present yourself and your solutions."

"Mr. Boxman," said Paul, "because I've done the preparation and have an in-depth understanding of the ideal profile, I've got a decent idea of how you want your representatives to present the value that Rocket Ocean Railroad offers. I had to present a value proposition on the battlefield. I had superiors to influence, and I had coworkers who needed to trust my opinions and recommendations. I had to get my guys to trust me.

"It's the same way you present your services to existing relationships and prospects. Your people are out there presenting your value proposition to those ideal customer profiles. They know and understand how to make their points to their audience, as I did on the battlefield. If you know what you're talking about, you can develop some trust and credibility, and people are more apt to give you an audience."

The Performance Equation: Performance= Process + Product + Pricing

"Mr. Boxman, my grandpa taught me never to buy anything from anyone or any place unless they have not just the proof of concept but also proof of performance. He said a company's value in an open marketplace could be broken down into three simple things: a process, a product, and a price. Even a product or service can be broken down in this way. A service, a solution, or any offering of any kind has differentiators that revolve around those simple words.

"He always told me that if you can offer a customer a **process** built for speed, ease, and continuity, and if it were designed for consistency, then you can separate yourself from most others. People are likely to return if they have good experiences. If you can offer a **product,** whether it's a widget or some type of service, that is comprehensive enough to satisfy the needs of your target base and ideal **profile,** and ultimately give them a **price** that makes sense and avoids opportunity cost, you will have an equation that equals **performance.**"

"**Performance = process + product + pricing.** That's the ultimate value proposition, Mr. Boxman. My grandpa told me that some companies can do one well, some may do two, but very few can really set themselves apart on all three."

Mr. Boxman was leaning forward, listening intently. "What sets us apart in the marketplace?"

"Well, Rocket Ocean Railroad has been providing transportation services at a high level for more than fifty years. It has a framework designed for success because it's rooted within a process that is repetitive in nature. It's a process built for speed, ease of use, and continuity, with a track record to prove it. It's a process that's designed to ensure people can rely on it, and it's why they stay with you and always come back.

"Rocket Ocean also has a comprehensive set of transportation solutions designed to meet the needs of almost any type of product. Its diversified set of boxcars and its state-of-the-art diesel-electric engines set its solutions apart from the rest. Your ability to deliver services on such a comprehensive web of railways makes you a primary choice to deliver goods coming from all directions. Your ability to negotiate price models that have the end users in mind makes you a strong and competitively priced option. Your organization's internal ability to price appropriately and fairly is a true differentiator.

"Mr. Boxman, Rocket Ocean Railroad has a history of performance in which I believe. I know it's been under government control, but based on everything I understand, I am confident your railroad is poised to come out of this on the other side stronger than ever. You have a process built for speed, ease, and continuity for your customers. Your clients understand and know that the process of Rocket Ocean will deliver their goods safely, reliably, and on time. You have a product line diversified enough to carry almost any form of good today, from grain to coal, and to destinations far and wide. Your railroad sets itself apart in carrying freight, and you have a desirable product line designed to serve the transportation needs of people in most of the major cities. With the company out of the hands of the U.S. railroad administrator, you will regain your ability to ensure your price competitiveness for your customers and the end users as well. Your sales professionals reputation for having the ability to discount where appropriate makes your pricing model a strong one.

"Mr. Boxman, you have an enormous amount of points with which to differentiate yourself on those three pillars of value and performance: **process, product,** and **pricing.** I understand that kind of value, though not because I have experience as a sales person at a railroad or any other company. It's because I understood it, lived it, and did my best to present it to the place I know needed it the most. That place was the battlefield, sir. It was my job to perform. I had to be the guy with a predesigned repetitive **process** or operating system who could provide speed, ease, comfort, and safety on a consistent basis. I had to offer my services and goods as a **product** line, and those services and goods had to be diversified enough to handle not just what I knew would be needed but also all the contingencies. My pricing was simple: I had to make the calculations and decisions in real time, and I had to make them every day with the ultimate opportunity cost at hand at every wrong turn. It was the **price** of life, sir. I pray to God today that what I provided was somehow priceless. And at the end of the day, I pray that what I presented on the battlefield to my soldiers was the highest and best form of **value proposition** that resulted in unparalleled **performance.**

"Mr. Boxman, I want to work for you. I am a match for what you need. I looked around, and I think I understand where things stand—my grandpa taught me that for anything to have a chance for success, it has to be **positioned** properly. It's like playing chess. Your sales people need to understand how Rocket Ocean Railroad is positioned in the marketplace so that at the end of the day, they will know how to position themselves to improve opportunities for successful outcomes.

"**Positioning** is the apex. It sits atop the others because everything that precedes it not only sits below it but also, more accurately, is part of it. The **preparation, planning, prospecting,** and **profiling** and the **presenting** of a **process,** a **product,** and the **price** all revolve around and are a part of **positioning.** It's the culmination of all those things that gives you the in-depth understanding of positioning, and if it's all done correctly it gives you the effective means to act upon that positioning.

"Mr. Boxman, I've done the homework. I know your railroad is positioned well to win not just today but, more important, from now on. I know that all I have communicated to you today has positioned me well to be a successful match for this job. I made sure to have that kind of positioning on the battlefield as well, and in my mind it's the same. Mr. Boxman, I hope your sales people in place today understand how they are in a position of strength. I hope they know and understand how to communicate it, and I hope they know exactly to whom they should be communicating it."

"I also want you to know that I know how to spend my time when I'm not in front of customers. I call that my off-peak time, and it's when I do all of my planning and preparation. I know that every day I'll be out there prospecting, profiling, and presenting. I know I'll be selling your value proposition as it relates to all the differentiators revolving around your process, your product, and your price. I'll know it's a winning formula, and as a representative of Rocket Ocean Railroad I'll be positioned to win because Rocket Ocean is uniquely positioned to ensure it.

"Mr. Boxman, I'll finish by saying I know that probably thousands of other men have some direct-match experience, and on the surface they may seem like better candidates than me. But I hope I have given you enough evidence today to help you understand that though you might not see my experience expressed on a piece of paper, I have in-depth, real-life transferable relevance for exactly what you need here. In addition to that relevance, whatever else I may lack can be made up for with passion. Mr. Boxman, I love the transportation business. I love the complexity involved in the strategy needed to make a difference for people as it relates to moving things around. I love repetitive processes, and I am a conceptual thinker by nature. I've always loved to look at the big picture of things because I can always naturally understand the dynamics for movement within that picture. Mr. Boxman, I'm a salesman."

"I've also always loved history because I love to understand patterns. I have a passion for understanding decisions and am fascinated by the impact of an opportunity cost on those decisions. For me the transportation business and the complexities involved provide a platform for my passions. It's my purpose in life, Mr. Boxman, to help guide the decisions for movement of goods and people in an efficient and effective way so everyone wins. I did that over in Europe. I know I can do it for you here at home, and I want to do it as a salesman."

Mr. Boxman had, by that time, sat back in his chair comfortably. He stared at Paul intently, with his brow furrowed. "You know, Paul, I've conducted many interviews and have had many discussions over the years about what makes business sense. I must say I have never heard anyone not only break down his own value points but also display so much evidence and understanding of what we do at the foundational level. I didn't come prepared for this conversation, and now that I've had it I'm not prepared to make a decision. I'm going to have to sleep on it. I will say I am more than impressed by the preparation you did in order to know and understand who Rocket Ocean is as an organization and how we are positioned in the marketplace. I've not been surprised by much in my years in business, but I must say I am today.

"Having said that, I've never given a thought to putting someone in the role of salesman without a background in the business. I see now that I have found comfort and safety in a somewhat myopic choice pattern. Maybe I have missed out on bringing in some folks who might have been better fits. You might be that out-of-the-box fit. I'm going to digest what we talked about today. I'm going to take a few days to think about all those P words you threw at me." He laughed as he began to get up. "Your grandpa must've been one hell of a guy."

Paul responded, "Yes sir, Mr. Boxman. He was one of a kind."

Paul said, "My grandpa told me that at some point, it wouldn't matter much how passionate a person might be about something or how qualified he might be to do it; nobody will ever see what you know unless you know how to communicate it and transfer that relevance over in a way people understand. He also said it wouldn't be enough just to be able to speak it; it needs to be rooted deep within your passions, and you have to match it with something that fulfills your purpose. In any case recognizing it, internalizing it, and finally communicating that transferable relevance with passion will be the key to fulfilling that purpose. Mr. Boxman, have I answered all of your questions?"

Rail answered, "Yes."

"Are there any questions or concerns you have that we haven't already covered?"

"No, Paul, I think we are good."

Paul responded, "Then I'll just say I am grateful to have had the opportunity to present myself, and I'm hopeful the presentation has given you enough evidence to see that I'm a value match for the job at every level, and the combination of my work ethic and attitude can help to ensure my success here."

Mr. Boxman reached his hand out, looked Paul in the eye, and said, "It's been my pleasure. You will hear from me soon, son." He turned and walked out the door.

Paul smiled to himself, pointed a finger to the sky, and said, "Thanks for the blood you gave me, Grandpa! And thanks for all those P words and lessons."

Paul got the job. He settled in Chicago. He eventually married and had ten kids—seven boys and three girls. He continued to work at the railroad with great success for years. However, as with most things in life, innovation arrived, and the landscape once again would change. People either changed or repositioned themselves within that change, or they didn't. As the years progressed, a lot of the unskilled labor jobs began to wane as railroads began to lose their share of the transportation market.

CHAPTER 16

THE RISE OF THE ROADS EVERYTHING IS EASIER THE SECOND TIME AROUND

I t was clear that change was at hand, and some were being left behind and some were not. Paul was determined to fight hard to make sure he wasn't going to be a casualty.

Roads existed in America well before Paul took his job at the railroad. But over time the roads went from 150,000 miles or so to more than 1.5 million miles by the end of World War II. The government had gotten into the road business, and the historical truth is that wherever the government decides to put its vast, tax-based resources, the landscape and the verticals associated with it are sure to rise as well. Those roads coincided with the rise of the automobile and the business of trucking. Paul understood that when the government decides to subsidize a sector of the economy, it might be good to make a shift toward it.

With the rise of the roads came new opportunities for some and despair for others. At Rocket Ocean Railroad, they still had a very comprehensive product line that included options for both freight and passengers. The rise of the roads, along with automobiles, buses, and trucks, began to take away that passenger product portion, and the trucking business began to erode the railroads' lock on the interstate transportation business. In any case the transportation vertical was becoming more competitive due to all the innovation. It simply became cheaper to go short distances by car or truck for people and for goods. Thus, two of the primary differentiators in the value proposition and performance equation—product and price—had noticeably eroded as meaningful.

The equation **performance = process + product + pricing** was no longer adding up for the railroad business by the 1940s. Route lines were being abandoned because they were no longer profitable; rates could no longer compete for many targets no matter how targeted or steep the discount would be. The Great Depression had really bitten into the passenger portion of transportation. If people didn't have jobs, they couldn't pay for train fares. Demand went down as bankruptcies and consolidations went up. Commercial airline transportation was another area from which innovation and technology put a dent into the transportation business. The railroads' stronghold on the transportation market share continued to erode.

Paul had always marveled at automobiles, and by the end of the 1920s the streets of Chicago were filled with them. Assembly lines were being put to full use, and it was obvious to Paul where things were going. There was no interstate highway in those early days, so the need for railway freight transportation between states over long distances was still strong, but Paul was excited about what the trucking business could do for the transportation of goods. In his mind, at the time, it was surely the next place to see growth, and he wanted to position himself to be a part of it.

Paul had seen firsthand what trucks could do during World War I. They could transport heavy loads. Trucks certainly would beat a wagon or a mule. Trucking was around in the 1920s but on a small scale. During the Great Depression in the 1930s, businesses suffered, like most other things. Paul saw one thing that might separate trucking from the railroads: regulation. Regulations were put in place in the 1930s to put some structure around the business of interstate traffic. The railroad business was still very heavily regulated. The trucking business, on the other hand, was not, thus the barriers to entry for businesses were much fewer in comparison to railroads.

Paul made the decision to do the things that had helped him find success in the past. He began the process of gathering information to set the stage for preparation and planning. He felt that trucking in general could be well positioned on the performance value proposition equation. That lack of regulation and a localized philosophy for local transport with the process designed for speed and ease would form the basis for performance. The unregulated atmosphere of the vertical made it possible for a wide-ranging pricing philosophy.

Paul was excited for the opportunity to find a company with a diversified product offering for a targeted and profiled customer list. It didn't matter that he didn't have any trucking experience or contacts. He had been down this road before. This time he would know how to make quicker use of the communication template to transfer his relevance.

The mid-1930s and the 1940s were good years for Paul except that his sons went to war in Europe. Going to war was the one unfortunate transferable part of his life he had hoped never to pass along. In all, three of his sons would go to fight World War II. Two would not return; one would. Patrick survived Guadalcanal and the Solomon Islands. He became a national war hero and would eventually be sent home to help the government sell war bonds.

Patrick did not share Paul's passion for transportation or love of sales in general. Instead he was a man of great courage and conviction, with a very strong independent streak—a man who would always be his own man. He was like his grandfather Phil, the builder, in that he had a passion for working with his hands. They both loved to build real and tangible frameworks, ones that housed, sheltered, and protected people. After all, that was what Patrick did best: He protected people. His heroics in combat would later be glorified in books and museums. He was a great man for many more reasons beyond his war service, and was idolized by his sons, his daughters, and his grandchildren. Paul was extremely proud of his son.

Patrick came home to the streets of Chicago and eventually the suburbs, where he would settle down in Hillside with the woman of his dreams and a huge brood of eleven children. Like many grandfathers, he too would become the idol of many of his own grandchildren. One in particular—Phoenix, the second son of his oldest—would spend days in his grandpa's basement looking at clippings and pictures, and retelling his grandfather's stories to anyone who might listen. Phoenix was proud to have the blood of his grandfather in him. He never forgot what he called the "silence" of his grandpa's war; it was the unwritten rule around the house that you didn't speak about the war to Grandpa. It was said that the faces of those he killed haunted him all the days of his life. Phoenix's grandfather always loved to tell stories that were funny and of a lighter nature. The family would only come to learn about the uglier details of his combat engagements through listening to the stories of Patrick's war buddies and reading the newspaper clippings and the books that were eventually released. But his descriptions of the reality of war would be forever imprinted on his grandson. It's one thing to watch a movie or to read a book, but really to try to put yourself in the shoes of someone you know and envision what the true-life experience must have been like hits home. Those of us who have never experienced combat can never really understand what it's like, but if you try to think about the reality through someone you know personally, you are likely to develop a greater appreciation for his or her sacrifice.

What Phoenix didn't have was his grandpa's ability to do anything with his hands. His grandfather Patrick was mechanically inclined in every way. No, this grandson was more like his great-grandfather Paul, the successful railway salesman, or his legendary great-great-grandfather, Pete the miner. His grandfather was mechanically inclined, his father was technically inclined, and Phoenix was conceptually inclined. He loved everything conceptual and philosophical. Phoenix loved history, its repetitive nature, and all of its complex patterns. He had a love for conceptual frameworks and that trait would serve him well for a career in sales. He had a love for educating others. It's what drove his passions. Phoenix did not know it right away, but he would eventually have to cross his own River Jordan and possess his own destiny. But he would not do so without learning the lessons that hardships so often bring, during which this grandson would be grateful to not only have the blood of his forefathers, but also the knowledge that was passed along in the form of a sales readiness template called Paul's Pyramid of P's.

PART IV: THE MULTI PURPOSE SALES READINESS TEMPLATE IN ACTION

CHAPTER 17

THE SALES ECOSYSTEM

T his section of the book and the description of the **sales grid**, the **self-audit** and internalization exercise is primarily geared for the job seeker needing to make sense of today's complex sales ecosystem in their quest to transfer job related relevance for highly desired sales positions of choice.

The river Phoenix had to cross lay before him in our modern era. I have told that story in describing myself and my personal experience in confronting the rise of the silos. They arose after the rise of the roads in the form of cyberspace highways and the associated technology. The entire globe has become connected, and our access to information is unparalleled, at speeds my forefathers never could have predicted.

Everything on its face is more connected, thus our abilities to maneuver within our spaces have become more complex. The ways goods and services are offered, secured, and delivered have become more complex; as a result, those who add value to those complex interactions must continuously find more meaningful ways to differentiate themselves. Methodology in sales has been evolving since people began writing about them in such books as *How to Win Friends and Influence People* by Dale Carnegie, written in 1936. In my opinion, nearly every sales based methodology book written since owes its inspiration and foundation from that book. In fact, some would argue that every sales book since is in some way simply offering a variation of what Mr. Carnegie's was teaching, but simply re-packaging the sales methodology to suit the times. As mentioned previously, I have been trained, and am a proponent, admirer, and indeed a user of many of today's most prominent methodologies. As much as I hold those teachings in high esteem, I remain convinced that methodology is fluid and that the art of it all must continuously be reconfigured to adapt to a changing environment. If you were to ask most sales leaders today what they struggle with the most as it relates to training, the common answer is sustainability. The trainers come in, the sales force learns the newest latest and greatest tricks, they leave highly motivated, they go back to their territories, the sales numbers jump, everything is great. Well, maybe for a little while. A lot of great performance improvement companies market themselves in being the one that can provide the methodology that is built to last. When it doesn't last, the common answer for why it doesn't usually revolves around poor adoption or lack of leadership. However, while that may be true to an extent, it is my contention, as I have described throughout this book, is that structure as I've brought them to life through the science of the P's, represent the only elements of sales that are universal, timeless, and permanent. It's the science and structure of things that are designed to last, not the art. The science, the structure, and the **sales education** has to come first, and only then can a prescription for sales performance methodology be administered properly. Too often, most organizations have the order backwards. With all of that in mind, lets look at some modern day performance methodology and take a 60k foot view of the entire sales ecosystem.

The Sales Grid

The rise of our current complexity brought upon the marketplace a divergent level of approach in methodology, from sources such as Questions Based Selling(QBS), Franklin Covey, Dale Carnegie, SPIN Selling, Sandler, Challenger, and Miller Heiman to name just a few. That rise in complexity also gives rise to the need to adhere to the kind of science and structure that my pyramid provides as a readiness template. The combined diversity and complexity of the modern day sales related economy created a demand for making sense of it all for individuals and for businesses. That demand for making sense of it all created a **sales ecosystem** by which sales types, sales formats, sales roles, sales titles, and the various sales methodologies prescribed to support them, have all become myopically categorized like everything else in the era of BIG DATA and analytics.

THE SALES GRID

GROUPING	FORMAT	METHODOLOGY	JOB ROLE	ROLE PORTRAYAL
__Retail	__Transactional	__Questions Based	__Entry Level	__Account Executive
__Wholesale	__Complex	__Spin Selling	__Telemarketing	__Business Development Manager
__B2B	__Consultative	__Conceptual	__Sales Support	__Regional Sales Manager
__B2C	__Relationship	__Strategic	__Regional Sales	__Corporate Account Manager
__Entry Level		__Solutions	__Enterprise Sales	__National Account Manager
__Short Cycle		__Negotiations	__National/Key Accounts	__Sales Executive
__Long Cycle		__Territory Management	__Vertical Sales	__Sales Manager
__Inside		__Funnel Management		__District Sales Manager
__outside		__Challenger		__Area Sales Executive
__Hunting				
__Farming				

Categories, groupings and **descriptions,** have developed over the years. Method, skill set, job role, job title, and sales format have been broadly split into either **Retail or Wholesale** oriented sales. These groupings are also more narrowly categorized into **B2B** versus **B2C, Hunter** versus **Farmer, Inside** versus **Outside** sales, and measured for being a **Short** or **Long Sales Cycle.**

Secondly, the **types** of wholesale or retail sales have been classified by type and method of the interaction or **Sales Format.** These sales formats broadly include **Transactional, Complex, Consultative,** and **Relationship.** These interactions and engagements can for example involve a range in both time span and in complexity. These interactions can comprise of just a single person of influence and a **Short Sales Cycle,** or one that involve multiple individuals and a **Long Sales Cycle.** These interactions are in addition often divided and classified based upon the location and method for that interaction. By that I mean the sales type and the subsequent engagement might be either **Inside versus Outside.**

And finally, the sales category is often defined broadly by the **job role** as either a **Hunter** or a **Farmer.** The hunter generates new business while the farmer expands existing business.

The sales target space and the target audience for all the categories, formats, sales types, sales roles, and the sales methodologies that support them are often vastly different. And for that reason, creating a sales readiness template built upon the universal and timeless fundamentals as has been described throughout this book are more important than ever if you want to understand where you belong within the world of sales, and if you hold any hope of having long term sustained success. Prescribing the right methodology for your sales interaction and engagement is important, but it's the adherence to sales structure that ensures sustained success.

The skill sets required within the broad context of the categories, sales types, formats, and the roles described above have different levels of perceived value in the open market space. The most complex roles are typically reserved for those with the greatest level of sales related experience, and those who have less experience are often siphoned into job profiles reserved for new and entry-level experience. Those more complex roles typically involve larger transaction dollar amounts that likely will have greater outcomes at stake while the less complex ones are typically associated with having less of an overall impact on an organization.

The entire world is connected. Information is available in a flash for anyone with access to a browser. Commerce has become a complex environment for both the offering side and the buying side of the equation. Sales have become an increasingly complex offering, and the ways organizations buy today have become just as complex. The job verticals, the roles, the titles, the methodologies, and the types of sales have become as numerous as the nighttime stars. Looking from the outside, it seems almost impossible to break it down and find out one's most optimal place. Some may say, "Why bother? I'll keep my job or take the next one that pays a little more and lets me ride out the guarantee until things get better."

Or you can stop, make the decision to internalize your foundational value, and pursue a job profile rooted within your passions so you can ultimately fulfill your purpose. You might say, "Yes, but it's too complex and too hard to do that!" Even if you understand your foundational value, how do you sift through the web of all those available job profiles and then somehow penetrate the talent silos in the land of Myopia, where nobody will talk to you and your resume floats through cyberspace?

Take a step back! Maybe the world of sales is really not that complex. At this point you might be thinking that showing transferable relevance through Paul's Pyramid of P's and moving from vertical to vertical and job to job looks easy. But it never has been easy. As we have seen, the 1840s and even the 1940s certainly had their shares of economic adversity; war; boom and bust cycles; and technological innovation that gave rise to the rivers, the rails, and the roads and forced workers to adapt or be left behind. Those decades also were the years of mass immigration and the entrance of women into the workforce, both of which created extra competitive pressure for jobs from a mere mathematical standpoint. There were simply more people fighting over the same jobs.

Adaptation is never easy—period! However, I do believe that the forces our forefathers had to overcome were part of a repetitive historical pattern—the same animal, so to speak, with different stripes at different points in time. Perhaps the barriers and obstacles brought upon us by a landscape dominated by the Internet coupled with a talent-acquisition space that is reliant upon "Big Data" micro-targeting analytics are truly unlike the repetitive patterns of the past. That does not necessarily mean adaptation is any harder today than it used to be. Let's take a look at how complicated it really is—or isn't.

The Self-Audit

If you're going to go through the exercise of internalization and perform a self-audit upon yourself, you first have to understand where you have been, where you want to go, and why you want to go there.

The world of sales has indeed become far busier, more complex, and, in a sense, more complicated because everything has become so much more categorized today. The categorization and types of sales have been like everything else in our modern-day world of employment—siphoned into silos—and the selection process, much like everything else, has become very myopic. The talent-acquisition process has certainly become more myopic, in part because of "Big Data" analytics and keyword algorithms. Job searchers face a variety of barriers never before seen from a historical perspective. We live in the era of "Big Data" and the talent-acquisition space has been no exception in its adoption. Hiring managers and recruiters have wasted no time in implementing various software-based analytical tools that help to continuously narrow the demographic profile for job candidates in an ever-increasing micro-targeted way. It's helped to create a very myopic approach to hiring people and never before have candidates had to overcome the barrier of "invisibility."

In my opinion, the world of sales in a larger macro sense is continuously changing as society changes. And the modern day changes have increasingly brought complexity to the sales ecosystem. In my opinion, it is indeed a tougher world out their for the sales professional seeking to make a job change and vertical migration. However, the role of the sales professional and the space from which he or she works has not really changed at all on the fundamental level as it relates to solutions, products, their offerings, and reasons for acceptance. You just have to take the time for some basic sales education to help you see through the cobweb of today's sales ecosystem. I believe the only things that have changed are the terms, the definitions, and the simple fact that the marketplace has created myopic categories and has forced the job seeker to sift through them.

So let's examine these categories. The first thing to do is make sense of them and their definitions. Once we do that, it'll be easier to understand how the talent broker community makes its decisions and implements its approaches to finding ideal candidates. Once we visualize what the landscape actually looks like and understand it, we can then begin the internalization process of understanding how to position ourselves within it, how to communicate our transferable relevance, and apply the science behind the Pyramid.

Categories, Groupings, & Descriptions

How do we make sense of modern-day sales formats, types, methodologies, roles, titles, job descriptions, and expectations? There are an endless number of titles that can make the act of sales out to be more complicated than it really is. Everyone wants a specialist of some sort, but when trying to make sense of the overall vertical called "sales jobs," it's best to start with a broad-based view within which I think every type of sale and sales position can fall.

Wholesale and Retail

As a sales professional today, you will be an advocate on behalf of someone or something for a tangible product or solution, and you will do this in either a retail or a wholesale capacity. Every interaction can be placed loosely into one of those two large buckets. In **retail** sales, you can expect to have direct interactions with the end users. In the **wholesale** format, you do not have interactions directly with the end users but offer and deliver your solutions to a third party that in turn has direct interactions with the end users. As an example, in the wholesale mortgage business I sold our products and solutions to mortgage brokers, who in turn utilized my services to offer mortgage products to end-user homeowners. Thus it was a wholesale job. Another example would be a manufacturer sales representative who offers solutions and products to channel resellers, who in turn sell products to end users in hospitals and surgery centers. Wholesalers are in effect "middlemen."

A sales professional working for a distributor would be working in a retail capacity because he or she would be interacting directly with the end user, while a manufacturer sales rep would be working in a wholesale capacity, selling to a third-party distributer. Now, I know some of you reading this will say, "I can think of a number of jobs that do both." And you're right. The division is not 100% absolute. But they are far more likely and typical than not. There are exceptions, but the vast majority of sales interactions can be divided into those two buckets: retail and wholesale.

B2B and B2C

Within those two primary buckets, we have a second primary categorization split between B2B and B2C roles. The distinction is simple. The term **B2B** refers to a sale between two or more business entities. It

187

doesn't matter if the sale is retail or wholesale. The term **B2C** is a sale (most often retail) between a business and the consumer.

Short Sales versus Long Sales Cycles

The third major categorization is defined and determined by the length of the sales cycle. In general there are just two categories: a short sales cycle and a long sales cycle. The length of time is not exact science, and it can often depend on the type of business. The first step in understanding the sales cycle is to take a measure of how long it typically takes between the act of prospecting for an opportunity, which often begins with introductions, and the time of acceptance and possession of the product or service. Sales can transpire in the same day, or they can take years.

As a general rule of thumb, a long sales cycle begins at about three months. You can make the distinction often by evaluating the typical process. To categorize it as a long sales cycle, the sale might involve multiple decision makers and have multiple tiers for approval and acceptance. On the other hand, if the process is simplified, with a limited number of people required for a conclusion, then it has a higher probability of being a short sales cycle. In any case it's not an exact science, and it's really just important that you recognize and understand what they are and that you have the ability to communicate your experience within those cycles.

Inside versus Outside Sales

This category is pretty self-explanatory. Inside sales involves a combination of phone, email, and webinars as the primary form of interaction, whereas outside sales can include those formats but also involve a lot of face-to-face live interactions.

Hunting versus Farming

The final primary categories to be defined are **hunting** and **farming.** These are common terms, if not a bit overused today. The term **hunter** refers to a sales professional who will have a primary focus on finding new business. A **farmer** is someone who maintains existing relationships and expands opportunities with existing clients. These roles can be inside or outside, and many existing roles today involve a measure of both hunting and farming. However, even if a role involves both, there will be a primary focus of activity within one or the other.

It's very common for organizations to have two defined, separate roles and separate teams for hunting and farming. The degree to which a job will entail hunting or farming depends very much on the organization's position in the marketplace, the type of product being offered, the sales cycle, whether it's B2B or B2C, and whether it's retail or wholesale in scope.

How many different Sales Types or Sales Formats are there?

Now that we have defined the primary categories for sales and described the types of interactions, we can begin to examine the primary sales types or formats a professional can expect to be involved in within the overall sales ecosystem. In my opinion, all sales will fall into one or more of the following four formats:

1. Transactional
2. Complex
3. Consultative
4. Relationship

Again, none of these categories is absolute, and there are crossovers everywhere throughout the sales arena. However, every type of sale can fall predominantly under one of these four headings. The important part of this exercise is to know how to recognize and understand the differences in each so you can internalize the differentiators properly as you commence your journey to create a sales readiness template or find a role for which you can communicate transferable relevance while finding passion and purpose in what you do every day.

Transactional

A transactional sale is an interaction between a person or a business offering a product or solution to a client or end user that involves a simple exchange of information and time with no long-term expectation of repeat or ongoing business. The client in this situation requires very little interaction or information because he or she understands the solution well, and typically the need is already realized prior to the interaction.

Buying and selling a car is a good example of a transactional sale. The customer comes to the lot with the idea that he needs and wants an automobile. The salesman, although he can be somewhat consultative, is more involved with offering choices as opposed to being a relied-upon expert. Transactional sales can be retail or wholesale, B2B or B2C, or inside or outside sales but are almost always in a hunter-style format involving a short sales cycle. The interaction is typically short and simple, involving just one to two people.

Complex

A complex sale is best described as one that has a multi-tiered decision process with multilevel decision makers. The sales interaction is likely to be a multi-tiered approach from introduction to conclusion. The interaction can involve all forms of communication—phone, email, in person—and may involve one or multiple meetings, presentations, and a continuous and planned set of action steps for follow-up.

The complex sale may involve multiple people for a decision on the purchasing end, and often there are multiple people involved on the offering end as well. For example, the sale of EMR software could typically involve not just the front-person sales professional but also his boss, perhaps someone from marketing, a clinical specialist, and a technical specialist.

It's not just the complex process that typifies a complex sale; it's also the complexity of the product or solution that is being sold. The decision to buy or not to buy is likely to affect the end users and decision makers not just for the short term but also typically for years. Entire careers can be affected positively or negatively by the outcome of the decision. This type of sale can be retail or wholesale, inside or outside, or hunting or farming. However, the complex sale is normally reserved for the B2B space and almost always involves a long sales cycle.

Complex sales and transactional sales as categories are mutually exclusive. You typically will not find any crossover traits, with the exception that a repeat or long-term relationship isn't necessarily expected with a complex sale. But otherwise these two pockets represent the biggest contrast of the four when making a comparison.

However, the same cannot be said for the next two: consultative and relationship sales.

Consultative

The consultative sale can be understood almost by definition. To consult is simply to offer advice. To be consultative, the advice has to be more than an offer; it has to be couched within the guardrails of trust and credibility as perceived by the end target, and the trust and credibility must be rooted legitimately within a level of expertise. In other words, the end target's general expectation is that the consultative sales professional is a subject-matter expert.

However, it goes further than that. It also involves an approach in which the consultant has to know and understand the unique needs of the client's target customer, the business target, and the overall big picture of the vertical for which he or she is consulting. The consultative approach is distinguished from a transactional approach in that the interaction involves a lot of information and typically involves multiple options from which a more customized solution is offered, as compared to the typical cookie-cutter solutions involved in a transactional sale.

Profiling your target with quality-level discovery is a primary key to success in consultative sales. The end target is in need of information and education. The end goal for the client is to make the optimal decision on an issue about which they may or may not be aware. The consultative sales professional simply helps his target audience understand and diagnose issues, understand available opportunities, and reach an optimal decision to satisfy a given need or set of needs.

A consultant's role can vary from a waiter in a restaurant to an insurance salesman, PEO sales professional, a sports agent, a healthcare provider, a business analyst, or a sales investment professional on Wall Street. The act of consulting can encompass an enormous area with much crossover. Consultative sales can include retail or wholesale, can be B2B or B2C, can be inside or outside sales, can have short- or long-term sales cycles, and can include aspects of both hunting and farming. It's typically not going to be a transactional sale, but it may be complex and can often involve aspects of relationship sales. If you ran a job search and typed in the words *consultative sales jobs*, you would probably get back an enormous list including multiple verticals, spaces, and job types with a very diverse set of options.

Relationship

Relationship sales are rooted within a process-based approach, but it is not a methodology. It's a sales category that can on its face often be confused with consultative sales. It does have crossover characteristics with consultancy, as they both have building trust and credibility for understanding a client's business, industry, and needs as an end goal in mind. The primary goal for the relationship salesperson is to establish a basis for repeat or ongoing business.

Whereas consultative sales often seeks to help its targets make the optimal choice, the primary goal of relationship sales is to create and maintain ongoing mutual concern and support. Therefore it's the primary goal that can often separate the two. Relationship sales often involve more account management. In some ways the sales professional in this capacity seeks to be almost an extension of the target's services and products. It's less about offering choices and more to do with merging a solution with a client's ongoing need to create an atmosphere of trust that will lead to repeat business.

In a typical relationship sale, there is a mutual concern for the solution and the need. Whereas consultative sales may involve an ongoing mutual concern, a relationship sale by its very definition is an ongoing mutual concern. Therefore, again, it's the primary goal that separates the definition of the two. Locating and creating true relationships can be an expensive investment, thus much emphasis is placed upon the ability to maintain those relationships. In a sense planting your flag in a prospect's backyard is the easiest portion of the sales interaction. Protecting your flank in maintaining or growing your relationship sale is often the most difficult.

Support is the key, and anticipating changes in the external environment for your clients is paramount to keep them. Things always change. For it to be an effective relationship, your value offering must be one that recognizes and adapts effectively to the changing conditions of the environment and your customer's positioning within it. Relationship sales are often associated with territory building and management.

All sales involve some level of relationship and rapport building, but what makes this bucket unique is that it's typified by the goal of creating an ongoing mutual concern with an ever-adapting value-added approach. Success is often in evidence by the sales professional's ability to become an extension of his or her client's solution, service, or product.

A relationship sale would certainly not be a transactional one. By nature, they are polar opposites. The sale can be retail or wholesale, B2B or B2C, inside or outside, and primarily a farming role. However, as stated before, the rules are not 100% absolute. A relationship sales professional would often be required to do more than just maintain and expand relationships; he or she would often be tasked with hunting for new opportunities as well.

As for the sales cycle, it could be a short or long one. The decision to create a long-term relationship doesn't necessarily need to be complex or involve multiple decision makers, nor does it necessarily mean a budget concern is involved in the process of opportunity creation, as would typify a long sales cycle. Rather, the cycle is more determinative of how long it takes a decision to be made. Therefore in relationship sales, the decisions can be long, short, and ongoing. The length of how long the relationship will last has nothing to do with the sales cycle.

Sales Methodologies – The Prescription after the Diagnosis

Now that we have a deeper understanding of how to separate the sales categories, the sales formats, the various definitions and descriptions of them, and their differentiators, it's very important to understand the methodologies we will use to support, win, and sustain our efforts in opportunity creation and conclusion. Now that you know what it means to be a transactional, consultative, relationship, or complex sales professional, you will need to understand which tactical approach works best with which category. In as much as I believe that structure in the form of a sales readiness template is the key to sustained success, today's job seeker has to understand how the talent acquisition world searches, measures, & evaluates sales talent. Today's talent search community begins by leveraging "Big Data" and all the available analytical tools and software to match their client's demand for a specific skill set and profile with a candidate's job history and experience based upon a set of keywords. The end result is that today's talent-acquisition space has become an extremely myopic one. Having a respected training outlet highlighted as part of a resume is helpful. I have been fortunate enough in my life to have had some outstanding professional sales training, including Miller Heiman, Challenger Sale, Gitomer's TrainOne, SPIN Selling, Franklin Covey's, and many others. There are a great number of additional high quality performance-improvement outlets, including (QBS) Questions Based Selling, Sandler, Richardson, and countless numbers of smaller boutique niche outfits. In 2014, Miller Heiman (MHI) merged with another group of performance improvement companies. That may be the continuing trend within the sales training industry as many of today's leading training outlets look to expand their value offering through combined synergy in an attempt perhaps to offer a more complete solution to the end user.

Knowing and understanding what these outlets are teaching can be key to knowing and understanding what you need to know for a particular vertical, job profile, and category. As an example, if you were in a transactional sales-related environment, it wouldn't help you a great deal to sign up for Miller Heiman's strategic selling, which specializes in complex sales with multiple buying influences and prolonged sales cycles. SPIN selling may be more appropriate for you, as it teaches the art of verbal give and take.

In any case it's not my objective to go through the offerings for each outlet. I list some of them in this book and I encourage all who are seeking performance improvement to look into one or more of those respected outlets. My goal here is to make sure you know, understand, and internalize the differences that exist.

Many methodologies revolve around asking good questions, such as SPIN Selling, Conceptual Selling, Strategic Selling, Solution Selling, and Negotiations. Others focus more upon the process, which can involve various techniques and best practices for funnel management and territory management. Others such as "The Challenger Sale" focus upon a sales persons value and ability in offering unique insights as the modern day magic for closing deals. There is a way to match the methodology with the sales types or formats (transactional, complex, consultative, relationships). They all can help in one capacity or more for every category, group, type, format, and role that we have listed. Even if you have not had any of the well known certified training, it is still important at least to understand what each of the methodologies represents on the surface level. Here is a list of some of those and my broad interpretation of what they offer. Some of the methodologies, tactics, and tools listed below such as QBS, Spin Selling, Miller Heiman, and the Challenger Sale are proprietary, and many more broadly offer the remaining. By example, I mean to say that even though Miller Heiman offers training for a complex sale and has a set of proprietary tools that nobody can use without being properly licensed, does not in turn mean that others do not offer solutions for complex sales. Because many most certainly do. They just use their own tools in doing so. My goal is just to highlight a few to give the reader a starting point for research, and thus the list below is in no way meant to be a complete listing of methodology. These are just few of the well known ones. My descriptions are just my basic interpretation for who some of the performance improvement companies are. I also highlighted a few basic tactics commonly taught and offered by many. I encourage you to explore each of these and others in depth.

1) **Question-Based Selling:** Simply the technique for advanced and engaging discovery and profiling that creates a high level of interaction, which in turn brings attention to true needs in an attempt to create an atmosphere for buying. It's designed to help you strategically ask questions that help uncover your prospect's

needs and strategically match your solutions to them. Tom Freese wrote the book *Secrets of Question Based Selling*, and he does offer training programs. www.Qbsresearch.com

2) **SPIN Selling:** Made famous by the book *SPIN Selling* by Neil Rackham, this is another question-based technique that teaches you a specific, sequential, and scientific approach designed to raise a client's needs so you can solve them. The concept is predicated on the assumption that asking "good questions" matter in the sales process. The questions are designed with a specific format in that your interactions should involve multiple types of questions strategically designed to surface deeply-held needs that can elicit the kinds of responses that help you close business. (Now part of the Miller Heiman merger). www.mhiglobal.com

3) **Strategic and Conceptual Selling:** Made famous by Miller Heiman, an organization that believes in the science of the sale and provides a very specific set of tools called Blue, Green, and Gold Sheets. Both strategic and conceptual selling are designed for the complex B2B sale with multiple buying influencers and typically a multi-tiered decision process. The strategic sale is geared more toward the overall opportunity objective, and the associated Blue Sheet is the tool designed to act as a centralized platform to be a shared as an interactive exercise for managing the complex opportunity. The conceptual sale is associated with the Green Sheet, and although it's part of an overall objective, it is geared more toward the interaction with the client; the techniques are geared toward client centricity. Client centricity is the philosophy of seeing things from the client's perspective. www.mhiglobal.com

4) **Solutions Selling:** Just as the name implies, it's a sale strictly designed to solve your customer's problems.

5) **Territory building and territory management:** This category is as much structural and fundamental as it is methodology. But it's an essential mix of both art and science and is taught as methodology by many performance improvement training outlets. Many sales roles today require you to be adept at effectively and efficiently creating, building, and managing geographical territories. This

methodology is more geared toward a sales professional's day-to-day geographical activity and focuses upon time management. It's a scientific and systematic approach that many respected outlets teach as part of their overall performance curriculum.

6) **Negotiation Sales**: Many sales roles require an ability to do more than just offer a solution at a price. There is a science and an art to deal making. The ideal is that all sides win. Many different respected performance improvement outlets teach this methodology in many different ways.

7) **Funnel Management**: This represents less of a methodology and more of a fundamental tactic. Nevertheless, it's an important enough of a component to be included as a form of methodology in terms of how it's practiced. Not all sales professionals understand how to manage the pipeline effectively and efficiently. There is a science to accomplishing it. The goal for sales professionals is to close business, not just find opportunities. Pulling your deal the final ten yards over the goal line can prove to be the most difficult stage, and a sales professional should understand how to allocate his or her time and resources effectively on a daily basis to ensure opportunities advance in the sales process as they should. Many sales outlets have programs for this, and there are a number of CRM tools that can help support sales professionals be effective.

8) **Challenger Sale**: This methodology in my opinion revolves around the idea that for a sales professional to find success in the complex and modern sales ecosystem they must have the means and the ability to offer unseen or unknown insight for their customers. The premise for the contention is that today's client no longer places an emphasis on uncovering problems and prescribing solutions. The idea is that in the era of BIG DATA. It's simply easier and faster to get access to information than in any previous generations. The people at Challenger believe that the customer still wants you to solve a problem but they really find value in helping them find one where they didn't know it existed. They believe that it's the insight and all the credibility that comes along with it that stands as the basis for winning or

losing a deal. In essence, they believe that to be successful a sales person has to be able to offer high-level insight in the capacity of a consultant. They also contend that the method cannot ultimately be successful without the supporting infrastructure of the organization itself. www.cebglobal.com

Some additional and highly respected performance improvement training outlets include:
1) Sandler www.sandler.com
2) Richardson www.richardson.com
3) Dale Carnegie www.dalecarnegie.com
4) Franklin Covey www.franklincovey.com
5) Gittomer www.gittomer.com

Each of these methodologies can be matched up with one or more of the sales types I listed: transactional, complex, consultative, and relationship. Matching up and prescribing the methodology with the sales type is key to having tactical and strategic success in not only finding a job that matches your relevance, but also ensures your long-term success in implementation once you're out there working your territory.

Job Roles

We now understand the broad-based categories of sales, the different types of sales in general, and the associated methodologies you will use in both a tactical and a strategic sense for creating your overall framework for success.

The next logical step in the equation as part of your internalization exercise is to match up all of those categories, types, and methods with the appropriate job role of your choice. Just as we separated sales categories, types, and methods, we make distinctions for job roles as well. Each role is unique as it relates to the demands and expectations for a position. By this time, you have completed the internalization exercise and self-audit. You recognize and understand all the relevant hard and soft skill elements of your work experience. You have a more finely tuned understanding for who you are, what you want to do, and you will know why you want to do it. And with some practice, you will be ready to use the pyramid as a communication template to transfer your relevance for a job role uniquely designed just for you.

Remember, many of your soft and hard skills may fall within multiple categories, types, and formats. The primary key is to recognize and understand why they fall into those buckets so you can communicate the relevance to your target hiring audience. The modern day sales ecosystem is filled with a whole range of job roles. The broad range of roles can typically fall into each of the following. They include entry level, telemarketing, sales support, regional sales, enterprise sales, national/key account sales, and vertical sales. These descriptions of roles can vary greatly and in many instances depend on the specific company and the vertical. If you have gone through the internalization exercise properly, at this point you should understand where and why you are matched up the best. It's important at least to have a basic understanding for how each of these types of roles are defined to help you spot some of the key characteristics.

1) **Entry level**: As the name implies, this is for a new or newer sales professional seeking a position in which to learn and gain experience. This is a place where a person can be molded. The typical job and its characteristics are likely noncomplex in nature. Work ethic and attitude are heavily coveted for this role along with some relatable experience within the offering.

2) **Telemarketing**: These roles are typically inside or home based, transactional and hunter in nature, with a heavy emphasis on phone work. It's often a role in which you would be involved in the pre-sale phase of an opportunity. By "pre-sale" I mean for example, it may often involve starting the sales process and then handing it off to a more seasoned sales professional. That more seasoned professional would then be expected to begin a deeper engagement phase within the sales cycle. In other words, it is often a setup function for a sales professional with more experience. The telemarketer would perform the cold call portion of the sales process and hand it off to someone with deeper

experience to handle the more complicated portions of the sale interaction. Today some telemarketing activities and interactions are presented through the webinar format as well. Typically the pre-sale or set-up portion of the sales process relies on a repetitive activity, such as reading from a sales script or giving a two-minute "elevator pitch." A transactional and questions-based background is likely coveted in this role.

3) **Sales support**: These roles can vary wildly in function depending on the company, the space, and the vertical. The sales support professional is typically either a pre-sales professional or post-sales professional. The pre-sales specialist is largely involved in the setup function, while the post-sales professional is largely involved at the implementation stage. They can range from a junior sales executive who works in a subordinate capacity to a more seasoned sales professional who is often in charge of a very specific component within the scope of the project. An example of this would be a technical solutions specialist in the software vertical or a clinical specialist in the capital medical sales space. In that type of instance the sales support professional is acting in a truly supportive capacity. In other cases, he or she may act typically in more of a hunter capacity and are responsible for finding the opportunity and setting it up. This is a typical format found in medical-related sales. In this type of instance the sales support rep would be acting more in the capacity of "junior sales rep."

The goal for the junior rep or sales support rep is typically a desire to be promoted to a full line rep once he or she has proven his or her ability and value. Sales support can also involve sales and marketing roles in which the support is in the form of administrative support for one or more senior sales professionals. Some sales support professionals might be in charge of helping manage opportunities for webinar's, presentations, lead generation, CRM management support, quoting, and proposals. The duties can vary greatly. The sales support may also come in the form of technical expertise.

These sales roles sometimes can be found in tech-related roles, in which there are individuals who have limited or no sales experience but have a high degree of technical expertise. As a good example, let's not forget our old friend Eric and the technical sales support role he worked while at Monroe Meadows. They act as technical advisors and then learn the science of the sales process in the interim, until such a time as they are ready for promotion and adopt the appropriate sales methodology. There are wide ranges of methodology types and categories that are applicable for these sales support roles. The precise details of the typical profile for a sales support professional depend largely on the vertical, the space, and the individual company.

4) **Regional sales**: Regional sales positions can include a wide variety of roles, types, and methodologies. However they can be categorized broadly as ones that have a defined geographical space to be covered. Experience types can vary from transactional to complex to consultative to relationship. They can be inside, outside, wholesale, retail, B2B, B2C, hunter, or farmer. All forms of methodologies may apply to these types of roles. It's a wide-ranging category.

5) **Enterprise sales**: These are typically complex in nature because the sales often encompass a broad-based set of solutions that affect multiple departments and individuals. The associated solutions and products are typically high in volume and dollar amount. The interactions tend to be complex in nature, and the associated process is typically multidimensional and lengthy.

An example of an enterprise sale would be an EMR (electronic medical record) for a hospital. An enterprise solution such as an EMR has a very broad-based and deep impact across the buying organization over the short and long term. The purchase of an EMR will affect the clinical workflow and patient outcomes across the continuum of care and ultimately the bottom line for the hospital for years to come. The results of the decision can in some cases make or break the careers of many of the influencers involved on the buying side. Complex sales experience, consultative, and strategic experience are highly coveted for these types of sales roles.

6. **National/key account sales**: This role is often associated with mature organizations with longstanding clientele. An account classified as national or key denotes a high level of importance. These roles are typically "fishbowl" roles, meaning they have high visibility because the success or failure of these relationships is deemed vital to the overall success of the selling organization. Subject matter expertise, consultancy, and relationship selling are highly valued for these roles.

7. **Vertical sales**: This relates to roles that have a designated industry group or target for which the sales professional will be responsible. As an example, a medical device company may offer patient monitors, anesthesia delivery systems, and ultrasound equipment. That organization may have designated sales professionals for just anesthesia delivery systems. In that case the sales professional's targets are just the operating room space and the anesthesiology groups.

Having a working knowledge of both the target vertical and the solution is highly coveted for a sales professional in a designated vertical. The nature of the role can vary from complex to relationship to consultative to transactional. The subsets can be hunting or farming, B2B or B2C, retail or wholesale, inside or outside. All forms of methodology training can apply depending on the particulars of the job profile, the company, and the specific vertical. It's a wide-ranging category.

Job Titles for Job Roles

We now understand the broad categories of sales formats, the various types, job roles, and some of the methodologies most often prescribed for working within those roles. We also now have an ability to recognize and understand the characteristics for those job roles, and how they are defined and segmented within the sales ecosystem. The final step for this section of the internalization and self-audit process is to be familiar with job titles. Everyone likes a cool-sounding, important title. However, the truth is a sales professional is a sales professional. This was true yesterday, it's true today, and it will be true tomorrow.

With that said, the marketplace loves to slice it up into segments. Common titles include:

- Account executive
- Business development manager/director
- Regional sales manager
- Corporate account manager/director
- National/key account manager/director
- Sales executive
- Account manager
- District sales manager
- Area sales manager

There are others. Some of the names indicate the associated type of role simply by its definition. If you are national/key account manager, it's likely you are responsible for interaction with key and national accounts. That is simple enough. But for an account executive, account manager, sales executive, or business development manager, your guess for the precise particulars of the role is as good as mine. The job profile and listing will typically spell it out.

In my opinion the key is to understand the company, the space, the solution, and the job profile and expectations. The point is that a title does not define the role in most instances, nor does it define your match for the role. Rather your match for the role is more determined by the elements of your transferable relevance combined with your internal recognition and understanding for how the job fits into your overall sense of passion and purpose.

CHAPTER 18

THE SELF-AUDIT & SALES-AUDIT IN ACTION
A CONVERSATION WITH STEFAN

The **self-audit** exercise for internalization, understanding, and recognition of the common elements that help define your sense of purpose and passion is only half over. As an example, I had a conversation with a friend of mine, Stefan. As with a number of people, he wanted to make a job change. He wanted to remain in sales and was looking for advice on what he should do next. The first thing we did was take a look at the illustrated categorized sales grid.

We started with getting an understanding of his hard skill experience. Stefan sold EMR software to hospitals and surgery centers on behalf of one of the world's leading organizations. He sold directly to the end user. The target customer utilized the solution on a wide scale, as it would apply to multiple departments.

The typical sales process, from prospecting through presentation to closing, was anywhere from three months to two years. The people involved were numerous and from multiple departments including clinical, engineering, IT, and C-Level administration. The decision process had multiple layers to it and often involved a budgetary process. The key to a sale was an ability not just to introduce his value proposition, but also to be deeply consultative. The typical sale involved multiple people from his own organization, including marketing, technical experts, and clinical solutions specialists. He was assigned a geographical territory that included multiple states, and his interactions with clients ranged from phone, email, webinar, to on-site face-to-face meetings. He was responsible for growing the existing account base as well as finding new business. His title was sales manager, although he did not actually manage employees.

So if we use the grid, Stefan was a B2B retail sales professional who was a mix of hunter and farmer and operated primarily in an external position with a long sales cycle. The type of sale was primarily a complex one, and his role could be categorized as a combination of enterprise and regional sales. His sales methodology would have to be one that revolved around a process-oriented plan for engagement that was both artful and scientific in its actions. The methodology would also include strategic, consultative, and conceptual elements to it. In other words, he had to have the comprehensive approach of a project manager while at the same time have the ability to artfully communicate a conceptual value proposition. He had to be able to offer unique insights with enough differentiators to secure the kind of across-the-board buy in that his customers would expect. The interactions required the ability to strategically utilize a questions-based platform and challenger approach designed to uncover complicated needs for which his prospects may or may not have been aware. The role demanded that he create and follow a template designed for efficiency and effectiveness as it related to working and building his territory. Stefan was an experienced and accomplished sales professional.

At first glance, it seemed pretty obvious that Stefan wouldn't face any heavy barriers to finding a new role in some form of capital medical sales. He had the experience, the relationships, and the proof of accomplishments. He had the entire DNA lottery keywords needed to enter the World of Myopia and crack the code of its talent silos. He was in a better position than most.

I asked Stefan what his problem was because I didn't see one on the surface. I thought he must have been getting calls from headhunters, and if he chose to pursue a position proactively he would likely find an audience willing to listen.

Stefan replied, "I just don't think I want to do this kind of role anymore. The money is pretty good, and I feel secure in my future, but I guess I just don't feel fulfilled. Something is missing in what I do every day. I'm not sure exactly what it is."

I asked him, "Do you mean you don't have a sense of passion or purpose?"

Stefan replied, "Yes, I guess that's it. I can't put my finger on it, but I just know I want to do something else."

I replied, "Stefan, I understand. What you want to do is take what you do well and what you like to do, and apply them to a position rooted within whatever sense of passion you have that can somehow fulfill a greater sense of purpose."

Stefan smiled and replied, "Yes, you're exactly right."

"Okay. I know how to help you, but you have to be open-minded. You have to be patient. You have to be serious about doing some introspection exercises. Are you ready to do that right now?"

"I'm ready, but let's schedule a date to meet and go through the exercise so I can give it my full attention and energy."

I smiled at that. "Perfect! I'll send you an invite for next Saturday, 8:30 a.m., at our favorite coffee joint."

The Grid Review with Stefan

THE SALES GRID				
GROUPING	**FORMAT**	**METHODOLOGY**	**JOB ROLE**	**ROLE PORTRAYAL**
___Retail	___Transactional	___Questions Based	___Entry Level	___Account Executive
___Wholesale	___Complex	___Spin Selling	___Telemarketing	___Business Development Manager
___B2B	___Consultative	___Conceptual	___Sales Support	___Regional Sales Manager
___B2C	___Relationship	___Strategic	___Regional Sales	___Corporate Account Manager
___Entry Level		___Solutions	___Enterprise Sales	___National Account Manager
___Short Cycle		___Negotiations	___National/Key Accounts	___Sales Executive
___Long Cycle		___Territory Management	___Vertical Sales	___Sales Manager
___Inside		___Funnel Management		___District Sales Manager
___Outside		___Challenger		___Area Sales Executive
___Hunting				
___Farming				

Finding the Passion and Purpose to Match Up with the Segments

"Good morning, Stefan," I said at our 8:30 meeting. "I prepared this grid for you. At first glance it looks complicated, but I believe that sales is sales, and the basic fundamentals of success have never changed. The only thing that changes is the ecosystem and the landscape from which sales operate. However, the basic operating system of sales is the same as it has always been. Paul's Pyramid of P's is proof of that.

"But what we are going after with this exercise is extracting not only the relevant elements of your work history, but also to understand where, and why your sense of passion and purpose reside within those elements. At this point we have already gone through the exercise of who you are from a hard-skill standpoint. We know what your resume says. I want to walk through what your resume may not be saying. It will be no problem for you to communicate your transferable relevance once you internalize it. The issue is to find out where your passions are and for what purpose. In order to do that, it's time to take a look inward, to discover what it is about the daily activities and interactions throughout your job history that you truly liked or disliked and why.

"The grid displays all the aspects of every type of sales position. We can find a way to fit any role or profile into these segmented categories. We know of what you are capable; let's find out what you really want to do and why. Imagine what you could accomplish if you could apply all of your relatable experience and put it all to use in a job you truly enjoy doing. A job that gives you satisfaction every day. A job that no longer feels like work for you. We can call it getting back to your lemonade stand.

"Let's start on the left side of the grid. Right now you work and have worked in the retail capacity, in that you sell directly to end-users. It's a B2B format with a long sales cycle, and you're an outside sales professional responsible for managing a territory through hunting and farming. Let's start with the first category, Stefan. Let me ask you: Do you like interacting with the end user on a day-to-day basis, and do you enjoy that the interactions are sometimes limited to a specific project?"

Stefan replied, "I do actually love working with the end user. The ability to offer solutions that affect the people I interact with is also something I love. I inherently like people, and I enjoy helping them solve problems. However, sometimes I wish I knew who my customers were going to be every day. I am envious of some of my friends who sell to distributors as third-party sales professionals because there is comfort and satisfaction in building a long-term relationship."

I asked him if he would be happier knowing who his customers were every day or offering solutions to the actual end user.

Stefan then replied, "I wish I could do both. However, if I had to choose one or the other, I would err on the side of interacting directly with the end user. It's just as important to me that my opinion matters to the people to whom I offer solutions."

"So, it's your opinion that matters the most?"

"Not necessarily just my opinion. It's also important to me if an end user takes action or doesn't take action because of the opinion I give. I am continuously curious to follow the results."

"Okay. What we have established so far is that the retail space where you interact with end users is an optimal place for you to be. You also wish you could have ongoing interactions with your prospects, and your favorite aspects of your job are that your opinion matters and that you get to witness the action steps the end users take and the results that follow."

Stefan answered, "Yes. That sounds exactly right. I also think I'd like to be more forthcoming with my prospects."

"What do you mean?"

"Oh, I don't think I'm dishonest in any way, but I wish I could say more. I believe in what I'm offering. It's just that sometimes I wish I could be more expansive in my opinions in terms of helping my clients see things on a bigger-picture level. I am always thinking about other options and different ways for them to accomplish even more than what my solutions can do. I don't mean at the expense of my solution. I just sometimes find myself wanting to be involved in other areas of their businesses that don't necessarily pertain to the scope of the project we work on together. However, I know I have a job to do and a fiduciary responsibility to stay focused on the solution we offer at XYZ Company."

I told Stefan that was an interesting point. We could table it for the time being and come back to it later. He was good with that.

"Stefan," I continued, "does it make any difference to you if you're in a B2B or B2C format?"

Stefan replied, "I don't think so."

"I think the interactions in this vertical require that it be B2B."

"Well, that makes sense because I'm not sure where else I could offer the same solutions to an individual consumer."

"Okay. Let's also table that for now. Stefan, I just want you to keep an open mind as to where it's possible to transfer your job profile to satisfy your passions that you might not have thought about yet." Stefan looked a little puzzled. "Okay. I'll keep an open mind, but I don't know of too many consumer customers that are in need of an EMR."

I reminded him, "The way you describe it, you might be right. However, perhaps there are multiple ways in which a B2B interaction might take place. For now let's just agree that you want to remain in retail B2B sales. Let's look at the sales cycles. Your job involves a long sales cycle. Would you rather it be shorter?"

"No, I don't think so. Of course I wish the decision would be made quicker and the commission would find its way to my bank quicker. However, I know that the reality for this vertical is that it will remain a long cycle because it's a complex process from end to end, and the decision is multi-tiered with a number of influential people. Besides, I enjoy the big-picture framework discussions involved in a long sales cycle. I like teaching people. I like painting pictures for them, and I like to be part of a process that has a long-lasting impact. I don't think a role in a shorter sales cycle could satisfy any of those desires."

I replied, "Interesting. So you enjoy teaching people things? You get satisfaction from teaching complex concepts, and you enjoy bringing to life things that spring forward from those concepts?"

Stefan replied enthusiastically, "I do! I take pride in being a subject-matter expert. I take pride in the investment I have made as a professional to learn and understand all of those things, and I take a great deal of satisfaction when I get the chance to share that knowledge."

"Perfect. You love a long sales cycle not because of the timeframe but more because it provides you an ample forum or platform from which you can help people understand the things you know and about which you feel strongly. And then, ultimately, you get to help implement those ideas into action."

"Yes, that's right, and don't forget the fact that I really enjoy seeing the results of those actions after the ideas have come to life." Stefan also went on to explain that he was comforted by the fact that his opinion, his input, and his solution made a difference in solving a problem that may or may not have been perceived.

I said, "So it sounds like you get your highest level of satisfaction in helping clients to surface needs of which they may not even be aware."

Stefan replied, "Absolutely. I really love it when during the discovery phase something comes up that they hadn't even thought about, and then perhaps I help them ultimately make a better decision because of it."

"Perfect. I think we're getting somewhere. Today you both hunt and farm. Which do you prefer?"

Stefan replied, "I enjoy doing both, quite honestly. It's fun to find new business, meet new people, and foster the process of forming new relationships. Besides that, it's really part of my job."

"Yes, but if you had to wake up tomorrow and decide whom you would rather interact with, would it be someone new or someone you already know?"

"If I had to choose, it would be the latter. I get so much satisfaction from being the established resource. I like the fact that I already know them. I understand their problems, they know me, they rely on me, and they trust me. And at the end of the day, they are going to rely on my opinions to make a decision. I am assured every day that what I say means something. I think if I had to wake up every day and start at the beginning stages of something, I would become dissatisfied."

"Okay. So, how much of your time is spent currently hunting and farming?"

Stefan replied, "I spend about 60% of my time out hunting, trying to generate new business, and 40% of my time on existing clients and projects. It has to be that way. I can't see how it's possible to make my quota off of my existing account base today any time in the near future."

"Clearly you enjoy farming for many of the same reasons you enjoy the retail space as a B2B rep working externally in a long sales cycle. You clearly enjoy being a part of things, and being a trusted part of the team clearly motivates you. You also appear to be passionate about having an opinion and offering a solution that can eventually be acted upon because it solves a problem or creates an opportunity."

"Yes, that's definitely the case."

I replied, "Now let's look at the type of sale. You work in complex sales. We already established that. I am pretty confident, based upon this discussion, that transactional sales would be an unsatisfying pursuit for you. Have you thought about relationship sales?"

"I think I'm already in relationship sales. I have existing clients, and I farm their business."

"You're right. You do. But how would you feel if you were in a job that required farming only, and it was your responsibility to manage those accounts from end to end on an ongoing basis?"

Stefan replied, "I would like that very much. It would satisfy my desire to know who my customer is every day. I would be a trusted and relied-upon resource for decisions, and I would be responsible for making sure we were in the right position to adapt to changes and challenges. Yes, I think a role in relationship sales would be ideal."

"I think it would be good for you as well. However, I'm still thinking in terms of something that's not just good, but great for you. The goal here is to find your passions."

Stefan looked confused again. "Yes, but I think that kind of role really suits me, and there are probably a ton of opportunities out there for me that pay well."

"You're right. However, earlier in our discussion, I asked you to table something. It was small, but I think it's the key to your passions. You mentioned that in your day-to-day interactions you wish you could go further outside of the box or the parameters of your existing solutions. You mentioned that you are at times frustrated by the constraints of those parameters. You mentioned you loved painting pictures for broader-based solutions and you wish you could be allowed to do so. You said you wished that you could leverage your broader knowledge to provide a deeper set of solutions that not just solves some of the problems for XYZ, but also the ones that fall outside of the narrow scope of work given to you. Stefan, perhaps those constraints are what is keeping you unfulfilled."

"Wow! I think you've really gotten somewhere with that."

I nodded. "I think we're starting to see where your passions reside. You want to be more than a relationship builder and manager. You want to be a *consultant* because only that can satisfy your needs for a deep and broad-based, unlimited offering that is not pigeonholed to a specific solution set or scope of work. Only a consultant can be allowed to offer his opinion as deeply and as broadly as the platform can allow. A consultant's role can satisfy your urge to teach, to create frameworks, to paint pictures for others. Only consultancy can satisfy your need to be relied upon for things that matter. You want to effect real change, and you want others to take action based upon your opinions. I think your deeper sense of passion in combination with your hard-skill relevance lies within a role that remains retail oriented, engaged with end users, is B2B with a long sales cycle, is outside oriented, and is within a farming consultant capacity.

"Stefan, there are jobs out there for consultants. We can begin doing research for those. It's clear that role requires a working knowledge of multiple sales methodologies, ranging from Challenger Sale, Question-Based Selling, to Strategic, Conceptual, Negotiations and Solutions Selling. I can recommend a number of outlets for training; however, you have already been to a number of them and are qualified enough from a hard-skill standpoint that there really is no need unless you feel compelled to take some refresher courses. Most often it's enough for your end-target employer to know that you can differentiate how all those methodologies are best applied."

Stefan replied, "This has been the most eye-opening set of exercises I've ever done. I'm so pumped up right now and cannot wait to begin the preparation and planning stage. I know that the medical field is a great vertical, with a ton of long-term upside and security. I have a passion for technology, and I am comfortable with hardware in my hands. Tomorrow I will begin to do my research. I'll choose an opportunity and profile that fit within all the parameters discovered by our exercises. I'm going to give them all the evidence they need to know that I'm a low-risk, can't-lose prospect. They are going to walk away knowing that I'm the perfect fit for the job profile and the organization as a whole. My passions and purpose will be aligned."

Stefan would eventually target a hospital-based consultant group that works with hospitals and surgery centers for the outsourcing and handling of buying capital equipment, disposable supplies, and talent acquisition for client organizations in transition in need of interim management personnel. A candidate would need to have a broad-based and deep-rooted set of skills and knowledge to do this sort of job well. Stefan was well positioned to make a case that he was indeed an ideal match for just such a profile.

There are health care consulting organizations all over the country of varying sizes and scopes. They provide consulting services on a fee or percentage basis. Some of these organizations are designed to help existing and struggling hospitals and major IDN's, and some are designed to help health care investment groups. They help negotiate pricing with GPO's, manufacturers, and distributors for everything from consumables and capital equipment to talent acquisition & enterprise-wide IT infrastructure. The consultant group can also help with new construction and expansion. These consultants act as buffers for their clients as needed. Some consultant organizations go beyond supplies, equipment, and construction to help broker human capital and fill job profiles for everything from the C level to clinical providers, even for things such as food and beverage.

The Sales Readiness Template serves as a Sales Audit

Stefan left the meeting extremely excited and could not thank me enough. Before he left, I shared with him a copy of a brief executive summary & business plan that a friend of mine put together and utilized in getting his last job. This friend of mine did a great job of incorporating the Pyramid of P's into it. I suggested that in addition to the research he would be doing for his role as a consultant, he could use it as a guide to building his own plan and sales readiness template. I told him that at a minimum it could help him focus by utilizing the parameters of the P's as a good communication template for his interview.

Stefan thought it was a fantastic idea. He knew that in order to relate his value to his targeted job of choice, he would have to first have a deep understanding for their value proposition and positioning in their market space. Stefan wanted his future employer to know that he understood the big picture and knew and understood how to research. It would be important if his future clients were going to rely upon him to make good choices. He wanted to demonstrate that he understood how & why to uncover information. The executive summary and business plan I gave Stefan was one designed to secure a job at a capital medical company that offered monitoring, telemetry, anesthesia delivery systems, disposables, beds, and portable ultrasound. The owner of that original template made it a point to highlight the positioning and performance equation from the Pyramid of P's, demonstrating it as a sales readiness tool and communication template during his job interview. The original owner also indicated that the same sales readiness template and summary had made such an impact upon the organization that he interviewed for that it subsequently served as the guideline for an eventual **sales-audit** it conducted upon itself. The organization thought the template could serve as the perfect guideline for evaluating its business model and sales related infrastructure and hoped that the assessment would be perfect for creating a gap analysis report. So, in effect the pyramid as a tool could serve multiple purposes. Stefan thought it was a great template and was excited to begin his research and make it his own. The document below is the original copy I gave to Stefan.

A LIVE SALES READINESS TEMPLATE
www.salesreadinesstemplate.com

Any descriptions, depictions, or likeness to any real company, persons, or events are unintended. The following executive summary/sales and action plan is meant to be for a fictional company and for illustrative purposes only.

SALES AND ACTION PLAN
SALES POSITION
Patient Monitoring and Beds Division
XYZ COMPANY
To:
HIRING MANAGER

Prepared by:
TRANSFER RELEVANCE CANDIDATE
XYZ COMPANY

Salesreadinesstemplate.com

XXX-XXX-XXXX

Table Of Contents

Executive Summary:

I have written this **on-boarding action plan** so that it can be adapted for use upon entry with **XYZ COMPANY**. The absence of specific volume projections is intentional in that I will be relying upon the direction and expectations of my superiors for proper context. The split percentages between hunting & farming have been inserted for illustration purposes as I expect to be doing a measure of both concurrently.

My action steps will be adjusted in accordance to the feedback from superiors, my predecessor, and peers as it relates to my marketing strategy for focusing on a target list in **(FICTIONAL STATE)** that includes more than 130 hospitals and surgical centers. I am assuming that the majority of my efforts will be spent cold calling purchasing directors, nursing managers, nursing directors, CIO's, CFOs, and anyone else working within my target base that can help me advance the ball with decision makers in a multi-department and multi-level environment. My target focus will be fashioned so that my efforts yield the highest level of impact and strategic value for **XYZ**. I am equally experienced and adept at both hunting and farming. **XYZ needs a sales professional like me** that knows how to build long-lasting, professional relationships and can **articulate** and present the **financial and value model at the C level.**

I will be **responsible** for all the **sales activity** for **anesthesia delivery systems, disposables, portable ultrasound, beds, and patient monitors** for **(FICTIONAL STATE).**

The needs and buying processes are different for almost every target. Therefore **a boilerplate approach to marketing is probably not the most effective way to go.** My action steps and marketing strategy will be supported by our product line & dependant upon the solutions they are designed to address.

The **WHATEVER series product line** will make an introduction in January 20XX and it is widely anticipated that it will create opportunities in areas we have with room for **growth** like **critical care.** My focus will be adapted to meet the **strategic demands** required for a **complex multilevel engagement** required for the larger group hospitals like **XXX**, and for a less complex target like a small for-profit independent hospital or surgical center.

The primary point I want to emphasize is that with the utilization of this action plan template, I will help you accomplish your broader long-term strategic objectives and **exceed the quota & expectations set upon me by TM and my other superiors** if I am given the opportunity to join your business development team as your **(FICTIONAL STATE)** sales representative for the Patient Monitoring & disposables division.

The **demographics,** according to some reports, are very favorable for the medical device industry. Demand is driven by population demographics. From 20XX to 20XX, the number of Americans **sixty-five** and older is projected to **increase by 35%.** In contrast the general population is expected to grow by just 10% over that same span of time. Medical device solutions designed to support the needs of the older population is positioned for growth. The bigger companies have advantages through economy of scale in manufacturing and R & D. Patient-monitoring technologies continue to evolve to meet the medical needs of the end user and the patient population. **Recent trends** indicate that the end user is burdened by **staff shortages** and **rising patient volumes.** The end users want advanced capabilities to handle the **aging baby boomers.** Patients are demanding more interaction with the management of their care and the end user demand requires solutions that are designed to be more **proactive** as opposed to reactive. Integrating clinical information with patient monitoring systems is becoming increasingly valued. **XYZ's** diversified product offering is designed to not just **improve patient outcomes** but have also been designed to add value to the end user by having a **net-positive effect** on **productivity, work flow, and efficiency.**

The patient-monitoring market is intensely **competitive. Business** and **financial concerns** are increasingly becoming **top of mind** for decision makers at hospitals. The **economy** is in a difficult situation, **healthcare reform** remains uncertain, and the fact that **reimbursements are down** is making a **low pricing** point a **primary differentiator.** XYZ's low-cost operating model and high-quality device offering for its monitoring equipment makes them **positioned well** to gain opportunity for a rapidly growing market segment.

I am seeking to add value to that growth by becoming a member of your team.

I am writing this to highlight and demonstrate an **action plan** I am confident will not only **lead to success** over my first ninety days but will also serve as the template and platform for a framework for **long-term** growth at **XYZ.**

My **goal is to exceed the volume and activity expectations** set upon me by my superiors. It should be noted that throughout this plan I am somewhat light on specifics as they relate to sales volume projections and the requirements in creating new business relationships, number of meetings with new and existing clients; number of presentations and demos; and phone, face-to-face, email and other advancement actions typically needed to create enough opportunities and successes to exceed quota. My activity level in creating positive opportunities will be fashioned upon leveraging the combination of the knowledge and best practices of my predecessor **JT, TM,** and my peers. My natural intensity, self-directed initiative, and my personal drive to become the **ultimate student of my environment** represent the added components necessary to ensure my long-term success at **XYZ.**

I come to **XYZ** with an enormous amount of **sales infrastructure** as it relates to my prior success and experience in creating and **building** long-lasting professional **relationships and territories from the ground up.** I am equally adept at both prospecting and creating new relationships and building upon an existing client base in delivering solutions enterprise wide. These skills will serve me well here.

If this plan is short on detailed volume specifics, it is on the other hand comprehensive in demonstrating the studied and serious approach I will pursue as your sales representative in **(FICTIONAL STATE).**

It is filled with my thought processes as I take you through not only my first ninety days but also provides you an overview of my strategy-oriented framework for success and sales process.

My Background:

I have more than ten years of experience and success hunting new business; building relationships; assessing the strategic objectives of prospects; diagnosing situational relevance; effectively influencing decision makers; prescribing solutions; presenting value propositions; and ultimately overseeing the timing, cost, and context of the delivery and implementation of solutions. I contribute much of my success to my ability and **willingness** to be the **consummate student** of my environment. I will do the same at **XYZ CORPORATION.**

I have a background filled with **direct and relatable experiences for the business-development framework** at **XYZ**. I am accustomed to building territories and developing long-term relationships in an intensely competitive and complex environment in which a sophisticated and consultative **multilevel engagement** is required for success. I am equally adept at both the **C-level** top-down approach to prospecting, and the **ground-up** campaign in which I have found ways to **leverage** internal champions to help me make my way to **decision makers.** Both skill sets are useful and I owe much of my success to my ability to demonstrate the flexibility to do both concurrently. I am confident that the combination of my skill, experience, work ethic, and attitude will represent a value proposition that **XYZ** can appreciate and will ultimately lead to results that exceed our mutual expectations.

Goals And Objectives:
The following goals and objectives will take you from a pre-hire agenda through my first ninety days.

Pre-Hire Agenda:
The **value proposition** at **XYZ** in my opinion has been **built upon a high-quality and low-cost strategy** model that not only improves patient outcomes but the solutions continue to be designed with the added objective of **improving** the **work flow, productivity, and efficiency for our end users..** That **heavy commitment to R & D is a key factor** in **XYZ's** ability to **differentiate itself** on multiple levels in its **processes, products,** and **pricing** going forward.

XYZ's ability to deliver and service its beds & patient-monitoring solutions at a gold-standard **process** level, offer a diversified **product** line with an ongoing and impressive pipeline, and be a **price** leader is in part the value platform that has helped them rise to number three in its market space and will continue to be what helps propel them to greater market share in areas of opportunity like critical care.

The **process** at **XYZ** has been built with keeping in mind that being close to the end user presents value. A process and system built for responsiveness, speed, and simplicity is vital to success in the medical device industry. The **brand for service and support** at the patient-monitoring division at **XYZ** and now **XYZ** has been **recognized** for being the **gold standard.** The process is supported by a service agreement offering, twenty-four-hour call center loaded with a team of clinical education specialists, clinical guidelines, service manuals, a national repair center for replacement and repair, and in **(FICTIONAL STATE)** the **field technician Bob** has twenty years of experience.

XYZ sells a diversified **product** line all around the world through a direct sales force and distributors. This plan is focused on creating opportunities within the patient-monitoring division. **This division provides the infrastructure needed to manage patient data.** It manufactures devices used in hospitals to keep track of patient's vital signs data, including cardiac output, blood pressure, and temperature. The product line includes anesthesia, ultrasound, and patient-monitoring devices & disposables. **The patient-monitoring devices account for the majority of the current sales.** The products are known for high quality and have been designed to both clinically improve patient outcomes, and at the same time address the administrative concerns of the end user by improving data-gathering accuracy along with the overall efficiency, productivity, and workflow of the staff. The Telemetry systems have the ability to effectively and efficiently acquire data, integrate data, and distribute data. The product line in the pipeline has been designed to **create opportunities** in areas such as **critical care** in which we **lag behind companies like XX and XXX.**

The **pricing** for our products is competitive across the board from what I understand at this point. The specific **pricing** differentiators require that I have a more detailed understanding of the needs of our prospects and also become familiar with the competition as I work through the on-boarding and pre-hire work agenda. I will become much more adept at understanding the differentiators of our **process** as I become accustomed to the delivery and support details in place and learn to position them against the competition and the status quo of our potential targets. The **product** and solutions will eventually become familiar to me, and the ability to absorb and master not just our specific applications and solutions but also those of our competition will take some self-direction and dedication. With that said, all things new take a measure of training, time, and require a good deal of self-study. Getting a firm understanding of **XYZ's** overall positioning is important. Therefore, my first action step should be to act prior to an official hire date as follows:

- Absorb any and all **XYZ** training material if available. Read and keep reading.
- Leverage **JT** and **TM** to learn and understand the history of where and why suites of products and solutions have been utilized in the past, and what products and solutions are in use today and most likely to be utilized going forward. Talk to existing sales reps and anyone else within the organization that can give me best-practice insight.
- Conduct in-depth industry research and also begin the process of creating a master target list for my territory. Create a prospect database.
- Create a master target list, which includes information passed along to me by my predecessor **JT, TM,** our customer service department, and **Bob, the field technician.** I will also concurrently be profiling for new prospects we have not yet had any success in penetrating yet. The list needs to include areas of opportunity for some of the bigger non-profits like XYZ hospital, the ABC Clinic, and all the other venues for critical care in which our new **BLANK series product line** can make an impact.
- Solicit feedback from future peers, leadership, and my professional network in order to get a good sense of our overall positioning.
- Research and understand the competition in depth: XX, XXX, and any others.

The **pre-hire agenda work will improve my familiarity with the overall value proposition and positioning** within the industry and I will begin the process of **understanding** the **physiological aspects** of our product line as well. **Terminology** and **clinical use knowledge** is very **important** in the medical device industry. The running start will also give me the credibility within the context of the conversations I will be having with my target customer base in those very important first thirty days. First impressions matter.

My First Thirty Days:
My extensive sales and business acumen means I **won't need a ton of hand holding.** I have a lot of transferrable experience and skills. I am accustomed to a lot of independent learning. My first thirty days will be a mixture of intense corporate training on my territory, equipment, and physiology study. I anticipate a lot of **"learn as you go"** and I expect that **JT** and **TM** will become my biggest sources for information and support. Where I spend my time will be influenced in large part by how I will be marketing my product. I will be doing **ride a longs** and gathering as much relevant information as possible as I go. I will be meeting with my existing client base for **introductions** to purchasing managers, nursing directors, CIO's, CFOs, and any other decision makers. From what I understand, we have a strong market presence in the surgical center market space in **(FICTIONAL STATE),** and I expect to utilize a heavy **farming** strategy to build upon **existing relationships** in those areas. Once I understand the depth of our penetration into the **(FICTIONAL STATE)** marketplace in areas we are hoping to grow like critical care I can be a lot more definitive on how and where I will spend my time **hunting.** I do fully expect that I will be spending **more than 50%** of my time prospecting and hunting for the **next opportunity.** I will also be gaining a working familiarity with **XYZ** personnel and support operations. Goals and objectives are as follows:

- Successfully complete all training requirements for new hires. Get in the field and begin having **meaningful conversations** right away.
- **Learn** and understand **XYZ's** delivery process, installation process, repair and replace process, and the overall internal web of operations. **Know to whom to go when, why, and where.** Get to know **JT, TM, and Bob** the field technician.

- Under the advisement of leadership and peers I will **begin the prospecting process** for new business. I will be using the target list I have been creating during my pre-hire agenda, my current **ride a longs,** our **client base, my personal network,** and from any other sources I gain as I continue. I want to engage as many warm referrals as possible alongside the cold ones, and I want to do so expeditiously. My plan is to **penetrate** my territory with a **concurrent and multilevel approach strategy.** My target list is a mix of warm clients and cold prospects with varying degrees of depth as it relates to their current relationship with us and the buying process in which they may or may not be currently engaged. In my opinion a boilerplate strategy would not be as effective as a concurrent multilevel marketing approach, because the needs may differ dramatically from prospect to prospect.
- Review samples of our existing entire account list. Review their case histories with my superiors and study the context of their purchases. This will give me a stronger understanding and sense for putting together a good plan for a relevant multilevel approach and introduction.

Leverage my predecessor **JT** in **(FICTIONAL STATE)** and **TM** for relevant information. I need to understand as much as possible as it relates to what point each target is at within the opportunity process. I **need to know details** and answers for questions such as "**have we had a conversation with the purchasing manager** about their **capital budget** and have we gained **support for a proposal?**"

- Create a **contact template** and be diligent in recording and updating relevant information. It's important to know and **understand the context** of every **conversation and engagement** I have with my clients and my prospects. It's important to **record activity** so you can measure results and access the information when needed for leverage. If you can measure results, you can make smart decisions as they relate to adjusting your activity. I want to know what is typical for creating winning opportunities. How many phone calls, email, conversations, demonstrations, PowerPoint presentations, conference calls, and client visits does it typically take to make advancements and ultimately sell our suite of products? I can then organize my days, weeks, and months on an ongoing basis accordingly. I will be doing this knowing that the buying time and buying process will be different with every single client and prospect.

- Become familiar with **the list of potential prospects** throughout my territory. With guidance from my superiors I will prioritize a contact plan for phone and face introductions. I will be conducting face-to-face multilevel prospecting as well with existing clients and I will be mindful of **geographical efficiency** as I do so.
- For purposes of this plan I will need a better understanding of my expectations set upon me in order to give volume projections at this time. **I can commit** to at a minimum **exceeding activity expectations.**

My First Sixty Days:

At this stage I will have a better understanding of my product line, and my overall value proposition. My goals include having meaningful and **evaluative conversations** with the decision makers at **XYZ Hospital and ABC Health** to begin breaking the hold **XXX** has on them. I will also be doing the same with the **EFG Clinic** to begin breaking the hold **XX** has on them. Our new product line **BLANK series** is going to help me create a high level of interest.

At this point I can now begin the **process of moving through the sales cycle more fluently,** start advancing solutions among multiple influencers, and getting introductions and referrals to the relevant decision makers. It's all in the process of building relationships and presenting our value proposition. I have a lot of experience in doing this.

- At this stage my **account list is growing** and I have begun to leverage my customers for warm referrals to other departments and customers.
- Because I have done the proper amount of research and had introductions, I have uncovered opportunities to **propose solutions**

for a growing prospect list both from our existing clients and for new prospects.

- I have begun the process of creating **new allies** and I have **identified** the **influencers** and decision makers within some of the larger target accounts.
- I continue hunting for new business and have identified targets in all areas of my territories throughout **(FICTIONAL STATE)** beyond just **DEF Town, HIJ City, and LMN County.**
- My product and physiology **knowledge has improved** and thus my approach at all levels of the sales cycle is **more crisp** and confident. I continue my training.
- My **routine is taking shape** and my level of phone, face, and email activity is gaining effectiveness and efficiency and thus my opportunity for meaningful discussions with decision makers at all levels is increasing. I am gaining access to the capital budget process, and with the help of **TM** I have done presentations and demonstrations at a level that **exceeds the typical expectation for a new hire.** At this point it would be hard to predict any sales made, as much of that depends on circumstances as they exist today. Because **XYZ** is only one of two companies in the territory that is on every single GPO for patient monitoring I am confident that at a minimum I have **made my way** into the **capital budget mix** for some **new business.**

My First Ninety Days:

At ninety days as an **XYZ** account executive, my workload and focus will be to place a greater emphasis on a wider hunting campaign into areas we have had little or no penetration. My focus will continue to be an optimal multilevel mix of calling on purchasing managers, nursing directors, nursing managers, CFOs and CIO's. I will be helping **TM** and my superiors achieve their strategic goals. My **pipeline** is now more **diverse** with opportunities at **varying stages** and levels of size and complexity.

After 90 days I am confident that I have built a platform upon which I can build. It is at this point in which I begin to leverage business from a wider network.

- I am **now comfortable with our overall positioning, product line, and the solutions** they provide financially, clinically, and administratively. I am **continuing** a **mix of self-directed and formalized training.** My diagnosis would be meaningless or negligent if I could not prescribe the right mixes of products to solve problems and present an attractive value proposition not just upon financial concerns but the clinical and administrative as well.
- My training is ongoing but my routine is in place. I am working from a set but flexible schedule, and my action steps are divided between a peak and off-peak hours.
- I am conducting **evaluations, demonstrations,** and **presentations** to new customers on a **consistent basis** and am traveling as needed throughout my territory. I am now more familiar with my **competition.** They include **XX** and **XXX** for the critical-care space and also involve companies like **XXXX,** against whom I compete for the patient-monitoring business in surgical centers.
- My **customer base is now more familiar with me** and they are helping to **channel new business** my way in other departments. My relationships are deepening and I am gaining trust and credibility. I am now having meaningful conversations with clients and prospects beyond simply the biggest accounts in the major cities in the area. My new **challenge** is **prioritizing** my time so that I am achieving maximum impact. **Geographical efficiency** is important.
- Find **innovative ways** to create **value to your customers.** Attend trade shows if any. Leverage trade groups and professional networks for contacts. I make it a habit to introduce my customers to trade groups and other professional networks that can provide a platform for them to gain value.
- I am continuing to research existing customers and potential prospects on a consistent weekly basis during my off peak hours.

- I am still spending **more than 50%** of my time **hunting for new business** or whatever level is appropriate to achieve the strategic goals of my superiors. The balance of my time is spent with continued training, demonstrations, presentations, profiling, evaluations, and proposals.
- I am now **attending trade-related offline networking events,** and have joined online related groups that will help yield new business and strengthen existing ones.
- At this time I have **a good funnel of business** in place at varying stages and am exceeding activity expectations set upon me.

Based upon my experience, the **master** of **building territories and relationships** is the one who remains a **student** of his environment and maintains a **hunger.** I have a long history of those things, and I am confident that this plan and my passion for success and excellence will ensure that I will do the same for my **XYZ** prospects and customers.

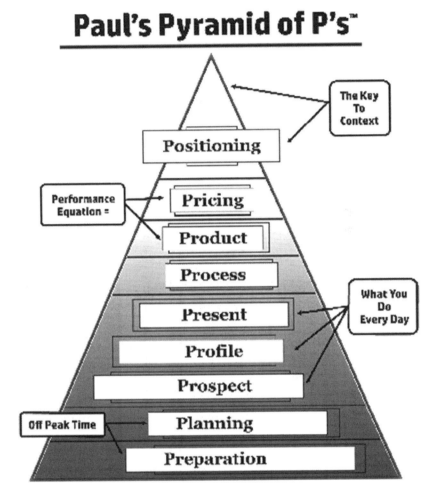

Paul's Pyramid of P's™

Sales Readiness Template:

This template is not only for my first ninety days at **XYZ CORPORATION,** but the following items are the action steps and building blocks for a long-term framework for success. In my opinion sales is **80% science and 20% art.** These following items represent the science I call **Paul's Pyramid of P's**

PEAK TIME: 10 a.m. to 4 p.m.

I am on the phone and in the field, doing presentations and demonstrations, evaluating needs, overseeing my existing projects, farming for wider solutions in multiple departments at multiple levels, and hunting for new relationships and opportunities. The idea behind peak time is simply that 10 a.m. to 4 p.m. represents the **optimal time for business-driving activity** because that is when people are most available. Upon feedback from my superiors and peers I will adjust my Peak Time to be fashioned for **maximum impact** according to whatever is more appropriate within the hospital vertical.

OFF-PEAK TIME: 7:30 a.m. to 10 a.m. & 4 p.m. to 6 p.m.

Off-peak time represents the hours that typically have the **least impact** and likelihood for customer contact. I will be using these hours for preparation: planning, evaluation, company meetings, training, self-study, CRM, research, and trade-related networking events. I want to take care of as much **administrative** detail during this time as possible, so I have more time to drive sales during peak hours.

Preparation

Before you can think about engagement with a prospect or a client you should first make sure it's **worthwhile engagement.** Preparation is simply self-directed study; taking the time to solicit information from your customers and network; and ultimately recording, evaluating, and leveraging that data to make advancements in the sales process. It is critical to conduct as much research as can be done so you can have a strong understanding of their past buying process; the context of their current situation; and their strategic objectives clinically, administratively, and financially for the future. I can then plan for a proper alignment of my solutions that match their objectives.

Knowledge is power. Preparation is the foundation for improving your chances for opportunities.

Planning

It's not only important to plan for the action steps you will take on a daily, weekly, and monthly basis, but you have to plan for a **multilevel concurrent sales approach** throughout the entire sales cycle. The sales at **XYZ** can range from the short to the long depending on the context and complexity of the prospect institution, its culture, and its particular needs. Every prospect has a different buying process and each will have different needs at different times. In either case, success is dependant upon having the **thought process of a project manager** to ensure that the sale will be advanced properly and the solution implemented.

Planning is important throughout the sales cycle. As I become accustomed to the support functions at **XYZ CORPORATION** I will be mindful of how to effectively leverage **TM, JT,** and any other people who will support the sales process. It's my job to know and understand how and when to schedule meetings, presentations, demonstrations, deliveries, implementations, follow up, etc. It will be part of my job to **set expectations and be accountable.** As an example, it will be my responsibility to be the go-to person for the full cycle of issues revolving around patient monitors but I will be acting more as a lead generator and coordinator for our anesthesia and ultrasound devices. That takes good planning skills.

Prospecting

Depending upon the feedback from my superiors and peers, I anticipate that prospecting for new business will occupy **more than 50% of my time** once my routine is in place and settled. I am very experienced at gaining entry to prospects. In addition to researching potential prospects, the key to success in a multilevel engagement is to leverage your relationships, your peers, and your network to create as much of a warm call as possible. **JT and TM** will be instrumental in helping this process.

My focus is to prospect for new business within our client base and throughout all of **(FICTIONAL STATE)**, not just the convenient locations.

Profiling

I make it a habit to **record** information and **organize** it in such a way that I can **retrieve** it when needed. Accessible information is a valuable opportunity creator. Information is power. I need to understand as much as possible about our clients and our prospects. I will make it a habit to know the buying history of our current clients and the history and processes of my prospects. I need to understand more than just the financial and clinical concerns. I need to understand how our telemetry solutions will integrate with their existing platforms, as every hospital might be different. I need to know to what extent our software and technology infrastructure interfaces with the various platforms of our clients and prospects. All indications indicate that our ability to **interface** and integrate is **not an issue today** to the extent it may have been in the past. If our clients have a need, we can provide a solution. Technical barriers are not an issue today according to the feedback I have gathered. It is important to know which **GPO** they belong to and to know if we are on the approved list for them to buy. In **(FICTIONAL STATE)** **we are just one of two** companies that are listed on every single GPO for patient monitors. We are the number **three player for GPO's** in the **anesthesia** space, the **disposables space**, and we are **solid** on **beds** and **ultrasound.** Selling to nonprofit organizations and for-profit organizations requires different marketing strategies because their buying concerns might be different. The point is that every client or prospect has different requirements and challenges. Every client or prospect has a different culture, mission, vision, and strategic and clinical objectives. This is the heavy **question-based selling stage.** My professional SPIN Selling training and professional experience in general presents the kind of sales infrastructure that will serve me well in this market space at **XYZ.** Good questions do more than just provide guidance for a solution match; they also establish strong credibility and build trust. **Knowledge creates value and value creates power.**

Presentations

I have a lot of experience presenting value propositions to both small and large audiences, in seminar format, PowerPoint, and the more informal elevator face-to-face and phone contexts. Public speaking and presentations are **strengths of mine.** I plan on being busy presenting the **XYZ** value proposition and solutions on a continuous basis. I excel at the both the casual relationship-building conversation and the higher impact value proposition talk tracks.

Performance = Process + Product + Pricing

In my opinion almost any value proposition is a function of the above equation. I call it the **PERFORMANCE EQUATION. XYZ** operates within a **low-cost model** that positions them as a **price** leader in the patient-monitoring space. Their reputation for having a **gold-standard** response model for repair, replace, and local field service support gives them a strong **process.** Their commitment and reputation for investing in **R & D** and their growing technical workforce will ensure that they continue to bring to market a **diversified** and **relevant** high-quality set of **products** like the upcoming **BLANK series.** That combination of strength will help to ensure **XYZ** continued success and **PERFORMANCE** in achieving its strategic long-term goals.

Process:

XYZ has a reputation for having a gold-standard process as it relates to its support functions from customer service, support, and repair. BOB Is the field service technician in **(FICTIONAL STATE)** and he has more than **twenty years** of experience. That field support is extremely important. Devices break and malfunction. **XYZ's** efficient service is a **competitive advantage.** Having a good experience and expectations met is what can help keep a customer coming back for more. Service, support, and delivery processes are major points for differentiation in the medical-device business. It will be **my job** to be the **full resource support for the patient monitors** and more of the overseer for our anesthesia, disposables, and ultrasound devices. My marketing strategy for the anesthesia and ultrasound machines will be more at the level of lead generator. The **sales force at XYZ** is a **primary differentiator** because have had to provide a high level of personal interaction in developing relationships in

233

order to compete with our larger competitors. I have a ton of experience and understand how to deliver the **added value** so important to developing and **deepening relationships.** Our competitors have an advantage of having more sites installed. That skill set is going to be what helps me drive through the barriers as we seek to expand our market share in **(FICTIONAL STATE).**

Product:

XYZ Global acquisition of **XYZ's** patient-monitoring division made **XYZ** the **third-largest competitor** in the global patient-monitoring device industry. **XYZ** continues to offer an impressive and diversified product line for the end user. **Diversity and innovation are key** to remaining relevant for existing clients and are what can help attract new prospects. The name **XYZ** does not have the brand recognition yet at the same level of a XX or XXX. However, **XYZ** is well known and has had a great reputation going back to its inception in **the early part of the 1920's.** Part of my responsibility will be to educate and provide **value linkage** from our past to our present to ensure that our prospective clientele understand that the quality and the brand are still intact. In fact, our commitment to R & D and quality has never been better. The pipeline of product and innovation that will be coming to market is impressive. Up until now our **legacy product line** such as the **"OLD FAITHFUL"** series didn't address the needs of a level-one surgery center. However, that is going to change with the introduction of the **BLANK series** due out in **January 20XX.** We also have a **new anesthesia machine** called **the NEWEST THING** that is very innovative. The **BLANK series** has been in the works for five years. It is coming with all the bells and whistles. It offers the **clinical-level solutions** to compete with XX and XXX for the **critical-care** business. Until now, we have sold the majority of our patient monitoring devices to the smaller surgical centers where our low-price model is more of a differentiator. **(FICTIONAL STATE)** is a great marketplace for surgical centers and **JT** has done very well here. **XYZ** had always committed an impressive amount of its revenue to R & D. The commitment to R & D has only gotten better, and I am confident that the organization will continue to find opportunities for newer and more innovate solutions. **XYZ** has continued to **close the gap** on some of the **historic disadvantages** revolving around **clinical solutions, GPO** network strength, and **technology.** The changes are in large part because of the acquisition. XYZ has gone from a handful of **technicians** to now having an impressive **300.** The opportunity for new and more innovative products is staggering. **XYZ** was able to come out with **35 new products in 20XX** alone. One of our primary differentiators is that unlike our competition we have full **vertical integration.** We don't outsource for any part of the building process from design to delivery. That integration is part of what helps us come to market with a **low-cost model** because we are in **full control** of our margins. None of our larger competitors can say the same. Another differentiator is the fact that we are **90% committed** to just the **medical-device** industry, unlike a XX or a XXX that have a number of different verticals in which they provide solutions. One challenge that remains a **barrier** for our competition is in the **government space.** Because none of our products are manufactured in **SOME OTHER COUNTRY** we are having great success in selling to venues like veterans' hospitals and Native American facilities. The same cannot be said for most of the competition.

The medical-device industry more than any other requires a mastery of the product line. I am an **insatiable student** and reader by nature and I am looking forward to knowing and understanding every single component of the devices as well as all the clinical, physiological, technical, systems, and administrative differentiators. Credibility and trust are important in every relationship. As a sales professional, I am a front-line representative of **XYZ** and it is crucial that I know and understand more than our conceptual value proposition but I also must be a **master** of the **equipment** as well if I am going to help the end user in a functional way in the OR. If our clients call me I have to **be a resource** for them and know how to help. It will be important to master the solution set of our product line, as the needs of our prospects are varied. A lack of product knowledge and understanding can reduce a salesman's credibility and lower the chances of success. Part of my job is to be a true master of my product line.

Pricing:

The overall economy is in poor condition and hospitals are not immune. XYZ is a **SOMEWHERE ELSE** manufacturer and has a **low-cost model** that comes to market with a significant price-point advantage over its competition. XYZ bought the patient-monitoring division of XYZ because it fit into their strategy of going after the end user by offering products of comparable or superior product at substantially lower prices. Our **vertical integration** gives us an edge because we have more control over the margins. The pricing gives me an advantage not just as an entry point but also leaves **room for negotiation.** Based upon my feedback, this company understands the value of flexibility. **"What will it take to get it done?"** is the prevailing attitude. There is more to pricing beyond the cost of equipment. The uncertainty of healthcare reform, reimbursement decreases, staff reductions, and rising patient prices are putting a **lot of price pressure on our end users.** XYZ's ability to provide not just clinical solutions for better patient outcomes but also its ability to remove some administrative burdens and improve workflow, productivity, and efficiency through its interactive technology will continue to be a factor in our strategy to gain market share and improve our position. The end user values a streamlined information flow and it has a positive effect on their bottom line. I am limited in my knowledge at the time of this writing as it relates to our specific pricing points for specific equipment but I am confident that we are **very price competitive across the board.** XYZ needs an experienced sales professional like me who knows how to have intelligent and **mature conversations with decision makers** not just at times when they have to buy, but also understands how to **create an atmosphere for change** by surfacing less obvious needs at **less obvious times.** My **sales and business acumen** will give me an **advantage.** I am confident I can be successful working within a framework that has been built upon a low-price model with the delivery of high-end devices. The ability to differentiate ourselves on the price of equipment that provides high-quality clinical outcomes while at the same time removes some administrative burdens by helping to improve workflow, productivity, and efficiency positions **XYZ as a multilevel differentiator as it relates to price and cost.**

Positioning:

None of the training, product knowledge, action plans, or utilization of the most artfully honed sales skills would translate into very many sales without a full understanding of **XYZ's** positioning within the marketplace.

Everything revolves around positioning. It is part of my job to know and understand not only the strengths and weaknesses of **XYZ** but I must also **know** the same for XX, XXX, and all the rest of **my competition.** To understand positioning is to understand how to **differentiate your-self** on a multitude of points as they relate to a value proposition and the **PERFORMANCE EQUATION.** I believe that I have highlighted the primary differentiators throughout this document. I will gain an ongoing working knowledge and understanding of our position within the marketplace starting with my pre-hire agenda and then at an accelerating rate as my career progresses at **XYZ. Complacency is your enemy.** Successful sales people understand that **positioning is a moving target** and we must always be chasing it to master it.

Summary:

In conclusion, I think this document represents a clear demonstration of my understanding of the sales process, the sales cycle, and the steps necessary to build a proper **framework for success.** I am confident that with support, direction, training, and my personal self-directed drive to not just learn but also become a master of my environment will translate into a quick and meaningful impact at **XYZ CORPORATION.** My history of success gives evidence that I have always found a way to create success even under the most difficult of circumstances.

Nothing sells itself. **XYZ** needs an experienced and aggressive hunter and relationship builder like me to **push through the barriers** and present a financial, clinical, and administrative value proposition that will make the case to justify the expenditure for mid- and long-term gains.

There are three things **you can't teach: attitude, work ethic, and desire.** My work ethic like everyone else's is born of the example set by those who raised me. You can't teach someone how to get out of bed every day, to make one more phone call, to see one more client, or to do one more thing when he or she doesn't feel like doing it. You can't teach someone or even convince some people that a glass is half full. The grass is always green from where I stand. You can't force someone to want something. The combination of my sales knowledge, skill, and experience along with my energy, hunger, and desire as they relate to a passion for providing solutions **makes me the perfect long-term candidate for this position and for XYZ.**

Stefan read through it and he loved it. He then proceeded to set about the work of making it his own. He told me he was confident that his prospective employer would be impressed by his going to this length as part of the preparation portion for a job he hadn't yet even secured.

Stefan told me, "You know, Paul, I think these templates, these exercises, these principles can apply to just about anything. For guys like us, it's all about sales because it's what we know. But I think for everyone else out there, it can be about so much more. It can be about anything and everything rooted in a passion or a purpose. It can be for any kind of job, for any kind of vertical. At the end of the day, we all want to do things well and find our own measures of what success means."

Those things will vary from person to person, but the common thread among all things is that we can all find an optimal level of happiness and satisfaction if we can find a way to do those things that are rooted the deepest within our own particular sets of passions and purpose. We each have an internal voice. We just have to find it. We can all communicate the relevant things that matter; we just sometimes need a little help in understanding how to do it effectively.

Call the Pyramid of P's a **sales readiness template**, use it as a **communication template,** use it as a **sales-audit**, or call it the **operating system** from which any and all sales methodologies can be applied upon it. Or call it something else if you think it applies. In any case, at the end of the day I hope you find a way to leverage the foundational principals to create your personal framework for success in business, in life, or both.

CHAPTER 19

PUTTING IT ALL TOGETHER

The World of Myopia can be a depressing place, but it doesn't have to be. I know that to be true because I lived it. As I mentioned at the beginning of this book, we are all a product of our experiences. I spent far to long in the world of Myopia.

The good news for you is that if you are in search of a job, you don't have to go to Myopia and stay as long as I did. The even better news is that if you decide you want to go there, you don't have to go blind, uninformed, and unarmed. You can arrive shielded by the Pyramid of P's and armed with the code and the keys to unlock the talent silos that litter the landscape.

I was inspired to write this book originally as a labor of love to share my incredibly frustrating experience in trying to find a job after being laid off in 2008. I had not had to actively look for a job since the mid-1990s; I was stunned by how much the job-search process had changed and by the daunting and unexpected barrier of being invisible. Everything felt so different. More than half of the people I knew were out of work at this time. All of our conversations with one another were centered upon these common threads: "Nobody will respond to my resume," "Nobody will call me back," and anyone lucky enough to speak to a human being was given a simple, "Sorry, but no thanks. You don't have the direct experience we are looking for."

I have an inherent passion for teaching and helping others. I wrote this book in part to share my experiences, since I know so many have gone through the same. I also sought to offer some insight on the tools and exercises that eventually helped me breach the seemingly insur-mountable talent-acquisition barriers that are so unique to this era of BIG DATA, Algorithms, and Analytics.

People stay in jobs, roles, and verticals they hate because they simply haven't yet discovered a way to understand, much less break through a myopic job-search landscape. They too often have not yet taken the time to look deep within themselves to truly understand what it is they have passion for. Too often they are stuck and dissatisfied with their work lives because they simply have not found a way to recognize their value, much less communicate that value in a relevant and meaningful way for jobs outside their current verticals. The people in charge of Myopia too often prefer the path of expediency to long-term value when it comes to choosing job candidates. Fortunately, there is a way out of the World of Myopia and even a way through it for anyone who wishes to enter. The Pyramid of P's points the way.

Ideas evolve. Even as I was writing this book, the application for my solutions went beyond the concept of transferable relevance for the job seeker. The book broadened into more of a sales based educational ex-amination and introduction of the basic structural fundamental prin-cipals for creating and sustaining sales success. The teachings were brought to life through the illustrative power of the sales readiness tem-plate Paul's Pyramid of P's. As you have read, the relevance and the use of the P's go far beyond just the job seeker. It includes sales profession-als, those who hope to be sales professionals, and businesses entities. For each of those entities, the solutions can be found and extracted from a structurally based sales readiness template.

The pyramid as has been described throughout this book is a multi-purpose tool for both individuals and businesses. There is much that can be learned and utilized throughout this book. However, if there is one concept you should take away from it all, it is transferrable relevance. The essence of that concept is that each of us possesses fundamental value in what we do every day—value that has far more relevance than most people are aware—and that with some focus, a few exercises, and the use of a strong communication and sales readiness template like the P's, that relevance can be effectively communicated for the job of your dreams. It means that if you have a job today and you want a job doing something for which you have no experience, you more than likely have more basic or fundamental relevance to that position than you are aware of. You simply need to first recognize the common relevance and then find a way to communicate those elements in an impactful way. Paul's Pyramid of P's is the tool you can use to do it. I want people to know that it's never too late to change, to start making decisions to do the hard things that get us to where we want to be in life. After all, passion means to suffer greatly for the things we love.

Regardless of your job, company, role, or vertical, you have skills that apply to all sorts of positions of which you may not have even previously thought. The majority of the workforce is dissatisfied with its job. What really matters is having passion and a purpose for what you do; the way you find that is by first through deep introspection, and then by relating your value-based relevance for a job that gives you a sense of fulfillment. If that choice is outside your current vertical and space, you have nothing to worry about. I am in the business of creating opportunities to help you relate your relevance and that's why I originally wrote this book. The Pyramid of P's was first created as a communication template for individuals like me seeking to find a tool that could help me communicate my fundamental sales-related value in order to land a job in a vertical and a space in which I had zero hard-skill experience. I wanted to share that with as many people as possible in hopes that in sharing, I could somehow mitigate the suffering of others.

But, as has been demonstrated throughout, it is relevant as a lot more than just a communication template for job seekers, or as a sales readiness template for sales professionals. It's just as applicable to any business entity willing to utilize it in performing an internal sales-audit exercise in order to ensure that its existing infrastructure is capable of creating a sustainable, portable, and flexible framework for success for its current and future sales force. In effect, this book hopefully has served as a basis for broad based introduction to sales education. Something our society and institutions are woeful in providing. I HOPE TO CHANGE THAT. Maybe a great topic for my next book, or at least a cause I'd like to champion?

I am a living, walking, and talking example of someone who successfully made multiple vertical migrations at the highest level of sales and have achieved success at those highest levels. My adherence to the fundamental principles of sales, my personal journey through multiple verticals, and my professional experiences helped me to recognize the common threads woven within those fundamentals, and how they applied to more than just sales. I created my Pyramid of P's to give you an easy way to recognize and understand those common threads for yourself. To be clear, the Pyramid is not a magic formula for success. Focus and implementation are key. Understanding how a tool works and using it are two different things. The Pyramid is no substitute for hard work or for implementing and acting upon the lessons learned.

What makes my readiness template different from many other sales performance solutions is that mine is more structure and science than it is art. It is the structure and science of things that last. There's no question that there is an art to sales, whether you are selling a concrete product, an abstract concept, or yourself as a job seeker worthy of a position; individual people require individual approaches. The Pyramid of P's puts you in touch with the science behind sales—the unchanging fundamental principles that form the basic foundational framework and structure for sales as a whole.

Most sales training outlets focus on methodology. They teach the latest and greatest way to walk, talk, and act to achieve success, focusing on trends that may be out of date within a year and leave you struggling to connect with whomever you're trying to sell anything to. Don't get me wrong: I am huge fan of performance improvement through the use of methodology. I have been lucky enough in my career to have been exposed to some of the best. However, methodology and art can be fleeting, it's the science of sales that is permanent and the tool for sustainability. In the same way that Apple's operating system allows millions of different applications to act within it, my Pyramid of P's acts as an operating system for any performance improvement based methodology. Think of the sales performance methodology such as "Spin Selling" in the same way you think of an application that runs on your iphone. No matter what methodology you choose, for whatever reason, it can be adapted to the Pyramid of P's for success. The integration is simple plug-n-play. It creates an intersection between the adaptable art of sales and the immutable science of sales to help you achieve your goals.

As a sales readiness template, the Pyramid is portable, flexible, and sustainable. It's portable in that you can take it with you to your current job or the next; if you're a business, it can be applied to your current group of salespeople or the next. It can serve you in whatever capacity you find yourself; in fact, if you like your current situation, it can help you focus upon the fundamentals that made you successful in the first place. It's flexible because it doesn't matter if your typical sales format, or type is complex, transactional, consultative, relational, hunting, farming, B2B, B2C, or a long or short sales cycle. The foundational principles of the Pyramid will apply. Finally, this template is sustainable because it was designed with that purpose in mind. It's a pyramid and thus it is built from the bottom up. A good modern-day example for any of you sports fans could be the Oakland A's and the Boston Red Sox. Both of these organizations are successful because they've positioned themselves from perennial losers to consistent winners by building from the bottom up in their minor league farm system. Even my beloved and often beleaguered Chicago Cubs at the time of this writing have adopted the philosophy. It's the bottom-up structural approach that creates a framework for sustained success, and the Pyramid of P's is a template that starts with preparation as its foundation. In other words it's a **"Foundation First" philosophy**. It adheres to universal fundamentals, is more science than art, and by its very nature as a live operating system has portability and flexibility. You can find success for years to come, no matter where you are or what you do, by applying the principles of the Pyramid of P's.

That portability, flexibility, and sustainability was on full display through the historical examples presented in this book. It was just as applicable to the mining and steamboat businesses in the 1800s as it was for Pete's descendants in the carriage, railroad, and trucking industries and on through to our modern day. They all found success in whatever job, role, etc. they tackled by applying the foundational principles of the Pyramid. Let's not forget our brave space traveler, either. The Pyramid and its principles were just as applicable for our spaces sales alien 1,000 years from now; they're what helped him become a success instead of keeping him stranded in the desert selling electric heaters to snakes. I used it myself as I migrated from banking to PEO, capital medical sales, and my current role in enterprise-wide software application sales. I have written this book as a personal testimony to help you succeed at whatever will make you happy.

Workers and job seekers have always had to adapt due to changes in technology, new entrants to the workforce such as immigrants and women, boom-and-bust cycles, economic fluctuation, and returning veterans from wars. Remember the hypothetical buggy-whip salesman and his classic inability to see what was coming? My theme throughout has been that these barriers for the workforce were primarily the same throughout our history, but the modern-day challenge is unlike any before it. Regardless of the cause, there has always been an upheaval, major or minor, to which the majority of the workforce was forced to adapt. Change is inevitable. However, in our modern era, the change workers could always count on was thrown into a ditch by the introduction of the Internet and the eventual adoption of BIG DATA, analytics, and algorithms as a means of recruiting and acquiring human capital across the entire talent-acquisition landscape. Actually, it's my contention that BIG DATA, analytics, and algorithms slicing and dicing their way through KEYWORD utilization are really the new gold, and every company in every vertical and space is constantly pushing to find more efficient and effective use of micro targeting.

I love technology. I use it and can't live without it personally or professionally. It's amazing in so many ways, and has allowed me personally, and society in general, to advance in degrees our friends in the 1800s would have found unthinkable. It has created jobs, roles, and even whole new verticals that only our space sales alien friend from 3035 could conceive. But once the talent-acquisition space of recruiters and hiring mangers adopted BIG DATA and all of its tools, the job-search landscape changed for the first time in a fundamental way. It has become detrimental to even the most adaptable workforce. And therefore, in my opinion, that is where the greatness ends. It's tough to overcome the barrier of **"invisibility."** It is no longer about people talking to people. Instead it's become an impersonal transaction-oriented process that values expediency over quality: short-term needs and satisfaction versus long-term mutually beneficial career-fulfillment objectives. In my opinion, it's creating a lost generation of workers and a huge opportunity cost for our nation's business community.

We still have to deal with all the traditional barriers, of course, but never before have we become invisible as we have today. Not even globalization has had that kind of impact on finding a job of choice. Micro targeting in recruiting has become a very myopic process and the result is that people just don't talk to people anymore. Companies no longer hire the person and train for the skill. They look only at the hard-skill keywords and ignore the individual worker's soft-skill applicability and relevance. They would rather hire someone who looks good on paper and deal with the consequences of whether or not that person is good at a particular job than invest in training someone who might actually be a better fit but may lack the hard-skill experience on his or her resume.

I created the World of Myopia with its locked talent silos to illustrate my points on this. Without the keys needed to unlock the gates of the ultra-secret, code-based algorithm filters splattered across the cyberspace universe, you can't be seen, you can't be heard, and you certainly can't get in to the talent silos. Those keys come in the form of keywords; if those keywords don't show up on your resume with a "hard-skill" stamp of approval, the door will most certainly be shut to you! No exact experience? Please don't bother applying.

There is a huge talent misalignment today, and the workers and companies suffer the opportunity cost. The tools presented throughout this book serve many purposes for which I am passionate about. I'm really an educator at heart. However, if I had to choose just one goal, it is to transform the talent-acquisition landscape and get people talking to people again. I want to help companies see the value in seeking candidates outside the box of those filtered talent silos. I want workers to break free from those silos and find jobs that fulfill the passion and purpose that gets them out of bed every day.

This is especially true for veterans. They have always had a difficult time coming home from war and transitioning into the private workforce. It is a jarring change of pace, setting, and atmosphere, and far too many get lost in the shuffle after returning home and trying to find opportunities to adapt to civilian life. Too often they have had to take jobs for which they are overqualified. If there is a single group of human beings I think make model employees, it's the highly disciplined U.S. soldiers who serve this country with their lives. I am passionate about their plight and want to help any of them who want to jumpstart careers for which they are uniquely qualified. I want to help veterans live the lives they want to lead and reap the benefits and rewards of high standards of living that jobs in other verticals and spaces might not allow. They are ideal targets that the Pyramid is designed to help. It is a repetitive, process-oriented operating system and soldiers definitely value process and discipline. They could easily adapt and succeed using the portability, flexibility, and sustainability of the Pyramid of P's.

I also want the lessons of this book to help educate existing sales professionals and anyone who wants to be one. This applies to new kids out of college, those working outside of sales, or just anyone who might be looking to change verticals or careers the way I did. The Pyramid of P's can be used as a communication template during the interview process for those who want to make vertical job migrations outside their hard-skill experiences. Quite simply, if you want a particular job, you need to understand how to make the case for why your experiences have relevance, and you need to understand how to relate them to what makes you passionate and purposeful. As a communication template, the Pyramid will help you translate your soft-skill value into a match for a position for which you may lack hard-skill experience.

Most people are simply unsure for what gives them a sense of passion and purpose. The self-audit internalization exercises mentioned in this book will work in tandem with the Pyramid to help you unlock what passions drive you, why it drives you, and lead you to the career you want. It all can help you gain the necessary recognition, understanding, and appreciation for your previous experiences and help you gain some insight into whatever sense of passion and purpose you might possess. This is how you can make decisions on what you really want to do with your life. It is what can lead the way for you in your professional life and gives you a greater sense of fulfillment for your personal life.

Remember my friend Stefan? He and I went through the internalization process together and discovered what it was that he really wanted to do with his life, leading him to make a strong and powerful case for a job for which he was uniquely qualified, even if he lacked the hard-skill experience for which overseers in the World of Myopia may have dismissed him.

The fictitious executive summary and sales readiness template that I reproduced for you in the last few pages is one more template you can follow to impress yourself upon people who may be on the fence about hiring you, but should. The Pyramid as a communication template, the self-audit internalization process, the use of the sales grid as a guide, and the creation of a strong executive summary and sales readiness template are all examples of end products for job seekers. I want to help you get the jobs you want, and these are tools to help you make that happen. The sales grid outlines all the categories, formats, methodologies, titles, etc. to help you identify and understand the modern day sales ecosystem. The self-audit internalization exercise will help you recognize and understand the qualities of your past to help you gain the focus you need to direct your future. Hopefully, these will perfectly align with your individual sense of passion and purpose to lead you to ultimate fulfillment. The executive summary and action plan are the culmination of putting it all together and putting it in on paper in a professional way

Finally, all the solutions I have established to efficiently and effectively help you have been presented here for you to take advantage of your strengths as an employee and as a person are just as applicable to a business. Paul's Pyramid of P's is more than a sales readiness template for just sales professionals. It's a multi purpose tool from which organizations willing to perform a **sales-audit** upon itself can use the pyramid as the guideline for evaluating and measuring it's existing infrastructure as it relates to it's ability to support and sustain its existing and future sales force. That exercise will help spot the gaps and also provide the kind of insight that taps into the depths of the performance equation and can help improve upon all their future sales related efforts. Those insights will serve as the basis for the adaptation of a sales readiness template that is optimally built for portability, flexibility, and sustainability.

The secret to all of this is the fundamental and structural principles on which they are all established. If we look closely enough at each level of the P's, we can all recognize some common threads and some sales-related relevance for what we do every day and for anything we aspire to do. We all tend to be a product of our experiences and my testimony gives evidence to that. The concepts, the exercises, and the tools I've created and outlined are not in and of themselves groundbreaking discoveries.

As human beings, our DNA has made it so that we are creatures that recognize patterns and through patterns we learn. The Pyramid of P's is simply a multipurpose focus tool for job candidates, sales professionals, those who want to be sales professionals, and business entities hoping to create sustained success. It is the pattern for which that Pyramid is designed that makes it such a useful tool, because it allows us as human beings to recognize the relevant value within ourselves in basic and fundamental ways. They were true a thousand years ago, they're true today, and they will be true one thousand years from now

As I explained at the beginning of this book, I entered into the World of Myopia with what I thought was plenty of money in the bank, a whole slew of free & clear assets, and a lot of confidence for my job related open market value. Well, I would eventually lose that money in the bank, I would be forced to sell those free and clear assets, and in that process my confidence would all but disappear. Actually, I lost even more than my confidence-I lost hope. However, the truth is, that while I thought I was losing all that I had, I would come to learn that I was actually gaining everything I would ever need. My favorite song has always been "Amazing Grace". The song has always pulled hard at my emotions even though I spent the majority of my life without any real relationship to God. I think there may have been a reason for loving that tune. But, it was not until I was lost, that I was finally able to see. Jesus said, "For what shall it profit a man, if he gain the whole world, and suffer the loss of his soul." I was invisible and mired down in the World of Myopia. It was not until the voice and the hand of God that came upon me that I would be set upon the path for which I was created. I have gained more than I ever dreamed possible. And I don't mean in terms of dollars or power. I have two things so much more valuable that I didn't have before. First and foremost I have Jesus, and I know that through him all things are possible. It has to begin there. The circumstances, the opportunities, the people, all the thoughts and the ideas for this book only came to me once I accepted him into my heart. The second most valuable thing I have today is a true self-awareness for my purpose and my passion. I know who I am today, I know what I love, and I know why I love it. This book was a labor of love and I believe my purpose is to help others learn.

At the end of the day, I'm simply an educator at heart and I love to help create frameworks of success for other people. My hope for you is that you walk away from this knowing that it's never too late to recognize and understand the differences within yourselves, and that you make the realization that you are unique, you are valuable, and that you indeed have all the relevance you will ever need as you make your migration to whatever it is that best fulfills your purpose and satisfies your passions.

Made in the USA
Middletown, DE
26 December 2015